Cuzco, La Paz & Lake Titicaca

Ben Box

Credits

Footprint credits
Editor: Alan Murphy
Layout and production: Emma Bryers,
Patrick Dawson, Elysia Alim, Danielle Bricker
Maps: Kevin Feeney

Managing Director: Andy Riddle
Commercial Director: Patrick Dawson
Publisher: Alan Murphy
Publishing Managers: Felicity Laughton,
Nicola Gibbs
Digital Editors: Jo Williams, Tom Mellors
Marketing and PR: Liz Harper
Sales: Diane McEntee
Advertising: Renu Sibal
Finance and Administration: Elizabeth
Taylor

Photography credits
Front cover: Neale Cousland / Shutterstock
Back cover: Jarno Gonzalez Zarraonandia /
Shutterstock

Printed and bound in the United States
of America

Every effort has been made to ensure that
the facts in this guidebook are accurate.
However, travellers should still obtain advice
from consulates, airlines, etc, about travel
and visa requirements before travelling.
The authors and publishers cannot
accept responsibility for any loss, injury
or inconvenience however caused.

Publishing information
Footprint *Focus Cuzco, La Paz & Lake Titicaca*
1st edition
© Footprint Handbooks Ltd
September 2011

ISBN: 978 1 908206 30 5
CIP DATA: A catalogue record for this book
is available from the British Library

® Footprint Handbooks and the
Footprint mark are a registered
trademark of Footprint Handbooks Ltd

Published by Footprint
6 Riverside Court
Lower Bristol Road
Bath BA2 3DZ, UK
T +44 (0)1225 469141
F +44 (0)1225 469461
www.footprintbooks.com

Distributed in the USA by Globe Pequot Press,
Guilford, Connecticut

The content of Footprint *Focus Cuzco, La Paz
& Lake Titicaca* has been taken directly from
Footprint's *South America Handbook*, which
was researched and written by Ben Box.

Contents

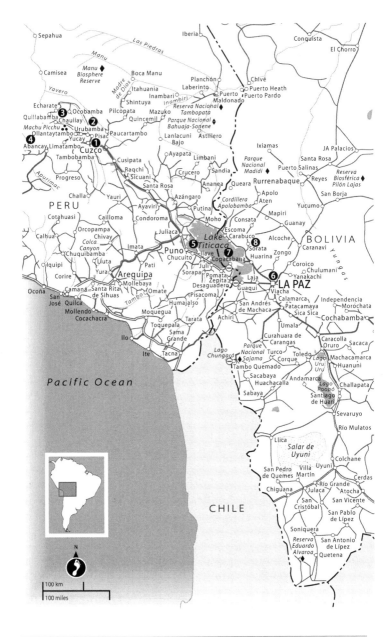

Can you imagine a city laid out in the shape of a puma; a stone to tie the sun to; a city of fleas? Are you willing to meet the Earth Changer, Our Lord of the Earthquakes and Mother Earth? If so, prepare to follow the pilgrimage to Cuzco, the place that every Inca endeavoured to visit once in a lifetime. Navel of the world, Spanish colonial showpiece, gringo capital of South America, Cuzco is all these things and more. The quintessential South American tourist site, Machu Picchu, is a mere train ride away from Cuzco – or a four-day hike along the Inca Trail. Also within easy reach of Cuzco are Andean markets selling essentials to the locals and handicrafts to the tourist, hot springs, charming places to stay and thrilling hikes that traverse 4000-m passes to reach lost cities.

Few cities can boast such an impressive setting as La Paz. Lying huddled at the bottom of a huge canyon, the first view of La Paz is a sight that leaves most visitors breathless – literally – for La Paz stands at over 3500 m. Airborne visitors touch down at the highest commercial airport in the world, and can then play golf at the highest golf course in the world, or ski (just about) on the highest ski slope in the world. Within striking distance of La Paz are an enormous variety of landscapes, extraordinary historical sites and potential for adventure. The most popular excursion is to the remarkable site of Tiahuanaco. Rising out of the vast flatness of the Altiplano are the remains of a great civilization that predated the Incas by a thousand years.

Straddling Peru's southern border with landlocked Bolivia are the deep, sapphire-blue waters of mystical Lake Titicaca, everyone's favourite school geography statistic. This gigantic inland sea covers up to 8500 sq km and is the highest navigable lake in the world, at an average 3810 m above sea level. Its shores and islands are home to the Aymara, Quechua and Uros peoples. Here you can wander through old traditional villages where Spanish is a second language and where ancient myths and beliefs are still held.

Planning your trip

When to go

Peru

In the sierra April-October is the dry season, hot and dry during the day, around 20-25°C, cold and dry at night, often below freezing. November-April is the wet season, dry and clear most mornings, some rainfall in the afternoon, with average temperatures of 18°C (15°C at night). Peru's high season is June-September, which is the best time for hiking the Inca trails or trekking and climbing elsewhere in the country. At this time the days are generally clear and sunny, though nights can be very cold at high altitude. The highlands can be visited at other times of the year, though during the wettest months of November-April some roads become impassable and hiking trails can be very muddy.

Bolivia

The dry season is May to September, July and August see the most tourists, while some of the best festivals, eg Carnival and Holy Week, fall during the wet season – generally December to March. On the Altiplano, the average temperature is 10°C, but above 4000 m may drop as low as -30°C at night from June to August. By day, the tropical sun raises temperatures to above 20°C. Rainfall on the northern Altiplano is 400-700 mm, much less further south. Little rain falls upon the western plateau between May and November, but the rest of the year can be wet. The Yungas north of La Paz, among the spurs of the Cordillera; altitude, 750-1500 m; average temperature 24°C. Rainfall in the Yungas is 700-800 mm a year, with high humidity.

Getting there

Air

There are direct flights to Peru and Bolivia from Europe. In many cases, though, the choice of departure point is limited to Madrid and one or two other cities (Paris or Amsterdam, for instance). Where there are no direct flights connections can be made in the USA (Miami, or other gateways), Buenos Aires, Rio de Janeiro or São Paulo. Main US gateways are Miami, Houston, Dallas, Atlanta and New York. On the west coast, Los Angeles has flights to several South American cities. If buying airline tickets routed through the USA, check that US taxes are included in the price. Flights from Canada are mostly via the USA. Likewise, flights from Australia and New Zealand are best through Los Angeles. Within Latin America there is plenty of choice on local carriers and some connections on US or European airlines.

Most airlines offer discounted fares on scheduled flights through agencies who specialize in this type of fare. Peak times are 7 December-15 January and 10 July-10 September. If you intend travelling during those times, book as far ahead as possible. Between February and May and September and November special offers may be available.

Peru has the most options for international flights and these land at Jorge Chávez **airport** in Lima, 16 km northwest of the city centre. Transport into town by taxi or bus is easy. If arriving in the city by **bus**, most of the recommended companies have their

Don't miss ...

terminals just south of the centre, many on Av Carlos Zavala. This is not a safe area and you should take a taxi to and from there.

Transport from the airport *Remise* taxis from desks outside International Arrivals and National Arrivals: **Taxi Green**, T484 4001, www.taxigreen.com.pe, US$8 to San Miguel, US$13 to the city centre, US$11.50 to San Isidro, US$15 to Miraflores and Barranco; **Mitsui**, T349 7722, remisse@mitsuiautomotriz.com, US$27 to centre, US$31 to San Isidro and Miraflores, US$36 to Barranco, and **CMVT**422 4838, cmv@exalmar.com.pe, a little cheaper. There are many taxi drivers offering their services outside Arrivals with similar or higher prices (more at night). The **Bus Super Shuttle**, T517 2556, www.supershuttleairport.com, runs from the airport to San Miguel, the centre, San Isidro, Miraflores and Barranco for US$15 (prices for 6 people sharing), US$25 for private hire. To get to Miraflores by combi, take the "Callao-Ate" with a big red "S" ("La S"), the only direct link from the airport to Miraflores. Catch it outside of the airport, on Av Faucett, US$0.45. From downtown Lima go to the junction of Alfonso Ugarte and Av Venezuela where many combis take the route "Todo aeropuerto – Avenida Faucett", US$0.35-0.45. At anytime other than very late at night or early in the morning luggage won't be allowed on public buses. For more detailed information including getting away from the airport, see Transport, page 74.

Airport information Arrivals or departures flight information T511 6055, www.lap. com.pe. **Jorge Chávez Airport**, 16 km from the centre of Lima. At the customs area, explain that you are a tourist and that your personal effects will not be sold in Peru; items such as laptops, cameras, bicycles, climbing equipment are exempt from taxes if they are not to be sold in Peru.

Information desks can be found in the national and international foyers. There is also a helpful desk in the international arrivals hall. It can make hotel and transport reservations. There are many smart shops, places to eat and drink, including Starbucks, and, in international arrivals, mobile phone rentals.

Global Net ATM (accepting American Express, Visa, MasterCard and the Plus, Maestro and Cirrus systems), Casas de Cambio (money changing kiosks) and a bank can be found in many parts of arrivals and departures. Exchange rates are marginally poorer than outside. There are public telephones around the airport and a Telefónica locutorio, open 0700-2300 daily. Internet facilities are more expensive than in the city. Most of the terminal has free Wi-Fi. There are postal services.

Hotels near Lima airport

$$$$ Ramada Costa del Sol, Av Elmer Faucett s/n, T711 2000, www.ramada.com. Within the airport perimeter. Offers day rates as well as overnights if you can't get into the city.

$$ Hostal Residencial Víctor, Manuel Mattos 325, Urb San Amadeo de Garagay, Lima 31, T01-569 4662, hostalvictor@terra.com.pe. 5 mins from the airport by taxi, or phone or email in advance for free pick-up, large comfortable rooms, with bath, hot water, cable TV, free luggage store, free internet and 10% discount for Footprint book owners, American breakfast, evening meals can be ordered locally, 2 malls with restaurants, shops, cinemas, etc nearby, very helpful.

$$ Pay Purix, Av Bertello Bolatti, Mz F, Lote 5, Urb Los Jazmines, 1ra Etapa, Callao, T484 9118, www.paypurix.com. 3 mins from airport, can arrange pick-up (taxi US$6, US$2 from outside airport). Hostel with doubles and dorms (**$** pp), convenient, with breakfast, Wi-Fi, washing machine, English spoken, CDs, DVDs, games and use of kitchen.

Getting around

Peru

Air Carriers serving the major cities are **Star Perú**, www.starperu.com, **LAN** *www.lan.com*, **Grupo Taca** *www.grupotaca.com*, and **Peruvian Airlines**, *www.peruvianairlines.pe*. For destinations such as Andahuaylas, Ayacucho, Cajamarca, Huancayo, Huánuco and Huaraz flights are offered by **LC Busre** *www.lcbusre.com.pe*. Flights start at about US$100 one-way anywhere in the country from Lima, but prices vary greatly between airlines, with LAN being the most expensive for non-Peruvians. Prices often increase at holiday times (Semana Santa, May Day, Inti Raymi, 28-29 July, Christmas and New Year), and for elections. During these times and the northern hemisphere summer, seats can be hard to come by, so book early. Flight schedules and departure times often change and delays are common. In the rainy season cancellations occur. Flights into the mountains may well be put forward one hour if there are reports of bad weather. Flights to jungle regions are also unreliable. Always allow an extra day between national and international flights, especially in the rainy season. Internal flight prices are fixed in US dollars (but can be paid in soles) and have 19% tax added. **Note** If possible travel with hand luggage only to avoid the risk of losing baggage. Flights must be reconfirmed at least 24 hours in advance. You can do this online or in the town you will be leaving from. Be at the airport well ahead of your flight.

Bus Services along the coast to the north and south as well as inland to Huancayo, Ayacucho and Huaraz are generally good, but since 2008 the number of accidents and hold-ups on buses has increased. On long-distance journeys it is advisable to pay a bit extra and take a reliable company. All major bus companies operate modern buses with two decks on interdepartmental routes. The first deck is called *bus cama*, the second *semi cama*. Both have seats that recline, *bus cama* further than *semi cama*. These buses usually run late at night and are more expensive than ordinary buses which tend to run earlier in the day. Many buses have toilets and show movies. Each company has a different name for its regular and *cama* or *ejecutivo* services. **Cruz del Sur** and **Ormeño** are bus lines covering most of the country. **Cruz del Sur**, generally regarded as a class above the others, accepts Visa cards and gives 10% discount to ISIC and Under26 cardholders (you may have to insist). There are many smaller but still excellent bus lines that run only to specific areas. An increasing number accept internet bookings. Take a blanket or warm jacket when travelling in the mountains. Where buses stop it is possible to buy food on the roadside. With the better companies you will get a receipt for your luggage, which will be locked under the bus. On local buses watch your luggage and never leave valuables on the luggage rack or floor, even when on the move. If your bus breaks down and you are transferred to another line and have to pay extra, keep your original ticket for refund from the first company. If possible, on country buses avoid the back seats because of the bumpiness, and the left side because of exhaust fumes.

Combis operate between most small towns on one- to three-hour journeys. This makes it possible, in many cases, just to turn up and travel within an hour or two. On rougher roads, combis are minibuses, while on better roads there are also slightly more expensive and much faster car colectivos, often called *autos*, or *cars*. These usually charge twice the bus fare. They leave only when full. They go almost anywhere in Peru; most firms have offices. Book one day in advance and they pick you up at your hotel or in the main plaza. Trucks are not always much cheaper than buses. Always try to arrive at your destination in daylight: much safer.

Note Prices of bus tickets are raised by 60-100%, 2-3 days before Semana Santa, 28 July (Independence Day – Fiestas Patrias), Christmas and special local events. Tickets are sold out 2-3 days in advance at this time and transport is hard to come by.

Hitchhiking Hitchhiking is difficult. Freight traffic has to stop at the police *garitas* outside each town and these are the best places to try (also toll points, but these are further from towns). Drivers usually ask for money but don't always expect to get it. In mountain and jungle areas you usually have to pay drivers of lorries, vans and even private cars; ask the driver first how much he is going to charge, and then recheck with the locals. Private cars are very few and far between.

Taxi Taxi prices are fixed in the mountain towns, about US$0.75-1.20 in the urban area. Fares are not fixed in Lima although some drivers work for companies that do have standard fares. Ask locals what the price should be and always set the price beforehand; expect to pay US$2-4 in the capital. The main cities have taxis which can be hired by phone, which charge a little more, but are reliable and safe. Many taxi drivers work for commission from hotels. Choose your own hotel and get a driver who is willing to take you. Taxis at airports are more expensive; seek advice about the price in advance. In some places it is cheaper to walk out of the airport to the main road and flag down a cab. Keep all hand luggage out of sight in taxis; smash-and-grab thieves are very quick. Another common form of public transport is the mototaxi, a three-wheel motorcycle with an awning covering the double-seat behind the driver. Fares are about US$1.

Train The main railways are Puno–Juliaca–Cuzco, Cuzco–Machu Picchu and Lima–Huancayo, with a continuation to Huancavelica in the Central Highlands. Details of services are given in the text below.

Bolivia

Air All of the following offer internal air services. **AeroSur** *www.aerosur.com*; also has various international flights, including Cuzco two to three times a week. **Boliviana de Aviación (BoA)**, *www.boa.bo*; also flies to São Paulo and Buenos Aires. **TAM**, the military airline, flies to main cities as well as several smaller and more remote destinations. **Aerocon** *www.aerocon.bo*, based in Trinidad, serves mostly the northen jungle. **Amaszonas** *www.amaszonas.com* flies between La Paz, Rurrenabaque and other lowland destinations. Many flights radiate from La Paz, Santa Cruz or Cochabamba. Note that a 'through' flight may require a change of plane, or be delayed waiting for a connecting flight coming from elsewhere. If your internal flight is delayed keep your baggage with you and do not check it in until the flight is definitely announced. Make sure you have adequate baggage insurance.

Bus Buses ply most of the roads. Inter-urban buses are called *flotas*, urban ones *micros* or *minibuses* (vans); *trufis* are shared taxis. Larger bus companies run frequent services and offer a/c, TV and other mod cons. You can usually buy tickets with reserved seats a day or two in advance. Alternatively, savings may sometimes be obtained by bargaining for fares at the last minute, although not at peak travel times like national holidays. A small charge is made for use of bus terminals; payment is before departure.

In the wet season, bus travel is subject to long delays and detours, at extra cost, and cancellations are not uncommon. On all journeys, take some food, water and toilet paper. It is best to travel by day, not just to enjoy the scenery and avoid arriving at night, but also for better road safety (also see Road Safety, page 19). Bus companies are responsible for any items packed in the luggage compartment or on the roof, but only if they give you a ticket for each bag.

Sleeping

Peru

Hotels All deluxe and first class hotels charge 19% in state sales tax (IGV) and 10% service charges. Foreigners should not have to pay the sales tax on hotel rooms. Neither is given in the accommodation listings, unless specified. By law all places that offer accommodation now have a plaque outside bearing the letters H (Hotel), Hs (Hostal), HR (Hotel Residencial) or P (Pensión) according to type. A hotel has 51 rooms or more, a hostal 50 or fewer; the categories do not describe quality or facilities. Many hotels have safe parking for motor cycles. All hotels seem to be crowded during Christmas and Easter holidays, Carnival and at the end of July; Cuzco in June is also very busy. **iPeru** advises that all accommodations registered with them are now listed on their web site: www.peru.info.

Camping Camping is easy in Peru, especially along the coast. There can be problems with robbery when camping near a small village. Avoid such a location, or ask permission to camp in a backyard or *chacra* (farmland). Most Peruvians are used to campers, but in some remote places, people have never seen a tent. Be casual about it, do not unpack all your gear, leave it inside your tent (especially at night) and never leave a tent unattended. Camping gas in little blue bottles is available in the main cities. Those with stoves designed for lead-free gasoline should use *ron de quemar*, available from hardware shops (*ferreterías*). White gas is called *bencina*, also available from hardware stores.

Sleeping and eating price codes

Sleeping

$$$$	over US$150	**$$$**	US$66-150
$$	US$30-65	**$**	under US$30

Price codes refer to the cost of two people sharing a double room in the high season.

Eating

$$$	over US$12	**$$**	US$6-12	**$**	under US$6

Prices refer to the average cost of a two-course meal for one person, not including drinks or service charge.

Youth hostels Contact Asociación Peruana de Albergues Turísticos Juveniles ① *Av Casimiro Ulloa 328, Miraflores, Lima, T446 5488, www.limahostell.com.pe or www.hostellingperu.com.pe.*

Bolivia

Hotels and hostales Hotels must display prices by law. The number of stars awarded each hotel is also regulated and is fairly accurate. The following terms likewise reflect the size and quality of an establishment (from largest and best, to smallest and simplest): *hotel, hostal, residencial*, and *alojamiento*. A *pensión* is a simple restaurant, not a place to sleep.

Camping Camping is best suited to the wilderness areas of Bolivia, away from towns, villages and people. Organized campsites, car or trailer camping does not exist here. Because of the abundance of cheap hotels you should never have to camp in populated areas

Youth hostels Youth hostels or self-styled 'backpackers' are not necessarily cheaper than hotels. A number of mid-range *residenciales* are affiliated to **Hostelling International** (HI), www.hostellingbolivia.org; some others just say they are. Another website listing hostels is www.boliviahostels.com, but they are not necessarily affiliated to HI.

Eating and drinking

Peru

Eating out A normal lunch or dinner costs US$5-8, but can go up to about US$80 in a first-class restaurant, with drinks and wine. Middle and high-class restaurants may add 10% service, but not include the 19% sales tax in the bill (which foreigners do have to pay); this is not shown on the price list or menu, check in advance. Lower class restaurants charge only tax, while cheap, local restaurants charge no taxes. Lunch is the main meal and most restaurants serve one or two set lunch menus, called *menú ejecutivo* or *menú económico* (US$1.50-2.50). The set menu has the advantage of being served almost immediately and it is usually cheap. The *menú ejecutivo* costs US$2 or more for a three-course meal with a soft drink and it offers greater choice and more interesting dishes. Chinese restaurants (*chifas*) serve good food at reasonable prices. For really economically minded people the *comedores populares* in most cities of Peru offer a standard three-course meal for US$1.

Peruvian cuisine The best **coastal** dishes are seafood based, the most popular being *ceviche*. This is a dish of raw white fish marinated in lemon juice, onion and hot peppers. Traditionally, *ceviche* is served with corn-on-the-cob, *cancha* (toasted corn), yucca and sweet potatoes. *Tiradito* is *ceviche* without onions made with plaice. Another mouth-watering fish dish is *escabeche* – fish with onions, hot green pepper, red peppers, prawns (*langostinos*), cumin, hard-boiled eggs, olives, and sprinkled with cheese (it can also be made with chicken). For fish on its own, don't miss the excellent *corvina*, or white sea bass. You should also try *chupe de camarones*, which is a shrimp stew made with varying ingredients. Other fish dishes include *parihuela*, a popular bouillabaisse which includes *yuyo de mar*, a tangy seaweed, and *aguadito*, a thick rice and fish soup said to have rejuvenating powers. A favourite northern coastal dish is *seco de cabrito*, roasted kid (baby goat) served with the ubiquitous beans and rice, or *seco de cordero* which uses lamb instead. Also good is *ají de gallina*, a rich and spicy creamed chicken, and duck is excellent. *Humitas* are small, stuffed dumplings made with maize. The *criollo* cooking of the coast has a strong tradition and can be found throughout the country. A dish almost guaranteed to appear on every restaurant menu is *lomo saltado*, a kind of stir-fried beef with onions, vinegar, ginger, chilli, tomatoes and fried potatoes, served with rice. Other popular examples are *cau cau*, made with tripe, potatoes, peppers, and parsley and served with rice, and *anticuchos*, which are shish kebabs of beef heart with garlic, peppers, cumin seeds and vinegar. *Rocoto relleno* is spicy bell pepper stuffed with beef and vegetables, *palta rellena* is avocado filled with chicken or Russian salad, *estofado de carne* is a stew that often contains wine and *carne en adobo* is a cut and seasoned steak. Two good dishes that use potatoes are *causa* and *carapulca*. On coastal menus *causa* is made with mashed potato wrapped around a filling, which often contains crabmeat.On other occasions, *causa* has yellow potatoes, lemons, pepper, hard-boiled eggs, olives, lettuce, sweet cooked corn, sweet cooked potato, fresh cheese, and served with onion sauce.

The staples of **highland** cooking, corn and potatoes, come in a variety of shapes, sizes and colours. A popular potato dish is *papa a la huancaína*, which is topped with a spicy sauce made with milk and cheese. The most commonly eaten corn dishes are *choclo con queso,* corn on the cob with cheese, and *tamales*, boiled corn dumplings filled with meat and wrapped in a banana leaf. Most typical of highland food is *pachamanca*, a combination of meats (beef, lamb, pork, chicken), potatoes, sweet potatoes, corn, beans, cheese and corn humitas, all slow-cooked in the ground, dating back to Inca times.

Meat dishes are many and varied. *Ollucos con charqui* is a kind of potato with dried meat, *sancochado* is meat and all kinds of vegetables stewed together and seasoned with ground garlic and *lomo a la huancaína* is beef with egg and cheese sauce.Others include *fritos*, fried pork, usually eaten in the morning, *chicharrones*, deep fried chunks of pork ribs and chicken or fish, and *lechón*, suckling pig. A delicacy in the highlands is *cuy*, guinea pig. Very filling and good value are the many soups on offer, such as *caldos* (broths): eg *de carnero, verde*, or *de cabeza*, which includes a sheep's head cooked with corn and tripe. Also*yacu-chupe*, a green soup made from potato, with cheese, garlic, coriander, parsley, peppers, eggs, onions, and mint, *and sopa a la criolla* containing thin noodles, beef heart, egg, vegetables and pleasantly spiced.

Peruvian fruits are of good quality: they include bananas, the citrus fruits, pineapples, dates, avocados (*paltas*), eggfruit (*lúcuma*), custard apple (*chirimoya*) which can be as big as your head, quince, papaya, mango, guava, the passion-fruit (*maracuyá*) and the soursop (*guanábana*).

Drink The most famous local drink is *pisco*, a clear brandy which, with egg whites and lime juice, makes the famous pisco sour. The most renowned brands come from the Ica valley. The best wines are also from Ica, *Tabernero*, *Tacama* (especially its Selección Especial and Terroix labels), *Ocucaje* and *Santiago Queirolo* (in particular its Intipalka label). Beer is best in lager types, especially the *Cusqueña* and *Arequipeña* brands (lager) and *Trujillo Malta* (porter). In Lima only *Cristal* and *Pilsen* are readily available. Other brands, including some Brazilian beers, are coming onto the market. Look out for the sweetish 'maltina' brown ale, which makes a change from the ubiquitous pilsner-type beers. *Chicha de jora* is a maize beer, usually homemade and not easy to come by, refreshing but strong, and *chicha morada* is a soft drink made with purple maize. The local rival to Coca Cola, the fluorescent yellow *Inca Cola*, is made from lemongrass. Peruvian coffee is good, but the best is exported and many cafés only serve coffee in liquid form or Nescafé. There are many different kinds of herb tea: the commonest are *manzanilla* (camomile) and *hierbaluisa* (lemon grass). *Mate de coca* is frequently served in the highlands to stave off the discomforts of altitude sickness.

Bolivia

Eating out Most restaurants do not open early but many hotels include breakfast, which is also served in markets (see below). In *pensiones* and cheaper restaurants a basic lunch (*almuerzo* – usually finished by 1300) and dinner (*cena*) are normally available. The *comida del día* is the best value in any class of restaurant. Breakfast and lunch can also be found in markets, but eat only what is cooked in front of you. Dishes cooked in the street are not safe. Llama meat contains parasites, so make sure it has been properly cooked, and be especially careful of raw salads as many tourists experience gastrointestinal upsets.

Food Bolivian highland cooking is usually tasty and *picante* (spicy). Recommended local specialities include *empanadas* (cheese pasties) and *humintas* (maize pies); *pukacapas* are *picante* cheese pies. Recommended main dishes include *sajta de pollo*, hot spicy chicken with onion, fresh potatoes and *chuño* (dehydrated potatoes), *parrillada* (mixed grill), *fricase* (juicy pork with *chuño*), *silpancho* (very thin fried breaded meat with eggs, rice and bananas), and *ají de lengua*, ox-tongue with hot peppers, potatoes and *chuño* or *tunta* (another kind of dehydrated potato). *Pique macho*, roast meat, sausage, chips, onion and pepper is especially popular with Bolivians and travellers alike. Near Lake Titicaca fish becomes an important part of the local diet and trout, though not native, is usually delicious. Bolivian soups are usually hearty and warming, including *chairo* made of meat, vegetables and *chuño*. *Salteñas* are very popular meat or chicken pasties eaten as a mid-morning snack, the trick is to avoid spilling the gravy all over yourself.

Ají is hot pepper, frequently used in cooking. *Rocoto* is an even hotter variety (with black seeds), sometimes served as a garnish and best avoided by the uninitiated. *Llajua* is a hot pepper sauce present on every Bolivian table. It's potency varies greatly so try a little bit before applying dollops to your food.

Bolivia's temperate and tropical fruits are excellent and abundant. Don't miss the luscious grapes and peaches in season (February-April). Brazil nuts, called *almendras* or *castañas*, are produced in the northern jungle department of Pando and sold throughout the country.

The popular tourist destinations have a profusion of cafés and restaurants catering to the gringo market. Some offer decent international cuisine at reasonable prices, but many seem convinced that foreigners eat only mediocre pizza and vegetarian omelettes. There must be a hundred 'Pizzería Italianas' in Bolivia's tourist towns.

Drink The several makes of local lager-type **beer** are recommendable; *Paceña* and *Auténtica* are the best-selling brands. There are also micro-brews in La Paz (see page 101). *Singani*, the national spirit, is distilled from grapes, and is cheap and strong. *Chuflay* is *singani* and a fizzy mixer, usually 7-Up. Good **wines** are produced by several vineyards near Tarija (tours are available). *Chicha* is a fermented maize drink, popular in Cochabamba. The hot maize drink, *api* (with cloves, cinnamon, lemon and sugar), is good on cold mornings. **Bottled water** is readily available. Tap, stream and well water should never be drunk without first being purified.

Essentials A-Z

Accident and emergency

Peru

Emergency medical attention T117. **Fire** T116. **Police** T105, www.pnp.gob.pe (Policía Nacional del Perú), for police emergencies nationwide. **Tourist Police**, Jr Moore 268, Magdalena, 38th block of Av Brasil, Lima, T01-460 1060, daily 24 hrs; for public enquiries, etc, Av España y Av Alfonso Ugarte, Lima, and Colón 246, Miraflores, T01-243 2190. Go there if you have had property stolen. They are friendly, helpful and speak English and some German.

Bolivia

Police T110. **Ambulance** T118. Robberies should be reported to the *Policía Turística*, they will issue a report for insurance purposes but stolen goods are rarely recovered. In La Paz: Calle Hugo Estrada 1354, Plaza Tejada Sorzano frente al estadio, Miraflores, next to Love City Chinese restaurant, T222 5016. In cities which do not have a Policía Turística report robberies to the *Fuerza Especial de Lucha Contra el Crimen (FELCC)*, Departamento de Robos.

Electricity

Peru 220 volts AC, 60 cycles throughout the country, except Arequipa (50 cycles). Most 4- and 5-star hotels have 110 volts AC. Plugs are American flat-pin or twin flat and round pin combined.
Bolivia 220 volts 50 cycles AC. Sockets usually accept both continental European (round) and US-type (flat) 2-pin plugs. Also some 110 volt sockets, when in doubt, ask.

Embassies and consulates

Visit www.embassy.goabroad.com for a full list of all Peruvian and Bolivian embassies and consulates abroad and for all foreign embassies and colnsulates in Peru and Bolivia.

Festivals and events

Two of the major festival dates are **Carnaval**, which is held over the weekend before Ash Wed, and **Semana Santa** (Holy Week), which ends on Easter Sun. Carnival is celebrated in most of the Andes and Semana Santa throughout Peru and Bolivia. In Cuzco, the entire month of Jun is one huge *fiesta*, culminating in **Inti Raymi**, on 24 Jun, one of Peru's prime tourist attractions. Another national festival is **Todos los Santos** (All Saints) on 1 Nov, and on 8 Dec is **Festividad de la Inmaculada Concepción**. A full list of local festivals is listed under each town.
Public holidays in Peru 1 Jan, New Year; 6 Jan, **Bajada de Reyes**; 1 May, Labour Day; 28-29 July, Independence (Fiestas Patrias); 7 Oct, Battle of Angamos; 24-25 Dec, Christmas.
Public holidays in Bolivia 1 Jan, New Year's Day; Carnival Week, Mon, Shrove Tuesday, Ash Wednesday; Holy Week: Thu, Fri and Sat; 1 May, Labour Day; Corpus Christi (movable May-Jun); 16 Jul, La Paz Municipal Holiday; 5-7 Aug, Independence; 24 Sep, Santa Cruz Municipal Holiday; 2 Nov, Day of the Dead; Christmas Day.

Money

Peru → *US$1 = S/2.74; €1 = S/3.93 (Aug 2011).*
Currency The new sol (s/) is divided into 100 céntimos. Notes in circulation are: S/200, S/100, S/50, S/20 and S/10. Coins: S/5, S/2, S/1, S/0.50, S/0.20, S/0.10 and S/0.05 (being phased out). Some prices are quoted in dollars (US$) in more expensive establishments, to avoid changes in the value of the sol. You can pay in soles, however.
Warning Forged US$ notes and forged soles notes and coins are in circulation. Always check your money when you change it, even in a bank (including ATMs). Hold sol notes up to the light to inspect the watermark and that the colours change

according to the light. The line down the side of the bill spelling out the bill's amount should appear green, blue and pink. Fake bills are only pink and have no hologram properties. There should also be tiny pieces of thread in the paper (not glued on). In parts of the country, forged 1-, 2- and 5-sol coins are in circulation. The fakes are slightly off-colour, the surface copper can be scratched off and they tend to bear a recent date. Posters in public places explain what to look for in forged soles. See also www.bcrp.gob.pe, under **Billetes y Monedas**. Try to break down large notes whenever you can as there is a shortage of change in museums, post offices, even shops. Taxi drivers are notorious in this regard – one is simply told 'no change'. Do not accept this excuse.

Credit cards, traveller's cheques (TCs), banks and ATMs Visa (by far the most widely accepted card in Peru), MasterCard, American Express and Diners Club are all valid. There is often an 8-12% commission for all credit card charges. Bank exchange policies vary from town to town, but as a general rule the following applies (but don't be surprised if a branch has different rules): **BCP** ① *Mon-Fri 0900-1800, Sat 0900-1300*, changes US$ cash to soles; cash advances on Visa in soles only; VíaBCP ATM for Visa/Plus, MasterCard/Cirrus, Amex. **BBVA Continental** changes US$ cash to soles, some branches change TCs at US$12 commission; B24 ATM for Visa/Plus. **Interbank** ① *Mon-Fri 0900-1815, Sat 0900-1230*, changes US$ cash and TCs to soles, TCs to US$ cash for US$5 per transaction up to US$500; branches have **Global Net** ATMs (see below). **Scotiabank** ① *Mon-Fri 0915-1800, Sat 0915-1230*, changes US$ cash to soles, cash advances on MasterCard; ATM for Visa, MasterCard, Maestro and Cirrus. There are also **Global Net** and **Red Unicard** ATMs that accept Visa, Plus and MasterCard, Maestro and Cirrus (the former makes a charge per transaction). Maximum allowed per transaction is US$140.

It is safest to use ATMs during banking hours. At night and on Sun there is more chance of the transaction going wrong, or false money being in the machine. ATMs usually give US$ if you don't request soles and their use is widespread. Availability decreases outside large towns. In smaller towns, take some cash. Businesses displaying credit card symbols, on the other hand, are less likely to take foreign cards. For credit card loss: **American Express** ① *Travex SA, Av Santa Cruz 621, Miraflores, Lima, T01-710 3900, info@ travex.com.pe*; **Diners Club** ① *Canaval y Moreyra 535, San Isidro, T01-615 1111, www.dinersclub.com.pe*; **MasterCard** ① *Porta 111, p 6, Miraflores, T01-311 6000, T0800-307 7309, www.mastercard.com/pe/ gateway.html*; **Visa** ① *T0800-890-0623.*

All banks' exchange rates are considerably less favourable than *casas de cambio* (exchange houses). Long queues and paperwork may be involved. US$ and euros are the only currencies which should be brought into Peru from abroad (take some small bills). There are no restrictions on foreign exchange. Few banks change euros. Some banks demand to see 2 documents with your signature for changing cash. Always count your money in the presence of the cashier. Street changers give the best rates for changing small amounts of US$ or euros cash, avoiding paperwork and queuing, but take care: check your soles before handing over your US$, check their calculators, etc, and don't change money in crowded areas. If using their services think about taking a taxi after changing, to avoid being followed. Street changers congregate near an office where the exchange 'wholesaler' operates; they will probably offer better rates than on the street. Soles can be exchanged into US$ at the exchange desks at Lima airport, and you can change soles for US$ at any border. US$ can also be bought at the various borders. **Note** No one, not even banks, will accept US$ bills that look 'old', damaged or torn.

Cost of travelling The average budget is US$35-50 pp a day for living comfortably, including transport, or US$15-20 a day for low budget travel. Your budget will be higher the longer you stay in Lima and Cuzco and depending on how many flights you take between destinations. Rooms range from US$5 pp for the most basic *alojamiento* to US$15-30 for mid-range places, to over US$90 for top-of-the-range hotels (more in Lima or Cuzco). Living costs in the provinces are 20-50% below those in Lima and Cuzco. The cost of using the internet is generally US$0.60-1 per hr, but where competition is not fierce, rates vary from US$1.50 to US$4.

Students can obtain very few reductions in Peru with an international students' card, except in and around Cuzco. To be any use in Peru, it must bear the owner's photograph. An ISIC card can be obtained in Lima from **Intej ①** *Av San Martín 240, Barranco, T01-247 3230. Also: Portal de Panes 123, of 304, Cuzco, T084-256367; Santo Domingo 123, of 401, Arequipa, T054-284756; Calle José Sabogal 913, Cajamarca, T076-362522; Av Mariscal Castilla 3909-4089, El Tambo, 7mo piso del Edificio de Administración y Gobierno de la UNCP, anexo 6056, Huancayo, T064-481081; Av Jorge Basadre Grohmann s/n, Pocollay, 4to piso del Edificio Facultad de Ciencias Empresariales (FACEM), Campus Capanique de la Universidad Privada de Tacna (UPT), Tacna, T051-981 084038, www.intej.org.*

Bolivia → *US$1 = Bs7.01; €1 = Bs10.09 (Aug 2011).*

The currency is the boliviano (Bs), divided into 100 centavos. There are notes for 200, 100, 50, 20 and 10 bolivianos, and 5, 2 and 1 boliviano coins, as well as 50, 20 and (rare) 10 centavos. Bolivianos are often referred to as pesos; expensive items, including hotel rooms, may be quoted in dollars.

Many *casas de cambio* and street changers (but among banks only **Banco Nacional de Bolivia**, BNB, www.bnb.com.bo) accept cash euros as well as dollars. Large bills may be hard to use in small towns, always carry some 20s and 10s. Small change may be given in forms other than money: eg, sweets. ATMs (**Enlace** network T800-103060) are common in all departmental capitals and some other cities but not in small towns, including several important tourist destinations. Copacabana, Samaipata, Sorata, Rurrenabaque and Tupiza, among others, have no ATM. ATMs are not always reliable and, in addition to plastic, **you must always carry some cash**. Most ATMs dispense both Bs and US$. Debit cards and Amex are generally less reliable than Visa/MC credit cards at ATMs. Note that Bolivian ATMs dispense cash first and only a few moments later return your card. Many tourists forget to take their card. In small towns without banks or ATMs, look for **Prodem**, which changes US$ cash at fair rates, and gives cash advances at tellers on Visa/MC for about 5% commission. (Prodem ATMs do not accept international cards.) **Banco Fie** is also found throughout the country, changes US$ cash at all branches and gives cash advances at some locations. ATM scams are worst in La Paz, but may occur elsewhere. For lost Visa cards T800-100188, MasterCard T800-100172.

Travellers' cheques (TCs) are of limited use in Bolivia. Most tourist establishments will not accept payment with TCs, or they may impose a surcharge of up to 20%. **Banco Bisa**, www.bisa.com, branches in most larger cities, will exchange US$ Amex TCs: approx 1% commission for Bs, US$6 flat fee for US$ cash (maximum 5 TCs); also Casa de cambio **Sudamer** in La Paz (see page 116), about 1.5% commission for Bs, 2% for US$ cash.

Cost of travelling Bolivia is cheaper to visit than most neighbouring countries. Budget travellers can get by on US$15-20 per person per day for two travelling together. A basic hotel in small towns costs as little as US$4-5 per person, breakfast US$1, and a simple set lunch (*almuerzo*) around US$1.50-3. For around US$35, though, you can find much better accommodation, more comfortable transport and a wider choice in food. Prices are higher in the city of La Paz; in the east, especially Santa Cruz and Tarija; and in Pando and the upper reaches of the Beni. The average cost of using the internet is US$0.40-0.60 per hr.

Opening hours
Peru
Shops: 0900 or 1000-1230 and 1500 or 1600-2000. In the main cities, supermarkets do not close for lunch and Lima has some that are open 24 hrs. Some are closed on Sat and most are closed on Sun. **Banks**: see under Money, above. Outside Lima and Cuzco banks may close 1200-1500 for lunch. **Offices**: 0900-1700; most close on Sat. **Government offices**: Jan-Mar Mon-Fri 0830-1130; Apr-Dec Mon-Fri 0900-1230, 1500-1700, but these hours change frequently.

Bolivia
Business hours Shops: Mon-Fri 0830-1230, 1430-1830 and Sat 0900-1200. Opening and closing in the afternoon are later in lowland provinces. Banks and offices normally open Mon-Fri 0900-1600, Sat 0900-1300, but may close for lunch in small towns.

Safety
The following notes on personal safety should not hide the fact that most South Americans are hospitable and helpful. Always use licensed taxis: anyone can stick a taxi label on the windscreen and pick up a fare, but "pseudo taxis" are not safe. The police presence in Lima and Cuzco, and to a lesser extent Puno, has been greatly stepped up. Nevertheless, be aware that aggressive assaults may occur in Lima and centres along the Gringo Trail. Also watch for scammers who ask you, "as a favour", to change dollars into (fake) soles and for strangers who shake your hand, leaving a chemical which will knock you out when you next put your hand to your nose. Outside the Jul-Aug peak holiday period, there is less tension, less risk of crime, and more friendliness.

Although certain illegal drugs are readily available, anyone carrying any is almost automatically assumed to be a drug trafficker. If arrested on any charge the wait for trial in prison can take a year and is particularly unpleasant. If you are asked by the narcotics police to go to the toilets to have your bags searched, insist on taking a witness. Drug use or purchase is punishable by up to 15 years' imprisonment.

Tricks employed to get foreigners into trouble over drugs include slipping a packet of cocaine into the money you are exchanging, being invited to a party or somewhere involving a taxi ride, or simply being asked on the street if you want to buy cocaine. In all cases, a plain clothes 'policeman' will discover the planted cocaine, in your money, at your feet in the taxi, and will ask to see your passport and money. He will then return them, minus a large part of your cash. Do not get into a taxi, do not show your money, and try not to be intimidated. Being in pairs is no guarantee of security, and single women may be particularly vulnerable. Beware also thieves dressed as policemen asking for your passport and wanting to search for drugs; searching is only permitted if prior paperwork is done.

Insurgency Until 2008 the activities of Sendero Luminoso and MRTA had seemed to be a thing of the past, but neither organization was completely non-functional. Reports indicate that Sendero Luminoso was mobilizing again in the areas where its remants had gone to ground, the drug-growing zones of the Huallaga Valley and the jungle east of Ayacucho. In 2011 it was still safe to travel to all parts of Peru except those just mentioned, but it is important to inform yourself of the latest situation before going.

For up-to-date information contact the **Tourist Police** (see Accident & emergency), your embassy or consulate, fellow travellers, or **South American Explorers**, who issue the pamphlet *How Not to Get Robbed in Peru* (Lima T444 2150, Cuzco T245484, or in Quito). You can also contact the **Tourist Protection Bureau** (Indecopi). As well as handling complaints, they will help if you have lost, or had stolen, documents.

Violent crime is less common in Bolivia than some other parts of South America but tricks and scams abound and fair precautions should be taken. The countryside and small towns throughout Bolivia are generally safe. Note however that civil disturbance, although less frequent in recent years, remains part of Bolivian life. It can take the form of strikes, demonstrations in major cities and roadblocks (*bloqueos*), some lasting a few hrs, others weeks.Try to be flexible in your plans if you encounter disruptions and make the most of nearby attractions if transport is not running. You can often find transport to the site of a roadblock, walk across and get onward transport on the other side. Check with locals first to find out how tense the situation is.

Road safety is an important concern for all visitors to Bolivia. Precarious roads, poorly maintained vehicles and frequently reckless drivers combine to cause many serious, at times fatal, accidents. Choose your transport judiciously and don't hesitate to pay a little more to travel with a better company. Look over the vehicle before you get on; if it doesn't feel right, look for another. If a driver is drunk or reckless, demand that he stop at the nearest village and let you off. Also note that smaller buses, although less comfortable, are often safer on narrow mountain roads.

Tax
Peru
Airport taxes US$31 on international flight departures, payable in US$ or soles; US$6.82 on internal flights, US$7.40 in Lima (when making a domestic connection in Lima, you don't have to pay airport tax; contact airline personnel at baggage claim to be escorted you to your departure gate). From 1 Jan 2011 both international and domestic airport taxes should be included in the price of flight tickets, not paid at the airport. 19% state tax is charged on air tickets; it is included in the price of the ticket.
VAT/IVA 19%.

Bolivia
Airport tax International departure tax of US$24 is payable in dollars or bolivianos, cash only. Airport tax for domestic flights, US$2.
IVA/VAT 13%.

Telephone
Peru → *Country code+51.*
The numbering system for digital phones is as follows: for Lima mobiles, add 9 before the number, for the departments of La Libertad 94, Arequipa 95, Piura 96, Lambayeque 97; for other departments, add 9 – if not already in the number – and the city code (for example, Cuzco numbers start 984). Note also that some towns are dominated by Claró, others by Movistar (the 2 main mobile companies). As it is expensive to call between the two you should check, if spending some time in one city and using a mobile, which is the best account to have.

Red Privada Movistar (RPM) and **Red Privada Claró** (RPC) are operated by the respective mobile phone companies. Mobile phone users who subscribe to these services obtain a 6-digit number in addition their 9-digit mobile phone number. Both the 6- and 9-digit numbers ring on the same physical phone. The RPM and RPC numbers can be called from anywhere in Peru without using an area code, you just dial the 6 digits, and the cost is about 20% of calling the 9-digit number. This 80% discount usually also applies when calling from *locutorios*. Many establishments including hotels, tour operators and transport companies have both RPM and RPC numbers.

Bolivia → *Country code +591.*
Equal tones with long pauses: ringing.
Equal tones with equal pauses: engaged.
IDD prefix: 00.

Time
Peru GMT -5.GMT-4 all year. **Bolivia** GMT -5.

Tipping
Peru
Restaurants: service is included in the bill, but tips can be given directly to the waiter for exceptional service. Taxi drivers: none (bargain the price down, then pay extra for good service). Cloakroom attendants and hairdressers (very high class only): US$0.50-1. Porters: US$0.50. Car wash boys: US$0.30. Car 'watch' boys: US$0.20. If going on a trek or tour, it is customary to tip the guide as well as the cook and porters.

Bolivia
Up to 10% in restaurants is very generous, Bolivians seldom leave more than a few coins. In general give a tip for a service provided, eg to a taxi driver who has been helpful (an extra Bs1-2), to someone who has looked after a car or carried bags (usual tip Bs1-2).

Tourist information
Peru
Tourism promotion and information is handled by **PromPerú** ① *Edif Mincetur, C Uno Oeste 50, p 13, urb Córpac, San Isidro, T01-224 3131, www.peru.info.* PromPerú runs an information and assistance service, **i perú** ① *T01-574 8000 (24 hrs).* Main office: Jorge

Basadre 610, San Isidro, Lima, T421 1627, iperulima@promperu.gob.pe, Mon-Fri 0830-1830. Also a 24-hr office at Jorge Chávez airport; and throughout the country.

There are tourist offices in most towns, either run by the municipality, or independently. Outside Peru, information can be obtained from Peruvian embassies/consulates. **Indecopi** ① *in Lima T224 7800, www.indecopi.gob.pe,* is the government-run consumer protection and tourist complaint bureau. They are friendly, professional and helpful. An excellent source of information is **South American Explorers**, in Lima (see page 50) and Cuzco. They have information on travellers held in prison, some for up to 1 year without sentencing, and details on visiting regulations. A visit will be really appreciated!

Bolivia
InfoTur offices are found in most departmental capitals (addresses given under each city), at international arrivals in El Alto airport (La Paz) and Viru Viru (Santa Cruz). In La Paz at Mariscal Santa Cruz y Colombia, T265 1778, www.turismolapaz.travel.

Visas and immigration
Peru
Tourist cards No visa is necessary for citizens of countries in the EU, most Asian countries, North and South America, and the Caribbean, or for citizens of Andorra, Belarus, Bulgaria, Croatia, Estonia, Finland, Iceland, Israel, Liechtenstein, Lithuania, Macedonia, Moldova, Norway, Russian Federation, Serbia and Montenegro, Switzerland, Ukraine, Australia, New Zealand and South Africa. A Tourist Card (TAM – Tarjeta Andina de Migración) is free on flights arriving in Peru, or at border crossings for visits up to 183 days. The form is in duplicate, the original given up on arrival and the copy on departure. A new tourist card must be obtained for each re-entry. If your tourist

card is stolen or lost, get a new one at
Migraciones ⓘ *Digemin, Av España 730,
Breña, Lima, T417 6900/433 0731,
www.digemin.gob.pe, Mon-Fri 0800-1300.*
Tourist visas For citizens of countries
not listed above (including Turkey), visas
cost US$32.50 or equivalent, for which you
require a valid passport, a departure ticket
from Peru (or a letter of guarantee from a
travel agency), 2 colour passport photos,
1 application form and proof of economic
solvency. Tourist visas are valid for 183 days.

Keep ID, preferably a passport, on you
at all times. You must present your passport
when reserving travel tickets. To avoid
having to show your passport, photocopy
the important pages of your passport –
including the immigration stamp, and have
it legalized by a 'Notario público'. We have
received no reports of travellers being asked
for onward tickets at the borders at Tacna,
Aguas Verdes, La Tina, Yunguyo or
Desaguadero. Travellers are not asked to
show an onward flight ticket at Lima airport,
but you will not be able to board a plane
in your home country without one.

Under Decree 1043 of Jun 2008, once in
Peru tourists may not extend their tourist
card or visa. It's therefore important to insist
on getting the full number of days to cover
your visit on arrival (it's at the discretion of
the border official). If you exceed your limit,
you'll pay a US$1-per-day fine.
Business visas If receiving money
from Peruvian sources, visitors must have
a business visa: requirements are a valid
passport, 2 colour passport photos, return
ticket and a letter from an employer or
Chamber of Commerce stating the nature
of business, length of stay and guarantee
that any Peruvian taxes will be paid. The visa
costs £20.70 (or equivalent) and allows the
holder to stay 183 days in the country. On
arrival business visitors must register with
the *Dirección General de Contribuciones* for
tax purposes.

Student visas These must be requested
from Migraciones (address above) once you
are in Peru. In addition to completing the
general visa form you must have proof of
adequate funds, affiliation to a Peruvian body,
a letter of consent from parents or tutors if
you are a minor. The cost is US$20. Full details
are on the Digemin website (in Spanish).

If you wish to change a tourist visa into
another type of visa (business, student,
resident, etc), you may do so without
leaving Peru. Visit Migraciones and
obtain the relevant forms.

Bolivia

A passport only, valid for 6 months beyond
date of visit, is needed for citizens of almost
all Western European countries, Israel, Japan,
Canada, South American countries, Australia
and New Zealand. Nationals of all other
countries require a visa. US citizens may
obtain a visa either in advance at a Bolivian
consulate, or directly on entry to the country
at airports and land borders. Requirements
include a fee of US$135 cash (subject
to change), proof of sufficient funds
(eg showing a credit card) and a yellow
fever vaccination certificate. Only the fee is
universally enforced. Some nationalities must
gain authorization from the Bolivian Ministry
of Foreign Affairs, which can take 6 weeks.
Other countries that require a visa do not
need authorisation (visas in this case take
1-2 working days). It is best to check current
requirements before leaving home. Tourists
are usually granted 30-60 days stay on entry
and can apply for a free extension
(*ampliación*) at immigration offices in all
departmental capitals, up to a maximum
stay of 90 days per calendar year. If you
overstay, the current fine is US$3 per day.

Weights and measures

Metric. Some old Spanish measures are
used for produce in markets in Bolivia.

Contents

Footprint features

Cuzco, Sacred Valley & Lake Titicaca

Cuzco

Cuzco stands at the head of the Sacred Valley of the Incas and is the jumping-off point for the Inca Trail and famous Inca city of Machu Picchu. It's not surprising, therefore, that this is the prime destination for the vast majority of Peru's visitors. In fact, what was once an ancient Inca capital is now the 'gringo' capital of the entire continent. And it's easy to see why. There are Inca ruins aplenty, as well as fabulous colonial architecture, stunning scenery, great trekking, river rafting and mountain biking, beautiful textiles and other traditional handicrafts – all within easy reach of the nearest cappuccino or comfy hotel room.

Since there are so many sights to see in Cuzco city, not even the most ardent tourist would be able to visit them all. For those with limited time, or for those who want a whistle-stop tour, a list of must-sees would comprise: the combination of Inca and colonial architecture at Qoricancha; the huge Inca ceremonial centre of Sacsayhuaman; the paintings of the Last Supper and the 1650 earthquake in the cathedral; the main altar of La Compañía de Jesús; the pulpit of San Blas; the high choir at San Francisco; the monstrance at La Merced; and the view from San Cristóbal. If you have the energy, catch a taxi up to the White Christ and watch the sunset as you look out upon one of the most fascinating cities in the world. If you visit one museum make it the Museo Inka; it has the most comprehensive collection.

Ins and outs → *Phone code: 084. Altitude: 3310 m.*

Getting there The **airport** is to the southeast of the city and the road into the centre goes close to Wanchac station, at which **trains** from Juliaca and Puno arrive. The **bus terminal** is near the Pachacútec statue in Ttio district. Transport to your hotel is not a problem from any of these places by taxi or in transport arranged by hotel representatives. ▶ *See also Transport, page 49.*

Getting around The centre of Cuzco is quite small and possible to explore on foot. Taxis in Cuzco are cheap and recommended when arriving by air, train or bus and especially when returning to your hotel at night. Cuzco is only slightly lower than Puno, so respect the altitude: two or three hours rest after arriving makes a great difference; avoid meat and smoking, eat lots of carbohydrates and drink plenty of clear, non-alcoholic liquid; remember to walk slowly. To see Cuzco and the surrounding area properly (including Pisac, Ollantaytambo, Chinchero and Machu Picchu) you need five days to a week, allowing for slowing down because of the altitude.

Tourist information Official tourist information ① *Portal Mantas 117-A, next to La Merced church, T263176, open 0800-1830.* There is also an i perú tourist information desk at the airport ① *T237364, open daily for flights,* and another at ① *Av Sol 103, of 102, Galerías Turísticas, T252974, iperucusco@promperu.gob.pe, daily 0830-1930.* Dircetur ① *Plaza Túpac Amaru Mz 1 Lte 2, Wanchac, T223761, open Mon-Fri 0800-1300,* gives out good map. Other information sources include **South American Explorers** ① *Atocsaycuchi 670, T245484, www.saexplorers.org, Mon-Fri 0930-1700, Sat 0930-1300.* It's worth making the climb up the steps to the large new clubhouse which has a garden. Sells good city map, members get many local discounts, has comprehensive recycling centre. As with SAE's other clubhouses, this is the place to go for specialized information, member-written trip reports and maps. Also has rooms for rent. Many churches close to visitors on Sunday. **Automóvil Club del Perú** ① *Av Sol 349, T224561, cusco@touringperu.com.pe,* has some maps. Motorists beware; many streets end in flights of steps. Apart from South American Explorers' comprehensive map, there are few good maps of Cuzco.

Visitors' tickets A combined entry ticket, called *Boleto Turístico de Cusco* (BTC), is available to most of the sites of main historical and cultural interest in and around the city, and costs as follows: 130 soles (US$45/€33.50) for all the sites and valid for 10 days; or 70 soles (US$24/€18) for either the museums in the city, or Sacsayhuaman, Qenqo, Puka Pukara and Tambo Machay, or Pisac, Ollantaytambo, Chinchero and Moray; the 70 soles ticket is valid for one day. The BTC can be bought at the offices of **Cosituc**, which issues the ticket, at ① *Av Sol 103, of 102, Galerías Turísticas, T261465, Mon-Sat 0800-1800, Sun 0800-1300, or Yuracpunku 79-A (east of centre, go along Recoleta), www.cosituc.gob.pe,* or at any of the sites included in the ticket. For students with an ISIC card the BTC costs 70 soles (US$24), which is only available at the Cosituc office upon presentation of the ISIC card. Take your ISIC card when visiting the sites, as some may ask to see it. Photography is not allowed in the churches, nor in museums.

    Entrance tickets for the Santo Domingo/Qoricancha, the Inka Museum (El Palacio del Almirante) and La Merced are sold separately, while the Cathedral (including El Triunfo and La Sagrada Familia), La Compañia, San Blas and the Museo de Arte Religioso del Arzobispado are included on a religious buildings ticket which costs 50 soles (US$17.75) and is valid for 10 days. Each of these sites may be visited individually. Machu Picchu ruins and Inca trail entrance tickets are sold at the **Ministerio de Cultura Cusco** ① *Av de la Cultura 238, Condominio Huáscar, T236061, www.drc-cusco.gob.pe, Mon-Fri 0715-1600, or electronically at http://boletajevirtual. drc-cusco.gob.pe or www.machupicchu.gob.pe.*

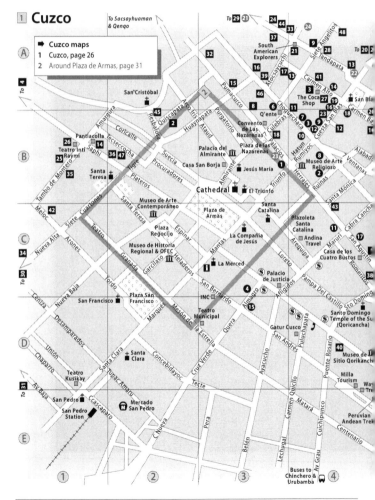

1 **Cuzco**

➡ **Cuzco maps**
1 Cuzco, page 26
2 Around Plaza de Armas, page 31

Security Police patrol the streets, trains and stations, but one should still be vigilant. On no account walk back to your hotel after dark from a bar or club, strangle muggings and rape do occur. For safety's sake, pay the US$1 taxi fare, but not just any taxi. Ask the club's doorman to get a taxi for you and make sure the taxi is licensed. Other areas in which to take care include San Pedro market (otherwise recommended), the San Cristóbal area, and at out-of-the-way ruins. Also take special care during Inti Raymi. The **Tourist Police**, C Saphi 510, T249665/ 221961. If you need a *denuncia* (a report for insurance purposes), which is available from the Banco de la Nación, they will type it out. Always go to the police when

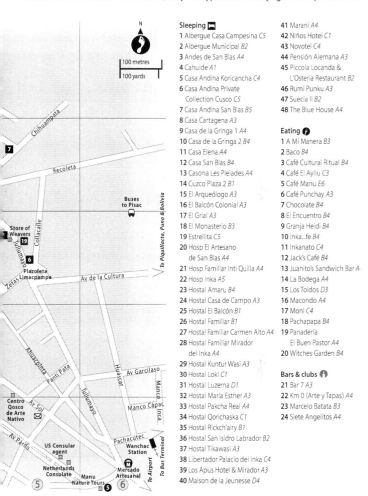

Sleeping 🛏
1 Albergue Casa Campesina *C5*
2 Albergue Municipal *B2*
3 Andes de San Blas *A4*
4 Cahuide *A1*
5 Casa Andina Koricancha *C4*
6 Casa Andina Private
   Collection Cusco *C5*
7 Casa Andina San Blas *B5*
8 Casa Cartagena *A3*
9 Casa de la Gringa 1 *A4*
10 Casa de la Gringa 2 *B4*
11 Casa Elena *A4*
12 Casa San Blas *B4*
13 Casona Les Pleiades *A4*
14 Cuzco Plaza 2 *B1*
15 El Arqueólogo *A3*
16 El Balcón Colonial *A3*
17 El Grial *A3*
18 El Monasterio *B3*
19 Estrellita *C5*
20 Hosp El Artesano
   de San Blas *A4*
21 Hosp Familiar Inti Quilla *A4*
22 Hosp Inka *A5*
23 Hostal Amaru *B4*
24 Hostal Casa de Campo *A3*
25 Hostal El Balcón *B1*
26 Hostal Familiar *B1*
27 Hostal Familiar Carmen Alto *A4*
28 Hostal Familiar Mirador
   del Inka *A4*
29 Hostal Kuntur Wasi *A3*
30 Hostal Loki *C1*
31 Hostal Luzerna *D1*
32 Hostal María Esther *A3*
33 Hostal Pakcha Real *A4*
34 Hostal Qorichaska *C1*
35 Hostal Rickch'aíry *B1*
36 Hostal San Isidro Labrador *B2*
37 Hostal Tikawasi *A3*
38 Libertador Palacio del Inka *C4*
39 Los Apus Hotel & Mirador *A3*
40 Maison de la Jeunesse *D4*
41 Marani *A4*
42 Niños Hotel *C1*
43 Novotel *C4*
44 Pensión Alemana *A3*
45 Piccola Locanda &
   L'Osteria Restaurant *B2*
46 Rumi Punku *A3*
47 Suecia II *B2*
48 The Blue House *A4*

Eating 🍴
1 A Mi Manera *B3*
2 Baco *B4*
3 Café Cultural Ritual *B4*
4 Café El Ayllu *C3*
5 Café Manu *E6*
6 Café Punchay *A3*
7 Chocolate *B4*
8 El Encuentro *B4*
9 Granja Heidi *B4*
10 Inka...fe *B4*
11 Inkanato *C4*
12 Jack's Café *B4*
13 Juanito's Sandwich Bar *A4*
14 La Bodega *A4*
15 Los Toldos *D3*
16 Macondo *A4*
17 Moni *C4*
18 Pachapapa *B4*
19 Panadería
   El Buen Pastor *A4*
20 Witches Garden *B4*

Bars & clubs 🍸
21 Bar 7 *A3*
22 Km 0 (Arte y Tapas) *A4*
23 Marcelo Batata *B3*
24 Siete Angelitos *A4*

Map labels:
N
100 metres
100 yards
Chihuampata
Recoleta
Buses to Pisac
Collacalle
Tullumayo
Zetas
Store of Weavers
Plazoleta Limacpampa
Av de la Cultura
Ahuacpinta
Panti Pata
Huascar
Av Garcilaso
Manco Cápac
Inka
Centro Qosco de Arte Nativo
Av Sol
Av Pardo
Manco Cápac
US Consular agent
Pachacutec
Wanchac Station
Netherlands Consulate
Manu Nature Tours
Mercado Artesanal
To Airport
To Bus Terminal
To Piquillacta, Puno & Bolivia
To Quillacta, Puno & Bolivia

robbed, even though it will cost you a bit of time. The Consumer Protection Bureau (**Indecopi**) is at Av Manco Inca 209, Wanchac, T252987, mmarroquin@indecopi.gob.pe. Toll free 0800-44040 (24-hour hotline, not available from payphones).

Sights → *For listings, see pages 33-53.*

The heart of the city in Inca days was *Huacaypata* (the place of tears) and *Cusipata* (the place of happiness), divided by a channel of the Saphi River. Today, Cusipata is Plaza Regocijo and Huacaypata is the Plaza de Armas, around which are colonial arcades and four churches. To the northeast is the early 17th-century baroque **Cathedral** ⓘ *US$9, open daily 1000-1800, Quechua mass is held 0500-0600.* It is built on the site of the Palace of Inca Wiracocha (*Kiswarcancha*). The high altar is solid silver and the original altar *retablo* behind it is a masterpiece of Andean wood carving. The earliest surviving painting of the city can be seen, depicting Cuzco during the 1650 earthquake. In the far right hand end of the church is an interesting local painting of the Last Supper replete with *cuy*, *chicha*, etc. In the sacristy are paintings of all the bishops of Cuzco. The choir stalls, by a 17th-century Spanish priest, are a magnificent example of colonial baroque art. The elaborate pulpit and the sacristy are also notable. Much venerated is the crucifix of El Señor de los Temblores, the object of many pilgrimages and viewed all over Peru as a guardian against earthquakes. The tourist entrance to the Cathedral is through the church of **La Sagrada Familia** (1733), which stands to its left as you face it. Its gilt main altar has been renovated. **El Triunfo** (1536), on its right of the Cathedral, is the first Christian church in Cuzco, built on the site of the Inca Roundhouse (the *Suntur Huasi*). It has a statue of the Virgin of the Descent, reputed to have helped the Spaniards repel Manco Inca when he besieged the city in 1536.

On the southeast side of the plaza is the beautiful **La Compañía de Jesús** ⓘ *US$3.55, or by religious buildings ticket, open daily 0900-1750*, built on the site of the Palace of the Serpents (*Amarucancha*, residence of Inca Huayna Capac) in the late 17th century. Its twin-towered exterior is extremely graceful, and the interior rich in fine murals, paintings and carved altars. Nearby is the **Santa Catalina** church ⓘ *Arequipa at Santa Catalina Angosta, daily 0900-1200, 1300-1700, except Fri 0900-1200, 1300-1600, joint ticket with Santo Domingo US$6*, convent and museum, built upon the foundations of the *Acllahuasi* (House of the Chosen Women). There are guided tours by English-speaking students; tip expected.

If you continue down Arequipa from Santa Catalina you come to Calle Maruri. Between this street at Santo Domingo is **Cusicancha** ⓘ *US$1.75, Mon-Fri 0730-1600, sometimes open at weekends*, an open space showing the layout of the buildings as they would have been in Inca times.

La Merced ⓘ *on Calle Márquez, church Mon-Fri 0800-1700, Sat 0900-1600; monastery and museum 1430-1700, except Sun, US$1*. The church was first built 1534 and rebuilt in the late 17th century. Attached is a very fine monastery with an exquisite cloister. Inside the church are buried Gonzalo Pizarro, half-brother of Francisco, and the two Almagros, father and son. The church is most famous for its jewelled monstrance, which is on view in the monastery's museum during visiting hours.

Much **Inca stonework** can be seen in the streets and most particularly in the Callejón Loreto, running southeast past La Compañía de Jesús from the main plaza. The walls of

Inca society

Cuzco was the capital of the Inca empire – one of the greatest planned societies the world has known – from its rise during the 11th century to its death in the early 16th century. (See John Hemming's *Conquest of the Incas* and B C Brundage's *Lords of Cuzco* and *Empire of the Inca*.) It was solidly based on other Peruvian civilizations which had attained great skill in textiles, building, ceramics and working in metal. Immemorially, the political structure of the Andean *indígena* had been the ayllu, the village community; it had its divine ancestor, worshipped household gods, was closely knit by ties of blood to the family and by economic necessity to the land, which was held in common. Submission to the ayllu was absolute, because it was only by such discipline that food could be obtained in an unsympathetic environment. All the domestic animals, the llama and alpaca and the dog, had long been tamed, and the great staple crops, maize and potatoes, established. What the Incas did – and it was a magnificent feat – was to conquer enormous territories and impose upon the variety of ayllus, through an unchallengeable central government, a willing spiritual and economic submission to the State. The common religion, already developed by the classical Tiwanaku culture, was worship of the Sun, whose vice-regent on earth was the absolute Sapa Inca. Around him, in the capital, was a religious and secular elite which never froze into a caste because it was open to talent. The elite was often recruited from chieftains defeated by the Incas; an effective way of reconciling local opposition. The mass of the people were subjected to rigorous planning. They were allotted land to work, for their group and

for the State; set various tasks (the making of textiles, pottery, weapons, ropes, etc) from primary materials supplied by the functionaries, or used in enlarging the area of cultivation by building terraces on the hill-sides. Their political organization was simple but effective. The family, and not the individual, was the unit. Families were grouped in units of 10, 100, 500, 1000, 10,000 and 40,000, each group with a leader responsible to the next largest group. The Sapa Inca crowned the political edifice; his four immediate counsellors were those to whom he allotted responsibility for the northern, southern, eastern and western regions (suyos) of the empire.

Equilibrium between production and consumption, in the absence of a free price mechanism and good transport facilities, must depend heavily upon statistical information. This the Incas raised to a high degree of efficiency by means of their quipus: a decimal system of recording numbers by knots in cords. Seasonal variations were guarded against by creating a system of state barns in which provender could be stored during years of plenty, to be used in years of scarcity. Statistical efficiency alone required that no one should be permitted to leave his home or his work. The loss of personal liberty was the price paid by the masses for economic security. In order to obtain information and to transmit orders quickly, the Incas built fine paved pathways along which couriers sped on foot. The whole system of rigorous control was completed by the greatest of all their monarchs, Pachacuti, who also imposed a common language, Quechua, as a further cementing force.

the *Acllahuasi* (House of the Chosen Women) are on one side, and of the *Amarucancha* on the other. There are also Inca remains in Calle San Agustín, to the east of the plaza. The stone of 12 angles is in Calle Hatun Rumiyoc halfway along its second block, on the right-hand side going away from the Plaza. The **Palacio Arzobispal** stands on Hatun Rumiyoc y Herrajes, two blocks northeast of Plaza de Armas. It was built on the site of the palace occupied in 1400. It contains the **Museo de Arte Religioso** ① *0800-1800, included on the religious buildings ticket, or US$5.35,* a collection of colonial paintings and furniture. The collection includes the paintings by the indigenous master, Diego Quispe Tito, of a 17th-century Corpus Christi procession that used to hang in the church of Santa Ana.

The **Palacio del Almirante**, just north of the Plaza de Armas, is impressive. It houses the **Museo Inka** ① *Cuesta del Almirante 103, T237380, Mon-Fri 0800-1900, Sat 0900-1600, US$3,* which is run by the Universidad San Antonio de Abad, the museum exhibits the development of culture in the region from pre-Inca, through Inca times to the present day: textiles, ceramics, metalwork, jewellery, architecture, technology. See the collection of miniature turquoise figures and other offerings to the gods. Weaving demonstrations are given in the courtyard. On the northwest side of the Plaza de las Nazarenas, No 231, is **Museo de Arte Precolombino** ① *www.map.org.pe, 0900-2200, US$7, US$3.50 with student card; under same auspices as the Larco Museum in Lima, MAP Café (see Eating, below),* housed in the **Casa Cabrera**. This beautiful museum is set around a spacious courtyard and contains many superb examples of pottery, metalwork (largely in gold and silver), wood carvings and shells from the Moche, Chimú, Paracas, Nazca and Inca cultures. There are some vividly rendered animistic designs, giving an insight into the way Peru's ancient people's viewed their world and the creatures that inhabited it. Every exhibit carries explanations in English and Spanish. Highly recommended. The **Convento de las Nazarenas**, also on Plaza de las Nazarenas, is now an annex of Orient Express' *Monasterio* hotel. You can see the Inca-colonial doorway with a mermaid motif, but ask permission to view the lovely 18th-century frescos inside. In the San Blas district, now firmly on the tourist map, the small church of **San Blas** ① *Carmen Bajo, 0800-1800, on the religious buildings ticket, or US$5.35* has a beautiful carved *mestizo* cedar pulpit, which is well worth seeing. See Shopping Local crafts, below.

Santo Domingo, southeast of the main Plaza, was built in the 17th century on the walls of the **Qoricancha**, **Temple of the Sun** ① *Mon-Sat 0830-1730, Sun 1400-1700 (closed holidays), US$3.55, or joint ticket with Santa Catalina US$6, English-speaking guides, tip of US$2-3 expected,* and from its stones. Excavation has revealed more of the five chambers of the Temple of the Sun, which shows the best Inca stonework to be seen in Cuzco. The Temple of the Sun was awarded to Juan Pizarro, the younger brother of Francisco, who willed it to the Dominicans after he had been fatally wounded in the Sacsayhuaman siege. The baroque cloister has been gutted to reveal four of the original chambers of the great Inca temple – two on the west have been partly reconstructed in a good imitation of Inca masonry. The finest stonework is in the celebrated curved wall beneath the west end of Santo Domingo. This was rebuilt after the 1950 earthquake, at which time a niche that once contained a shrine was found at the inner top of the wall. Below the curved wall was a garden of gold and silver replicas of animals, maize and other plants. Excavations have revealed Inca baths below here, and more Inca retaining walls. The other superb stretch of late Inca stonework is in C Ahuacpinta outside the temple, to the east or left as you enter.

② Around Plaza de Armas

➡ Cuzco maps
1 Cuzco, page 26
2 Around Plaza de Armas, page 31

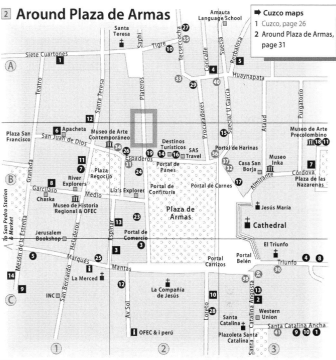

Plateros detail

50 metres
50 yards

Sleeping 🛏
1 Andean Wings A1
2 Casa Andina Catedral C3
3 Casa Andina Plaza C2
4 El Procurador del Cusco A2
5 Hostal Resbalosa A3
6 Hostal Royal Frankenstein B1
7 La Casona Inkaterra B3
8 Marqueses B1
9 Pariwana C1
10 Pensión Loreto C2
11 Royal Inka I B1
12 Royal Inka II A1
13 Sonesta Posadas del Inca B2
14 The Point C1

Eating 🍴
1 Al Grano C3
2 Amaru Plateros detail
3 Bembos C2
4 Bistrot 370 C3
5 Café El Ayllu B3
6 Café Hallíy Plateros detail
7 Chicha, El Truco & Taberna del Truco B1
8 Cicciolina C3
9 Dolce Vita C3
10 El Encuentro A2, C3
11 Fallen Angel B3
12 Fusiones & Maikhana C2
13 Incanto & Greens Organic C3
14 Inka Grill B2
15 Kusikuy B3
16 La Retama B2
17 Limo B3
18 MAP Café B3
19 Pachacútec Grill & Bar B2
20 Pucará Plateros detail
21 The Muse Plateros detail
22 The Real McCoy Plateros detail
23 Trotamundos B2
24 Tunupa B2
25 Tupananchis C1
26 Varayoc B2
27 Víctor Victoria A2
28 Witches Garden C2
29 Yaku Mama A2

Bars & clubs 🍸
30 Cross Keys Pub A2
31 El Garabato Video Music Club B2
32 Extreme B3
33 Indigo A2
34 Kamikaze B2
35 Los Perros A2
36 Mama Africa B2
37 Mythology B3
38 Norton Rat's Tavern C3
39 Paddy Flaherty's C3
40 Roots A2
41 Rosie O'Grady's C3
42 Ukuku's Plateros detail

Museo de Sitio Qorikancha (formerly Museo Arqueológico) ① *Av Sol, Mon-Sat 0900-1200, 1300-1700, Sun 0800-1400, entrance by BTC* is under the garden below Santo Domingo. It contains a limited collection of pre-Columbian items, Spanish paintings of imitation Inca royalty dating from the 18th century, and photos of the excavation of Qoricancha. The palace called **Casa de los Cuatro Bustos**, whose colonial doorway is at San Agustín 400, is now the **Hotel Libertador**. The general public can enter the Hotel from Plazoleta Santo Domingo, opposite the Temple of the Sun/Qoricancha.

Museo de Historia Regional ① *in the Casa Garcilaso, Jr Garcilaso y Heladeros, 0730-1700, entrance by BTC* tries to show the evolution of the Cuzqueño school of painting. It also contains Inca agricultural implements, colonial furniture and paintings. **San Francisco** ① *on Plaza San Francisco, 3 blocks southwest of the Plaza de Armas, 0600-0800, 1800-2000,* is an austere church reflecting many indigenous influences. Its monastery is being rebuilt and may be closed. **San Pedro** ① *in front of the San Pedro market, Mon-Sat 1000-1200, 1400-1700,* was built in 1688. Its two towers were made from stones brought from an Inca ruin.

Above Cuzco, on the road up to Sacsayhuamán, is **San Cristóbal**, built to his patron saint by Cristóbal Paullu Inca. The church's atrium has been restored and there is a sidewalk access to the Sacsayhuamán Archaeological Park. North of San Cristóbal, you can see the 11 doorway-sized niches of the great Inca wall of the **Palacio de Colcampata**, which was the residence of Manco Inca before he rebelled against the Spanish and fled to Vilcabamba.

Sacsayhuaman
① *Daily 0700-1730; free student guides, give them a tip.*
There are some magnificent Inca walls in this ruined ceremonial centre, on a hill in the northern outskirts. The Incaic stones are hugely impressive. The massive rocks weighing up to 130 tons are fitted together with absolute perfection. Three walls run parallel for over 360 m and there are 21 bastions. Sacsayhuaman was thought for centuries to be a fortress, but the layout and architecture suggest a great sanctuary and temple to the Sun, which rises exactly opposite the place previously believed to be the Inca's throne – which was probably an altar, carved out of the solid rock. Broad steps lead to the altar from either side. The hieratic, rather than the military, hypothesis was supported by the discovery in 1982 of the graves of priests, who would have been unlikely to be buried in a fortress. The precise functions of the site, however, will probably continue to be a matter of dispute as very few clues remain, owing to its steady destruction. The site is about a 30-minute walk up Pumacurco from Plaza de las Nazarenas.

Along the road from Sacsayhuaman to Pisac, past a radio station, is the temple and amphitheatre of **Qenqo** with some of the finest examples of Inca stone carving *in situ*, especially inside the large hollowed-out stone that houses an altar. On the same road are **Puka Pukara** (Red Fort, but more likely to have been a *tambo*, or post-house), wonderful views; and the spring shrine of **Tambo Machay**, which is in excellent condition. Water still flows by a hidden channel out of the masonry wall, straight into a little rock pool traditionally known as the Inca's bath. Take a guide to the sites and visit in the morning for the best photographs. Carry your multi-site ticket, there are roving ticket inspectors. You can visit the sites on foot, a pleasant walk of at least half a day through the countryside; take water, sun protection, and watch out for dogs. Alternatively, take the Pisac bus up to Tambo Machay (US$0.70) and walk back, or arrange a horseback tour with an agency.

Cuzco listings

For Sleeping and Eating price codes and other relevant information, see pages 10-14.

● Sleeping

Cuzco *p24, maps p26 and p31*
In Jun and other busy times, double-booking occurs so double-check reservations. Book more expensive hotels well in advance, particularly for the week or so around Inti Raymi, when prices are greatly increased. Prices given are for the high season in Jun-Aug. When there are fewer tourists hotels may drop their prices by as much as half. Always check for discounts. Be wary of unlicensed hotel agents for medium-priced hotels who are often misleading about details; their local nickname is *jalagringos* (gringo pullers), or *piratas*. Taxis and tourist minibuses meet new arrivals and (should) take you to the hotel of your choice for US$1, but be insistent. Since it is cold here and many hotels have no heating, ask for an *estufa*, a heater which some places will provide for an extra charge. Many places will store your luggage when you go trekking, but always check valuables and possessions before and after depositing them with hotel/hostel staff.

Around the Plaza de Armas
$$$$ Andean Wings, Siete Cuartones 225, T243166, www.andeanwingshotel.com. In a restored 17-th century house, in the same group as Casa de la Gringa and Another Planet, 5-star, intimate, suites, some with jacuzzi, are individually designed (one is accessible for the disabled), restaurant and bar.
$$$$ The Fallen Angel Guest House, Plaza Nazarenas 221, T258184, www.fallen angelincusco.com/theguesthouse. A 4-room luxury hotel above the restaurant of the same name. Each suite is decorated in its own lavish style (with living room, dining room,

bathroom, feather duvets, heating), very comfortable and a far cry from the usual adaptation of colonial buildings elsewhere in the city.With all amenities, including Wi-Fi, excellent service.
$$$$ La Casona Inkaterra, Plazoleta Las Nazarenas 113, T223010, www.inkaterra.com. A private, colonial-style boutique hotel in a converted 16th-century mansion, built on the site of Manco Cápac's palace. 11 exclusive suites, all facilities, concierge service with activities and excursions, highly-regarded and the height of luxury (prices from US$600).
$$$ Brituvian Inn, Suecia 345, T245858, www.brituvianinn.com. Boutique hotel in the former residence of Gonzalo Pizarro. Rooms have flat screen cable TV, heating, minibar, safe, some even have the only water beds in Cuzco, with coffee shop and piano bar.
$$$ Casa Andina Classic – Cusco Plaza, Portal Espinar 142, T231733, www.casa-andina.com. 40-room hotel near plaza, cable TV, private bathroom, internet access, ATM and safe deposit box. Equally recommendable are **Casa Andina Koricancha**, San Agustín 371, T252633, **Casa Andina Catedral**, Santa Catalina Angosta 149, T233661, and the **Casa Andina San Blas**, Chihuampata 278, San Blas, T263964, all of which are in the same vein.
$$$ Loreto Boutique Hotel, Pasaje Loreto 115, T226352, www.loretoboutique hotel.com. Price includes buffet breakfast. Great location; 12 spacious rooms with original Inca walls, upgraded to "boutique" status. Laundry service, will help organize travel services including guides and taxis, free airport pick-up.
$$$ Sonesta Posadas del Inca, Portal Espinar 108, T227061, www.sonesta.com. Includes buffet breakfast, warmly decorated rooms with heating and cable TV, safe, some rooms on 3rd floor with view of Plaza, very helpful, English spoken, restaurant with Andean food, excellent service.

$$ Marqueses, Garcilaso 256, T264249, www.hotelmarqueses.com. Recently restored in Spanish colonial style, with 16/17th-century style religious paintings and 2 lovely courtyards. Rooms have heavy curtains and some are a little dark; luxury rooms have bath. Buffet breakfast.

$ pp EcoPackers, Santa Teresa 375, T231800, www.EcoPackersperu.com. Ecologically friendly, well-regarded hostal in a colonial casona, double rooms with en suite or dorms for 4-18 people, communal kitchen, games room, bar, large-screen TV room, Wi-Fi, garage for bicycles or motorcycles.

$ Hostal Resbalosa, Resbalosa 494, T224839, www.hostalresbalosa.com. Cheaper without bath, hot water in the mornings and evenings, ask for a room with a view, luggage stored, laundry facilities, full breakfast extra.

$ Hostal Royal Frankenstein, San Juan de Dios 260, 2 blocks from the Plaza de Armas, T236999, www.hostal-frankenstein.net. Eccentric place but a frequent favourite, cheaper with shared bath, hot water, safe, kitchen, free Wi-Fi, small charge for internet and laundry, German-owned, German and English spoken.

$ pp Pariwana, Mesón de la Estrella 136, T233751, www.pariwana-hostel.com. Variety of rooms in a converted colonial mansion with courtyard, from doubles with bath to dorms sleeping 11 or more, also girls only dorm, restaurant, bar/lounge, with breakfast, kitchen, internet and Wi-Fi, lockers, English spoken, lots of activities.

$ pp Pirwa Hostels, T244315, www.pirwa hostelscusco.com. This chain of hostels offers a range of rooms from private doubles with bath to dorms, in colonial buildings, breakfast included, internet, use of kitchen, 24-hr reception: **Pirwa Suecia**, Suecia 300, the B&B branch; **Pirwa Posada del Corregidor**, Portal de Panes 151 (Plaza de Armas); **Pirwa Backpackers San Blas**, Carmen Alto 283, and **Pirwa Backpackers Colonial**, Plaza San Francisco 360.

$ pp The Point, Mesón de la Estrella 172, T252266, www.thepointhostels.com. Dormitory accommodation, also has doubles, includes breakfast, free internet, hot showers, good party atmosphere.

Beyond the Plaza, including San Blas
$$$$ Casa Andina Private Collection
Cusco, Plazoleta de Limacpampa Chico 473, T232610, www.casa-andina.com. The most upmarket and comfortable in this group, in a 16th-century mansion with 4 courtyards, enriched oxygen available in the rooms, plus a gourmet restaurant serving local cuisine and a bar with an extensive pisco collection.

$$$$ Casa Cartagena, Pumacurco 336, T261171, www.casacartagena.com. In a converted monastery and national heritage building, super-deluxe facilities with Italian design and colonial features, 4 levels of suite from US$700 to US$1,800 a night, La Chola restaurant, extensive Qoya spa, enriched oxygen system, Wi-Fi, and all services to be expected in a Luxury Properties group hotel.

$$$$ El Monasterio, C Palacios 136, Plazoleta Nazarenas, T604000, www.monasteriohotel. com. 5-star, beautifully restored Seminary of San Antonio Abad (a Peruvian National Historical Landmark), including the Baroque chapel, spacious comfortable rooms with all facilities (some rooms offer an oxygen-enriched atmosphere to help clients acclimatize), very helpful staff, price includes buffet breakfast (open to non-residents, will fill you up for the rest of the day), good restaurants, lunch and dinner à la carte, business centre with internet for guests.

$$$$ Libertador Palacio del Inka, Plazoleta Santo Domingo 259, T231961, www.libertador.com.pe. 5-star, price includes buffet breakfast, good, especially the service, warm and bright, *Inti Raymi* restaurant, excellent, live music in the evening.

$$$$ Novotel, San Agustín 239, T581033, www.novotel.com. 4-star, cheaper in modern section; price includes buffet breakfast, converted from colonial house with beautiful glass-roofed courtyard, spacious rooms, cable TV, central heating, 2 restaurants and a French chef.

$$$ Casa San Blas, Tocuyeros 566, just off Cuesta San Blas, T237900, www.casasanblas.com. An international-standard boutique hotel with bright, airy rooms decorated with traditional textiles. Breakfast, served in the **Tika Bistro** downstairs, and Wi-Fi are included. Pleasant balcony with good views, attentive service.

$$$ Casona Les Pleiades, Tandapata 116, T506430, www.casona-pleiades.com. Small guesthouse in renovated colonial house, cosy and warm, generous hosts, hot water, cable TV, Wi-Fi, roof terrace, video lounge and book exchange, café, free airport pickup with reservation, lots of info.

$$$ El Arqueólogo, Pumacurco 408, T232569, www.hotelarqueologo.com. Includes breakfast, hot water, heating extra, helpful, French and English spoken, will store luggage, garden, cafeteria and kitchen. Also has a B&B hostal t Carmen Alto 294, T232760, **$$$-$$**. Vida Tours, Ladrillo 425, T227750, www.vidatours.com. Traditional and adventure tourism.

$$$ Hostal El Balcón, Tambo de Montero 222, T236738, www.balconcusco.com. With breakfast, homely atmosphere, very welcoming, quiet, laundry, sauna, bar, meals on request, English spoken, wonderful views, beautiful garden.

$$$ Los Apus Hotel & Mirador, Atocsaycuchi 515 y Choquechaca, San Blas, T264243, www.losapushotel.com. Includes breakfast and airport transfer, full of character, very smart, central heating, disabled facilities.

$$$ Piccola Locanda, Resbalosa 520, T252551, www.piccolalocanda.com. Steep walk up from the Plaza de Armas, colourful Peruvian/Italian run B&B. Rooftop terrace with 360º views, excellent restaurant **L'Osteria**, a TV room, pleasant courtyard. Some rooms without bath. Associated with

Perú Etico tour company and 2 children's projects. Recommended.

$$$ Rumi Punku, Choquechaca 339, T221102, www.rumipunku.com. A genuine Inca doorway leading to a sunny courtyard, comfortable rooms, helpful staff, safe. Highly recommended.

$$$ Sonesta Hotel Cusco, Av Sol 954, T581200, www.sonesta.com/cusco/. Sonesta has refurbished the old Hotel Savoy, with modern, comfortable rooms, views of the city and surrounding mountains, cable TV,Wi-Fi, restaurant serving classic Peruvian cuisine and bar.

$$$-$$ Andenes al Cielo, Choquechaca 176, T222237, www.andenesalcielo.com. At tht foot of the San Blas district, 15 rooms in renovated historic home, all with either balconies or patios, flat screen TV and heating. Buffet breakfast incuded, free airport pick up, Wi-Fi, luggage storage, gym. Recommended.

$$$-$$ Cahuide, Saphi 845, T222771, www.hotelcahuide-cusco.com. Discount for long stay, hot water, good rooms, quiet, good laundry service, storage facilities, helpful, good value breakfasts.

$$$-$$ Hostal Tikawasi, Tandapata 491, T231609, www.tikawasi.com. Includes breakfast, heating, family-run, lovely garden overlooking the city. Stylish rooms with good views, comfortable beds.

$$ Andes de San Blas, Carmen Alto 227, T242346, www.andesdesanblas.com. Family run, excellent location with good views from rooftop terrace and some rooms. Basic breakfast included, internet access, can arrange budget tours. Generally good.

$$ Casa Elena, Choquechaca 162, T241202, www.casaelenacusco.com. French/Peruvian hostel, very comfortable, good choice, breakfast.

$$ El Grial, Carmen Alto 112, T223012, www.hotelelgrial.com. Family-run, 2 star hostel, in a 17th-century building, all rooms with cable TV, coffee shop, internet, laundry service and free luggage storage.

$$ Flying Dog Hostel, Choquechaca 469, T253997, www.flyingdogperu.com. Shared and private rooms and family suites, kitchen facilities, bar, living room with TV and DVD, buffet breakfast included.

$$ Goldie's Guest House, Saphi 456, T01-242 5534, www.goldiesguesthouse.com. Self-contained accommodation (preferably long-term for a week or a month) in a pleasant and safe environment, 250 m from Plaza de Armas.

$$ Hostal Amaru, Cuesta San Blas 541, T225933, www.amaruhostal.com. (**$** with shared bath). Price includes breakfast and airport/train/bus pick-up. Oxygen, kitchen for use in the evenings, laundry, book exchange. Rooms around a pretty colonial courtyard, good beds, pleasant, relaxing, some Inca walls. Also has **$$ Hostal Amaru II**, Chihuampata 642, San Blas, www.amaruhostal2.com, and **Hostería de Anita**, Alabado 525-5, T225933, amaruhostal3@speedy.com.pe, safe, quiet, good breakfast.

$$ Hostal Casa de Campo, Tandapata 296-B (at the end of the street), T244404, www.hotel casadecampo.com. Some of the highest rooms have a *lot* of steps up to them, hot water, includes Continental breakfast and airport/bus/rail transfer with reservations, discount for longer stays, 10% discount for Footprint book owners, safe deposit box, sun terrace, quiet and relaxing, all rooms have great views, Dutch and English spoken, take a taxi there after dark.

$$ Hostal Kuntur Wasi, Tandapata 352-A, San Blas, T227570, www.kunturws.com. Great views, cheaper without bath, use of kitchen and laundry (both extra), owner speaks a bit of English and is very helpful and welcoming, a pleasant place to stay.

$$ Hostal Loki, Cuesta Santa Ana 601, T243705, www.lokihostel.com/en/cusco. Huge hostel in a restored viceroy's residence on the steep Cuesta Santa Ana, dorms and rooms set around a beautiful courtyard, comfortable beds, hot water, free internet. A great meeting place.

$$ Hostal María Esther, Pumacurco 516, T224382, http://hostalmariaesther. free.fr/. Very comfortable, helpful, includes breakfast, garden.

$$ Marani, Carmen Alto 194, San Blas, T249462, www.hostalmarani.com. Full of character, set around a courtyard, breakfast available, Dutch-owned hostel associated with Hope Foundation (www.stichtinghope.org), which builds schools, helps teachers and hospitals, good value.

$$ Niños Hotel, Meloc 442, T231424, www.ninos hotel.com. Hot water, excellent breakfast extra, restaurant, laundry service, luggage store, Dutch, English, German and French spoken, run as part of the Dutch foundation *Niños Unidos Peruanos* and all profits are invested in projects to help street children. Also has *Niños 2*, on C Fierro, with all the same features, and the **$$$ Niños Hacienda** in Huasao, 25 mins from Cuzco, with rooms and bungalows, breakfast and dinner included, also weekend packages.

$$ Pensión Alemana, Tandapata 260, San Blas, T226861, www.cuzco.com.pe. Swiss owned, welcoming, price includes American breakfast, comfortable, discount in low season.

$$-$ Hostal Qorichaska, Nueva Alta 458, some distance from centre, T228974, www.qoricha skaperu.com. Includes breakfast, use of well-equipped kitchen, internet and safe. Also has dorms, mixed and women only, **$** pp without breakfast. Laundry service. Rooms are clean and sunny, the older ones have traditional balconies.

$$-$ The Walk on Inn, Suecia 504, T235065, www.walkoninn.com. 2 blocks from the Plaza, private or shared bathrooms, breakfast US$2, free internet and Wi-Fi, laundry service, free airport and bus station pick up.

$ Albergue Casa Campesina, Av Tullumayo 274, T233466, www.cbc.org.pe/ casacampesina.com Includes breakfast, shared bath, lovely place, funds support the Casa Campesina organization (www.cbc.org. pe/casacamp/), which is linked to local campesina communities (see also Store of the Weavers under Shopping, below). 23% discount for SAE members.

$ pp The Blue House, Kiskapata 291 (parallel and above Tandapata), T242407, www.aschisite02.activesbs.co.uk. Cosy hostal, good value. Reductions for longer stays, includes breakfast, DVDs, shared kitchen, great views.

$ Casa de La Gringa 1, Tandapata y Pasñapacana 148, T241168, www.casa delagringa.com. Also **Casa de la Gringa 2**, Carmen Bajo 226, both in San Blas, with each room individually decorated, lots of art and colour, 24-hr hot water, Wi-Fi, cable TV, DVD, CD player in the common areas, heaters in the main lounges. See also **Another Planet** (Tour operators), below.

$ El Balcón Colonial, Choquechaca 350, T238129, balconcolonial@hotmail.com. Accommodation for 11 people in this family house, hot showers, breakfast, kitchen and laundry facilities all extra, comfortable, safe, generous hosts.

$ Estrellita, Av Tullumayo 445, parte Alta, T234134. Includes breakfast, basic kitchen for guests, most rooms with shared bath, 2 with private bath, basic but excellent value, safe parking available for bikes.

$ Hospedaje El Artesano de San Blas, Suytucato 790, San Blas, T263968, mano sandinas@yahoo.com. Many bright and airy rooms, taxis leave you at Plaza San Blas, then it's a steep walk uphill for 5-10 mins.

$ Hospedaje Inka, Suytuccato 848, T231995, http://hospedajeinka.weebly.com. Taxis leave you at Plaza San Blas, walk steeply uphill for 5-10 mins, or phone the hostal. Cheaper without bath, breakfast included in price. Wonderful views, spacious rooms, very helpful owner, Américo.

$ Hostal Familiar, Saphi 661, T239353. Popular hostal in a colonial house, hot water, good beds, luggage store extra.

$ Hostal Familiar Mirador del Inka, Tandapata 160, off Plaza San Blas, T261384, www.miradordelinka.info. Cheaper without bath, hot water, laundry, the son Edwin rents trekking equipment.

$ Hostal Killipata, Killichapata 238, just off Tambo de Montero, T236668, www.cusco. net/killipata/. Cheaper in shared rooms. Family-run lodging with good showers, hot water and fully equipped kitchen. Breakfast is US$2 extra.

$ Hostal Pakcha Real, Tandapata 300, San Blas, T237484, www.hostalpakchareal.com. Family run, hot water, relaxed, cheaper without bath. Breakfast, cooking and laundry facilities extra. Airport/train/bus pick-up, but call ahead if arriving late.

$ Yamanyá Backpackers, San Andrés 269, T224473, www.yamanya.com. New hostal with shared and private rooms, breakfast included, Wi-Fi, common areas with HD TV and DVD and – a rarity in Cuzco –a swimming pool.

Youth hostels

$ Albergue Municipal, Quiscapata 240, San Cristóbal, T252506, albergue@ municusco.gob.pe. Dormitories and double rooms, great views, bar, cafeteria, laundry, discount for members, luggage store.

$ El Procurador del Cusco, Coricalle 440, Prolongación Procuradores, T243559, http://hostelprocuradordelcusco.blogspot.co m. Price includes use of the basic kitchen (no fridge) and laundry area, cheaper without bath, basic rooms, but upstairs is better, helpful, good value. Recommended.

$ Maison de la Jeunesse (affiliated to HI), Av Sol, Cuadra 5, Pasaje Grace, Edif San Jorge (down a small side street opposite Qoricancha) T235617, www.hostelling cuscoperu.com. Price is for a double room and includes bath and breakfast. A bed in a dorm with shared bath is cheaper, breakfast included; HI discount. TV and video room, internet, Wi-Fi, lockers, cooking facilities and hot water.

Cuzco *p24, maps p26 and p31*
Around the Plaza de Armas
There are many good cheap restaurants on Procuradores, Plateros and Tecseccocha.

$$$ Bistrot 370, Triunfo 370, p 2, T224908. 'Fusion' cuisine, menu with Peruvian and Oriental touches, smart and highly regarded, good bar and wine list, cosy seating areas.

$$$ Chicha, Plaza Regocijo 261, p 2 (above El Truco), T240520, daily 1200-2400. Specializes in regional dishes created by restaurateur Gastón Acurio (see under Lima, Eating), Peruvian cuisine of the highest standards in a renovated colonial house, at one time the royal mint, tastefully decorated, open-to-view kitchen, bar with a variety of pisco sours, good service.

$$$ Cicciolina, Triunfo 393, 2nd floor, T239510. Sophisticated cooking focusing largely on Italian/ Mediterranean cuisine, impressive wine list. Good atmosphere, great for a special occasion.

$$$ El Truco, Plaza Regocijo 261. Open 0900-0100, buffet lunch 1200-1500. Excellent local and international dishes, nightly folk music at 2045, next door is **Taberna del Truco**.

$$$ Fallen Angel, Plazoleta Nazarenas 320, T258184. International and Novo Andino gourmet cuisine, great steaks, genuinely innovative interior design, worth checking out their events. Sun from 1500.

$$$ Fusiones, Av El Sol 106, T233341, in the new commercial centre La Merced, 2nd floor. Open 1100-2300. Novo Andino and international cuisine in a chic contemporary setting, fine wines.

$$$ Incanto, Santa Catalina Angosta 135, T254753. Open daily 1100-2400. Under same ownership as Inka Grill and with the same standards, restaurant has Inca stone work and serves Italian dishes (pastas, grilled meats, pizzas), and desserts, accompanied by an extensive wine list. Also Peruvian delicatessen.

$$$ Inka Grill, Portal de Panes 115, Plaza de Armas, T262992. Specializing in Novo Andino cuisine, also homemade pastas, wide vegetarian selection, live music, excellent coffee and homemade pastries 'to go'.

$$$ Kusikuy, Suecia 339, T292870. Open 0800-2300 Mon-Sat. Local, national and international dishes, good service, set lunch unbeatable value at only US$2.

$$$ La Cosa Nostra, Plateros 358A, p 2, T232992, open 1200-2300. Sicilian/Peruvian owned Italian place with good food and service, à la carte, wine list, unpretentious and intimate.

$$$ La Retama, Portal de Panes 123, 2nd floor, T226372. Good food (also Novo Andino) and service, live music and dance, art exhibitions.

$$$ Limo, Portal de Carnes 236, T240668. On 2nd floor of a colonial mansion overlooking the Plaza de Armas, Peruvian cuisine of the highest standard, with strong emphasis on fish and seafood, fine pisco bar, good service and atmosphere.

$$$ MAP Café, in Museo de Arte Precolombino, Plaza de las Nazarenas 231. Café by day (1000-1830), from 1830 to 2200 serves superb international and Peruvian-Andean cuisine, innovative children's menu, minimalist design and top-class service.

$$$ Pachacútec Grill and Bar, Portal de Panes 105, Plaza de Armas. International cuisine, seafood and Italian specialities, folk music nightly.

$$$ Pisku'o, Portal Belén 115, T231782. Entrance near the Gato's Market on Plaza de Armas, on 2nd floor with great views from the balcony of the colonial churches, trendy new restaurant, nice selection of piqueos, wines and cocktails.

$$$ Tunupa, Portal Confiturias 233, p 2, Plaza de Armas. Large restaurant, small balcony overlooking Plaza, international, Peruvian and Novo Andino cuisine, good buffet US$15, nicely decorated, cocktail lounge, live music and dance at 2030.

$$$ Tupananchis, Portal Mantas 180, T245159. Tasty Novo Andino and Fusion cuisine in a sophisticated atmosphere. Recommended.

$$ Al Grano, Santa Catalina Ancha 398, T228032. Authentic Asian dishes, menu changes daily, excellent food, excellent coffee, vegetarian choices, open 1000-2100, closed on Sun.

$$ El Batan del Inka, Hatun Rumiyoc 487, p 2, T601304, www.bookingbox.org/ elbatandelinka. Specializes in Peruvian food, also good vegetarian and international menu.

$$ Greens Organic, Santa Catalina Angosta 135, upstairs, T243379. Exclusively organic, but not wholly vegetarian, ingredients in fusion cuisine and a fresh daily buffet, very good.

$$ Pucará, Plateros 309. Mon-Sat 1230-2200. Peruvian and international food (no language skills required as a sample plate of their daily menu is placed in the window at lunchtime), nice atmosphere.

$$ The Real McCoy, Plateros 326, 2nd floor, T261111. A retreat for homesick Brits and Aussies, the full English and good value breakfast buffet, English classics for dinner, puddings too. Wi-Fi, comfy sofas and well stocked book exchange.

$$ Sara, Santa Catalina Ancha 370, T261691. Vegetarian-friendly organic café bistro, stylish and modern setting, menu includes both traditional Peruvian dishes as well as pasta and other international dishes.

$$ Two Nations, Huaynapata 410 y Suecia, T240198. Comfortable restaurant run by an Australian/Peruvian couple. Fresh food, cooked to order, from alpaca steaks to burgers or pizza, good value, large portions. Second location at Arequipa 265 has a courtyard open for lunch in the restored Túpac Inca Yupanqui Cultural Centre, which shows contemporary local art.

$$-$ Circus Restobar, Santa Teresa 351, T222461. Great food, tasty cocktailss, games and lots of 'toys', even the bathrooms are fun! Themost entertaining dining option in Cuzco,

games for kids make this a great spot for families as well as couples.

$ El Encuentro, Santa Catalina Ancha 384, Choquechaca 136 and Tigre 130. One of the best value eateries in Cuzco, 3 courses of good healthy vegan food and a drink for US$2, very busy at lunchtime.

$ El Fogón, Plateros 365. Huge local *menú del día*, good solid food at reasonable prices. Very popular.

$ Víctor Victoria, Tecseccocha 466, T252854. Israeli and local dishes, first-class breakfasts, good value.

Cafés

Amaru, Plateros 325, p 2. Limitless coffee and tea, great bread and juices, even on ´non-buffet´ breakfasts, colonial balcony. Also has bar.

Café El Ayllu, Almagro 133,T232357, and Marqués 263, T255078. Classical/folk music, good atmosphere, superb range of milk products, wonderful apple pastries, good selection for breakfast, great juices, quick service.

Café Halliy, Plateros 363. Popular meeting place, especially for breakfast, good for comments on guides, has good snacks and 'copa Halliy' (fruit, muesli, yoghurt, honey and chocolate cake), also good vegetarian *menú* and set lunch.

Café Perla, Santa Catalina Ancha 304, on the plazoleta, T774130. Extensive menu of light meals, sandwiches, desserts and coffee, including beans for sale roasted on the premises. Popular.

Dolce Vita, Santa Catalina Ancha 366. Delicious Italian ice cream, open 1000-2100.

La Bondiet, Márquez y Heladeros and Plateros 363. Clean, simple café with a huge selection of sweet and savoury pastries, empanadas, good sandwiches, juices and coffee.

La Tertulia, Procuradores 44, p 2. Open until 2300. Breakfast served 0630-1300, includes muesli, bread, yoghurt, eggs, juice and coffee, all you can eat for US$3, superb value, vegetarian buffet daily 18-2200, set dinner and salad bar for US$3.50, also fondue and gourmet meals, book exchange, newspapers, classical music.

Trotamundos, Portal Comercio 177, p 2. Open Mon-Sat 0800-2400. Balcony overlooking the plaza, nice atmosphere, especially at night with open fire, good coffees and cakes, safe salads, internet service.

Yahuu Juice Bar, Marqués 200. Fresh inexpensive juices and smoothies as well as sandwiches.

Yaku Mama, Procuradores 397. Good for breakfast, unlimited fruit and coffee.

Beyond the Plaza, including San Blas

$$$ A Mi Manera, Triunfo 393, T222219. Imaginative Novo Andino cuisine with open kitchen. Great hospitality and atmosphere.

$$$ Baco, Ruinas 465, T242808. Wine bar and bistro-style restaurant, same owner as *Cicciolina*. Specializes in BBQ and grilled meats, also veggie dishes, pizzas and good wines. Unpretentious and comfy, groups welcome.

$$$ Pachapapa, Plazoleta San Blas 120, opposite church of San Blas, T241318. A beautiful patio restaurant in a colonial house, good Cusqueña and other dishes, at night diners can sit in their own, private colonial dining room, attentive staff. Recommended.

$$$-$$ Divina Comedia, Pumacurco 406, T437640. Open daily 1230-1500, 1830-2300. An elegant restaurant just 1 block from the Monasterio hotel, diners are entertained by classical piano and singing. Friendly atmosphere with comfortable seating, perfect for a special night out, reasonable prices.

$$ Inka Panaka, Tandapata 140, T235034. Artistic flair, gallery of local artists' work. Novo Andina cuisine, and tasty innovative treats. Several vegetarian options, also breakfast.

$$ Inkanato, San Agustín 280, T222926. Good food, staff dressed in Inca outfits and dishes made only with ingredients known in Inca times, calls itself a "living museum".

$$ Jack's Café, Choquechaca y San Blas, T806960. Excellent varied menu, generous portions, relaxed atmosphere, can get very busy at lunchtime, expect a queue in high season.

$$ Justina, Palacios 110. Open Mon-Sat from 1800. Good value, good quality pizzería, with wine bar. It's at the back of a patio.

$$ La Bodega, Carmen Alto 146, San Blas. Snug Dutch and Peruvian-owned café/restaurant, good food, salads, drinks.

$$ Los Toldos, Almagro 171 and San Andrés 219. Grilled chicken, fries and salad bar, also *trattoria* with homemade pasta and pizza, delivery T229829.

$$ Macondo, Cuesta San Blas 571, T229415. Interesting restaurant with an imaginative menu, good food, well-furnished, gay friendly.

$$-$ Aldea Yanapay, Ruinas 415, p 2. Good café serving breakfast, lunch and dinner. Run by a charity which supports children's homes (www.aldeayanapay.org).

$ Café Punchay, Choquechaca 229, T261504, www.cafe-punchay.de. German-owned vegetarian restaurant, with a variety of pasta and potato dishes, good range of wines and spirits, large screen for international sports and you can bring a DVD for your own private movie showing.

$ Inka...fé, Choquechaca 131-A and Espaderos 142, T258073. Great food and value in a nice setting, English spoken.

Cafés

Chocolate, Choquechaca 162. Good for coffee and cakes, but don't miss the gourmet chocolates.

Cositas Café y Arte, Pasaje Inca Roca 108 and 110, T236410. Inventive local cuisine in a small, art-filled café. Profits support local social projects such as arts and crafts which are on sale in the café.

Granja Heidi, Cuesta San Blas 525, T238383. Delicious yoghurt, granola, ricotta cheese and honey and other great breakfast options, vegetarian dishes.

Juanito's Sandwich Café, Qanchipata 596. Great grilled veggie and meaty burgers and sandwiches, coffee, tea and hot chocolate. Juanito himself is a great character and the café stays open late.

Manu Café, Av Pardo 1046. Good coffee and good food too.

Panadería El Buen Pastor, Cuesta San Blas 579. Very good bread, *empanadas* and pastries, proceeds go to a charity for orphans and street children.

Cuzco *p24, maps p26 and p31*
Bars
Bar 7, Tandapata 690, San Blas, T506472. Good food and drinks in a trendy bar which specializes in local ingredients.

Cross Keys Pub, Triunfo 350 (upstairs), T229227, www.cross-keys-pub-cusco-peru.com. Open 1100-0130, run by Barry Walker of **Manu Expeditions**, a Mancunian and ornithologist, cosy, darts, cable sports, pool, bar meals, plus daily half price specials Sun-Wed, great pisco sours, very popular, great atmosphere, free Wi-Fi.

The Frogs Restaurant and Lounge, Huarankallqui 185, just off Ruinas, T221762. Roomy, modern, chic bar in historic building, with music, movies, pool table, football, a hookah room and good food as well.

Hierba Buena Lounge, Suytuccato 715-B, T260685. Restaurant and bar with live music, comfortable seats and hammocks on different levels with some private 'nooks', DVD library, cool ambience.

Indigo, Tecseccocha 2, p 2, T260271. Shows 3 films a day. Also has a lounge and cocktail bar and serves Asian and local food. A log fire keeps out the night-time cold.

Km 0 (Arte y Tapas), Tandapata 100, San Blas. Mediterranean themed bar tucked in behind San Blas, good snacks and tapas, with live music every night (around 2200).

La Chupitería Shots Bar, Tecseccocha 400. A fun bar with an amazing list of different shots and the widest variety of liquors in Cuzco. Cool music, lively atmosphere, a great evening.

Los Perros Bar, Tecseccocha 436. Open 1100-0100. Great place to chill out on comfy couches, excellent music, welcoming, good coffee, tasty meals available (including vegetarian), book exchange, English and other magazines, board games. Has a take-away only branch at Suecia 368, open 2400 midnight to 0600 for good quality, post-club food.

Lost City, Tecseccocha 429, T224349. Bar showing international sports on wide screen TVs. Super friendly, great pizzas, happy hour drink specials and free popcorn. Closed Mon.

Marcelo Batata, Palacio 121, p 3, T222424, www.cuzcodining.com. Bar/restaurant offering sandwiches and international food, slow service but worth going to sit on the rooftop for the great 360° panorama and enjoy the Cuzco sunshine.

Norton Rat's Tavern, Santa Catalina Angosta 116, www.nortonrats.com. On the corner of the Plaza de Armas, fine balcony, open 0700-0230, also serves meals, cable TV, popular, English spoken, pool, darts, motorcycle theme with information for motorcyclists from owner, Jeffrey Powers. Also has **Hostal Gocta Cusco** here.

Paddy's Pub, Triunfo 124 on the corner of the plaza. Irish theme pub, deservedly popular, open 1300-0100, good grub.

Rosie O'Grady's, Santa Catalina Ancha 360, T247935. Good music, tasty food, English and Russian spoken, good value, open 1100 till late (food served till 2400).

Clubs
El Garabato Video Music Club, Espaderos 132, p 3. Open daily 1600-0300, dance area, lounge for chilling, bar, live shows 2300-0030 (all sorts of styles) and large screen showing music videos.

Extreme, C Suecia. Movies in the late afternoon and early evening, but after midnight this place really gets going with an eclectic range of music, from 60s and 70s rock and pop to techno and trance. **Kamikaze**, Plaza Regocijo 274, T233865. *Peña* at 2200, good old traditional rock music, candle-lit cavern atmosphere, entry US$2.50. **Mama Africa**, Portal de Panes 190. Cool music and clubber's spot, good food with varied menu, happy hour till 2300, good value. **Mythology**, Portal de Carnes 298, p 2. Mostly an early 80's and 90's combination of cheese, punk and classic, popular. Food in served in the jungle-themed **Lek Café**. They also show movies in the afternoons.

Night Sky Disco, Av del Sol 106, Galería La Merced Int 208, p 3. One of the latest 'in' places to drink and dance.

Roots, Huaynapata 194 (just off Suecia). Plays mostly reggae, but there are other styles too, good atmosphere and popular. **Siete Angelitos**, Siete Angelitos 638. Tiny club, just a couple of rooms, but spectacular cocktails, a friendly owner by the name of Walter and an awesome atmosphere when things get going. **Ukuku's**, Plateros 316. US$1.35 entry, very popular, good atmosphere, good mix of music including live shows nightly. Also has a **restaurant** at Carmen Alto 133, good value and fabulous views.

⚙ Entertainment

Cuzco *p24, maps p26 and p31*
Folklore Regular nightly folklore show at **Centro Qosqo de Arte Nativo**, Av Sol 604, T227901. Show from 1900 to 2030, entrance on BTC ticket. **Teatro Inti Raymi**, Saphi 605, nightly at 1845, US$4.50, well worth it. **Teatro Kusikay**, Unión 117, T255414, www.kusikay.com (tickets from the theatre Mon-Sat 0900-2100 or, out of hours, **Inka Grill** or **Incanto** restaurants, or at the **Mayu Café** at Ollantaytambo train station). Mon-Sat 1930, US$35, thriliing show with spectacular dances based on the Mamacha Carmen festival of Paucartambo, with lavish

costumes, special effects and a troupe of 30. **Teatro Municipal**, C Mesón de la Estrella 149 (T227321 for information 0900-1300 and 1500-1900). Plays, dancing and shows, mostly Thu-Sun. They also run classes in music and dancing from Jan to Mar which are great value.

⚙ Festivals and events

Cuzco *p24, maps p26 and p31*
Carnival in Cuzco is a messy affair with flour, water, cacti, bad fruit and animal manure being thrown about in the streets. **Easter Monday**: procession of **El Señor de los Temblores** (Lord of the Earthquakes), starting at 1600 outside the Cathedral. A large crucifix is paraded through the streets, returning to the Plaza de Armas around 2000 to bless the tens of thousands of people who have assembled there. **2-3 May**: Vigil of the Cross takes place at all mountaintops with crosses on them, a boisterous affair. **Jun**: Q'Olloriti, the Snow Star Festival, is held at a 4700 m glacier north of Ocongate (Ausangate) 150 km southeast of Cuzco. Several agencies offer tours. (The date is moveable.) On **Corpus Christi** day, the Thu after Trinity Sunday, all the statues of the Virgin and of saints from Cuzco's churches are paraded through the streets to the Cathedral. The Plaza de Armas is surrounded by tables with women selling *cuy* (guinea pig) and a mixed grill called *chiriuchu* (*cuy*, chicken, *tortillas*, fish eggs, water-weeds, maize, cheese and sausage) and lots of Cusqueña beer. **24 Jun**: the pageant of **Inti Raymi**, the Inca festival of the winter solstice, is enacted in Quechua at 1000 at the Qoricancha, moving on to Sacsayhuaman at 1300. Tickets for the stands can be bought a week in advance from the Emufec office, Santa Catalina Ancha 325, US$80, less if bought Mar-May. Travel agents can arrange the whole day for you, with meeting points, transport, reserved seats and packed lunch. Those who try to persuade you to buy a ticket for the right to film or take

photos are being dishonest. On the night before Inti Raymi, the Plaza de Armas is crowded with processions and food stalls. Try to arrive in Cuzco 15 days before Inti Raymi. **28 Jul**: Peruvian Independence Day. Prices shoot up during these celebrations. **Aug**: on the last Sun is the **Huarachicoy** festival at Sacsayhuaman, a spectacular re-enactment of the Inca manhood rite, performed in dazzling costumes by boys of a local school. **8 Sep**: **Day of the Virgin** is a colourful procession of masked dancers from the church of Almudena, at the southwest edge of Cuzco, near Belén, to the Plaza de San Francisco. There is also a splendid fair at Almudena, and a free bull fight on the following day. **1 Nov**: All Saints Day, celebrated everywhere with bread dolls and traditional cooking. **8 Dec**: Cuzco day, when churches and museums close at 1200. **24 Dec**: Santuranticuy, 'the buying of saints', with a big crafts market in the plaza, very noisy until early hours of the 25th.

○ Shopping

Cuzco *p24, maps p26 and p31*
Arts and crafts
In the Plaza San Blas and the surrounding area, authentic Cuzco crafts still survive. A market is held on Sat. Many leading artisans welcome visitors. Among fine objects made are Biblical figures from plaster, wheatflour and potatoes, reproductions of pre-Columbian ceramics and colonial sculptures, pious paintings, earthenware figurines, festive dolls and wood carvings.

Cuzco is the weaving centre of Peru and excellent textiles can be found at good value. Be very careful of buying gold and silver objects and jewellery in and around Cuzco.
Agua y Tierra, Plazoleta Nazarenas 167, and Cuesta San Blas 595, T226951. Excellent quality crafts from rainforest communities.
Apacheta, San Juan de Dios 250, T238210, www.apachetaperu.com. Replicas of Pre-Inca and Inca textiles, ceramics, alpaca goods,

contemporary art gallery, books on Andean culture.
Inkantations, Choquechaca 200. Radical baskets made from natural materials in all sorts of weird and wonderful shapes. Also ceramics and Andean weavings. Interesting and original.
Mercado Artesanal, Av Sol, block 4, is good for cheap crafts.
Pedazo de Arte, Plateros 334B. A tasteful collection of Andean handicrafts, many designed by Japanese owner Miki Suzuki.
La Pérez, Urb Mateo Pumacahua 598, Huanchac, T232186. A big co-operative with a good selection; they will arrange a free pick-up from your hotel.
Seminario, Portal de Carnes 244, Plaza de Armas, sells the ceramics of Seminario-Behar (see under Urubamba, page 56), plus cotton, basketry, jewellery, etc.

Bookshops
Centro de Estudios Regionales Andinos Bartolomé de las Casas, Av Tullumayo 465, T233472, www.cbc.org.pe. Good books on Peruvian history, archaeology, etc, Mon-Sat 1100-1400, 1600-1900.
Jerusalem, Heladeros 143, T235408. English books, guidebooks, music, postcards, book exchange (3 for 1).
Special Book Services, Av El Sol 781-A, T248106.
Book exchange, 1 for 1, at **The Sun**, Plazoleta Limacpampa Chico 471, café/restaurant, run by an Aussie.

Camping equipment
For renting equipment, there are several places around the Plaza area. Check the equipment carefully as it is common for parts to be missing. A deposit of US$100 is asked, plus credit card, passport or plane ticket. White gas (*bencina*), US$1.50 per litre, can be bought at hardware stores, but check the purity. Stove spirit (*alcoól para quemar*) is available at pharmacies; blue gas canisters,

costing US$5, can be found at hardware stores and camping shops. You can also rent equipment through travel agencies.

Edson Zuñiga Huillca, Mercado Rosaspata, Jr Abel Landeo P-1, T802831, 993 7243 (mob). 3 mins from Plaza de Armas, for repair of camping equipment and footwear, also equipment rental, open 24 hrs a day, 7 days a week, English and Italian spoken.

Tatoo, C del Medio 130, T254211, www.tatoo.ws. High-quality hiking, climbing and camping gear, not cheap, but western brand names and their own lines.

Fabrics and alpaca clothing

Alpaca Golden, Portal de Panes 151, T251724, alpaca.golden@terra.com.pe. Also at Plazoleta Nazarenas 175. Designer, producer and retailer of fine alpaca clothing.

The Center for Traditional Textiles of Cuzco, Av Sol 603, T228117, www.textiles cusco.org. A non-profit organization that seeks to promote, refine and rediscover the weaving traditions of the Cuzco area. Tours of workshops, weaving classes, you can watch weavers at work. Over 50% of the price goes direct to the weaver. Recommended.

Hilo, Carmen Alto 260, T254536. Fashionable items designed individually and hand made on-site. Run by Eibhlin Cassidy, she can adjust and tailor designs.

Josefina Olivera, Portal Comercio 173, Plaza de Armas. Sells old textiles and weavings, expensive but worth it to save pieces being cut up to make other items, open daily 1100-2100.

Kuna by Alpaca 111, Plaza Regocijo 202, T243233, www.kuna.com.pe. High quality alpaca clothing with outlets also in hotels *El Monasterio, Libertador* and *Machu Picchu Sanctuary Lodge*.

Store of Weavers (Asociación Central de Artesanos y Artesanas del Sur Andino Inkakunaq Ruwaynin), Av Tullumayo 274, T233466, www.cbc.org.pe/tejidosandinos. Store run by 6 local weaving communities,

some of whose residents you can see working on site. All profits go to the weavers themselves.

Food and natural products

Casa Ecológica Cusco, Triunfo 393 and Portal de Carnes 236, interior 2, Plaza de Armas. Organic foods, wild honey, coffee, granola. Casa Ecológica also offers natural medicines, indigenous art and weavings.

La Cholita, Portal Espinar 142-B and at airport. Special chocolates made with local ingredients.

The Coca Shop, Carmen Alto 115, San Blas, T260774, www.thecocashop.com. Tiny shop selling an interesting selection of sweets and chocolates made using coca leaf flour. There is also plenty of information about the nutritional values of coca leaves.

Jewellery

Calas, Siete Angelitos 619-B, San Blas. Hand-made silver jewellery in interesting designs and alpaca goods from the community of Pitumarca.

Ilaria, Portal Carrizos 258, T246253. Branches in hotels *Monasterio, Libertador* and at the airport. For recommended jewellery and silver.

Inka Treasure, Triunfo 375, T227470, www.inkatreasure.com.pe. With branches at Av Pardo 1080, Plazoleta Nazarenas 159 and Portal de Panes 163. Also at the airport and the airport in Juliaca. Fine jewellery including goldwork, mostly with pre-Columbian designs, and silver with the owner's designs. Tours of workshops at Av Circunvalación, near Cristo Blanco. The stores also incorporte the work of famed jeweller Carlos Chakiras.

Mullu, Triunfo 120, T229831. Contemporary silver jewellery with semi-precious stones and cotton clothing with interesting designs, open Mon-Sat 1000-2100.

Spondylus, Cuesta San Blas 505 and Plazoleta San Blas 617, T226929. A good selection of interesting gold and silver jewellery and fashion tops with Inca and pre-Inca designs.

Music
Taki Museo de Música de los Andes,
Hatunrumiyoc 487-5. Shop and workshop
selling and displaying musical instruments,
owner is an ethno-musicologist.
Recommended for anyone interested
in Andean music.

Markets
Wanchac, Av Garcilaso (southeast of centre)
and **San Pedro Market**, opposite Estación
San Pedro, sell a variety of goods.

▲ Activities and tours

Cuzco *p24, maps p26 and p31*
There are many travel agencies in Cuzco. The
sheer number and variety of tours on offer is
bewildering and prices for the same tour can
vary dramatically. Always remember that you
get what you pay for and that, in a crowded
market, organization can sometimes be a
weak point. In general you should only deal
directly with the agencies themselves. You
can do this when in town, or you can raise
whatever questions you may have in advance
(or even in Cuzco), and get replies in writing,
by email. Other sources of advice are visitors
returning from trips, who can give the latest
information, and the trip reports for members
of the South America Explorers. Students will
normally receive a discount on production
of an ISIC card. Do not deal with guides who
claim to be employed by agencies listed
below without verifying their credentials.
City tours cost about US$7-15 for 4 hrs;
check what sites are included and that
the guide is experienced.

Only a restricted number of agencies are
licensed to operate **Inca Trail** trips. Sernanp,
Av José Gabriel Cosio 308, Urb Magisterial,
1 etapa, T229297, www.sernanp.gob.pe,
verifies operating permits (see Visitors'
tickets, above, for Ministerio de Cultura
office). Unlicensed agencies will sell Inca
Trail trips, but pass clients on to the
operating agency. This can cause confusion

and booking problems at busy times.
Current advice is to book your preferred
dates as early as possible, between 2
months and a year in advance, depending
on the season when you want to go, then
confirm nearer the time. There have been
many instances of disappointed trekkers
whose bookings did not materialize. Don't
wait to the last minute and check your
operator's cancellation fees. **Note** See
page 70, under Inca Trails, for regulations
governing the Trail. Note also that many
companies offer treks as alternatives to
the Inca Trail and its variations to Machu
Picchu. Unlike the Inca Trail, these treks
are unregulated. Ensure that the trekking
company does not employ the sort of
practices (such as mistreating porters,
not clearing up rubbish) which are now
outlawed on the trails to Machu Picchu.

Inca Trail and general tours
Amazing Peru, C Yépez Miranda C-6,
Magisterio (9 Alma Rd, Manchester M19 2FG,
T0808 2346805), www.amazingperu.com.
Highly recommended, professional and
well-organized, "perfect tour",
knowledgeable guides.
Amazon Trails Peru, Tandapata 660,
T437374, or 984 714148, www.amazon
trailsperu.com. Trekking tours around the
area, including the Inca Trail, Salkantay
and Choquequirao. Also trips to Manu.
Andean Treks, Av Pardo 705, T225701,
www.andeantreks.com. Manager Tom
Hendrickson uses high-quality equipment
and satellite phones. This company organizes
itineraries, from 2 to 15 days with a wide variety
of activities in this area and further afield.
Andina Travel, Plazoleta Santa Catalina
219, T251892, www.andinatravel.com.
Specializes in trekking and biking, notably
the Lares Valley, working with traditional
weaving communities.
Big Foot, Triunfo 392 (oficina 213), T238568,
www.bigfootcusco.com. Tailor-made hiking

trips, especially in the remote corners of the Vilcabamba and Vilcanota mountains; also the Inca Trail.

Ch'aska, Garcilaso 265 p 2, of 6, T240424, www.chaskatours.com. Dutch-Peruvian company offering cultural, adventure, nature and esoteric tours. They specialize in the Inca Trail, but also llama treks to Lares, treks to Choquequirao.

Culturas Peru, Tandapata 354A, T243629, www.culturasperu.com. Swiss-Peruvian company offering adventure, cultural, ecological and spiritual tours. Also specialize in alternative Inca trails.

Destinos Turísticos, Portal de Panes 123, oficina 101-102, Plaza de Armas, T228168, www.destino sturisticosperu.com. The owner speaks Spanish, English, Dutch and Portuguese and specializes in package tours from economic to 5-star budgets. Advice on booking jungle trips and renting mountain bikes. Very helpful.

EcotrailPeru, Av El Sol 106, no 205, 2 p, T233357, www.ecotrailperu.com. Operates treks, tours and adventure trips throughout Peru for all fitness levels. Committed to sustainable travel.

Enigma Adventure, Jirón Clorinda Matto de Turner 100, Urb Magisterial 1a Etapa, T222155, www.enigmaperu.com. Run by Spaniard Silvia Rico Coll. Well-organized, innovative trekking expeditions including a luxury service, Inca Trail and a variety of challenging alternatives. Also cultural tours to weaving communities, Ayahuasca therapy, climbing and biking.

Explorandes, Av Garcilaso 316-A (not to be confused with C Garcilaso in the centre), T238380, www.explorandes.com. Experienced high-end adventure company. Arrange a wide variety of mountain treks; trips available in Peru and Ecuador, book through website also arranges tours across Peru for lovers of orchids, ceramics or textiles. Award-winning environmental practices.

Fertur, C San Agustín 317, T221304, www.fertur-travel.com. Mon-Fri 0900-1900, Sat 0900-1200. Cuzco branch of the Lima tour operator, see page 73.

Gatur Cusco, Puluchapata 140 (a small street off Av Sol 3rd block), T223496, www.gatur cusco.com. Esoteric, ecotourism, and general tours. Owner Dr José (Pepe) Altamirano is knowledgeable in Andean folk traditions. Excellent conventional tours, bilingual guides and transportation. Guides speak English, French, Spanish and German. They can also book internal flights.

Hiking Peru, Portal de Panes 109, of 6, T247942, 984 651414, www.hiking peru.com. 8-day treks to Espíritu Pampa; 7 days/6 nights around Ausangate; 4-day/3-night Lares Valley Trek.

Inca Explorers, Ruinas 427, T241070, www.inca explorers.com. Specialist trekking agency for small group expeditions in socially and environmentally responsible manner. Also 2-week hike in the Cordillera Vilcanota (passing Nevado Ausangate), and Choquequirao to Espíritu Pampa.

InkaNatura Travel, Ricardo Palma J1, T255255, www.inkanatura.com. Offers tours with special emphasis on sustainable tourism and conservation. Knowledgeable guides.

Liz's Explorer, Medio 114B, T246619, www.lizexplorer.com. 4-day/ 3-night Inca Trail trek (minimum group size 10, maximum 16), other lengths of trips available. Reports of good trips but haphazard organization.

Llama Path, San Juan de Dios 250, T240822, www.llamapath.com. A wide variety of local tours, specializing in Inca Trail and alternative treks, involved in environmental campaigns and porter welfare. Many good reports.

Machete Tours, Nueva Alta 432, Int B, T224829, T984 631662, www.machete tours.com. Peruvian and Danish owners. Tours cover all Peru and also Bolivia and Chile. All guides speak good English. Adventure tours arranged using local accommodation or family camping areas. Tours are eco-friendly and benefit the local community.

Peru Planet, Suecia 318, T251145, www.peru-planet.net. Peruvian/Belgian owned agency offering tours of Inca Trail, other treks around Cuzco and packages within Peru, also Bolivia and Patagonia.

Peru Treks, Av Pardo 540, T222722, www.perutreks.com. Trekking agency set up by Englishman Mike Weston and his wife Koqui González. They pride themselves on good treatment of porters and support staff and have been consistently recommended for professionalism and customer care, a portion of profits go to community projects. Treks offered include Salkantay, the Lares Valley and Vilcabamba Vieja.

Q'ente, Choquechaca 229, p 2, T222535, www.qente.com. Their Inca Trail service is recommended. Also private treks to Salkantay, Ausangate, Choquequirao, Vilcabamba and Q'eros. Horse riding to local ruins costs US$35 for 4-5 hrs. Very good, especially with children.

SAS Travel, Garcilaso 270, Plaza San Francisco, T249194, www.sastravelperu.com. Discount for students. Inca Trail and a variety of alternatives. Also Manu, family tours, mountain bike, horse riding and rafting trips can be organized. All guides speak some English. They can book internal flights at cheaper rates than from overseas. Recent reports increasingly mixed.

Sky Travel, Santa Catalina Ancha 366, interior 3-C (down alleyway near Rosie O'Grady's pub), T261818, www.skyperu.com. English spoken. General tours around city and Sacred Valley. Inca Trail with good-sized double tents and a dinner tent (the group is asked what it would like on the menu 2 days before departure). Other trips include Vilcabamba and Ausangate (trekking).

Tambo Tours, 4405 Spring Cypress Rd, Suite 210, Spring, TX 77388, USA, T1-888-2-GO-PERU (246-7378), T001-281 528 9448, www.2GO PERU.com. Long established

adventure and tour specialist with offices in Peru and the US. Customized trips to the Amazon and archaeological sites of Peru, Bolivia and Ecuador.

T'ika Trek, Suytu Qhatu 766, T254183, www.tikatrek.com. New in 2011, high-quality customized tours and treks, including Inca Trail, Vilcabamba, Pongo de Mainique, cultural tours, Galápagos, for small groups, families. Also on sale here, eco-friendly soaps, oils and beauty products made from local ingredients, www.tikasoapperu.com.

Trekperu, Av República de Chile B-15, Parque Industrial, Wanchac, T261501, www.trekperu.com. Experienced trek operator as well as other adventure sports and mountain biking. Offers 'culturally sensitive' tours. Cusco Biking Adventure includes support vehicle and good camping gear (but providing your own sleeping bag).

Tucan Travel, T241123, cuzco@tucan travel.com. Offer adventure tours and overland expeditions.

United Mice, Plateros 351, T221139, www.unitedmice.com. Inca Trail and alternative trail via Salkantay and Santa Teresa, well-established and reputable. Good guides who speak languages other than Spanish. Discount with student card, good food and equipment. City and Sacred Valley tours and treks to Choquequirao.

Wayki Trek, Av Pardo 510, T224092, www.waykitrek.net. Budget travel agency with a hostel attached, recommended for their Inca Trail service. Owner Leo knows the area very well. Treks to several almost unknown Inca sites and interesting variations on the 'classic' Inca Trail with visits to porters' communities. Also treks to Ausangate, Salkantay and Choquequirao.

Rafting, mountain biking and trekking

When looking for an operator please consider more than just the price of your tour. Competition between companies in

Cuzco is intense and price wars can lead to compromises in safety. Consider the quality of safety equipment (lifejackets, etc) and the number and experience of rescue kayakers and support staff. On a large and potentially dangerous rivers like the Apurímac and Urubamba (where fatalities have occurred), this can make all the difference.

Amazonas Explorers, Av Collasuyo 910, Miravalle, PO Box 722, www.amazonas explorer.com. Experts in rafting, inflatable canoeing, mountain biking, horse riding and hiking. English owner Paul Cripps has great experience. Most bookings from overseas (in UK, T01874-658125, Jan-Mar; T01437-891743, Apr-Dec), but they may be able to arrange a trip for travellers in Cuzco with advanced notice. Rafting and inflatable canoeing includes Río Urubamba, Río Apurímac, Río Tambopata (including Lake Titicaca). Also 5-day/4-night Inca Trail, alternatives to the Inca Trail and Choquequirao to Machu Picchu, an excellent variation of the Ausangate Circuit and a trek to Espíritu Pampa. Multi-activity and family trips are a speciality. Mountain biking trips all use state-of-the-art equipment, expert guides and support vehicles where appropriate. All options are at the higher end of the market and are highly recommended. Amazonas Explorer are members of www.onepercentfortheplanet.org, donating 1% of their turnover to a tree-planting project in the Lares watershed.

Apumayo, Jr Ricardo Palma N-5, Santa Mónica, Wanchaq, T246018, www.apumayo. com. Mon-Sat 0900-1300, 1600-2000. Urubamba rafting (from 0800-1530 every day); 3- to 4-day Apurímac trips. Also mountain biking to Maras and Moray in Sacred Valley, or from Cuzco to the jungle town of Quillabamba. This company also offers tours for disabled people, including rafting.

Apus Perú, Cuichipunco 366, T232691, www.apus-peru. com. Conducts most business by internet, specializes in alternatives to the Inca Trail, strong commitment to sustainability, well-organized. Associated with **Threads of Peru** NGO which helps weavers.

Camp Expeditions, Triunfo 392, of 202, T431468, www.campexpedition.net. All sorts of adventure tours, but specialists in climbing, for which they are recommended as most reliable, and trekking.

Cusco Adventure Team, Santa Catalina Ancha 398 (under Al Grano), T228032, www.CuscoAdventureTeam.com. Utilizing the experience of **Amazonas Explorers** (see above), CAT offer half-day to 3-day bike rides and rafting and canoe trips for small groups or individuals, state of the art equipment, adventurous, safe and environmentally aware. Part of **Grupo Inca**, www.grupo-inca.com.

Eric Adventures, Urb Santa María A1-6, San Sebastián, T272862, www.eric adventures.com. Specialize in many adventure activities. They clearly explain what equipment is included in their prices and what you will need to bring. They also rent motorcross bikes for US$70-90 per day, mountain bikes and cars and 4WDs. Prices are more expensive if you book by email. A popular company.

Medina Brothers, contact Christian or Alain Medina on T225163 or 984 653485/984 691670. Family-run rafting company with good equipment and plenty of experience. They usually focus on day rafting trips in the Sacred Valley, but services are tailored to the needs of the client.

Pachatusan Trek, Psje Esmeralda 160, Santiago, T231817, www.pachatusantrek.com. Offers a wide variety to treks, as alternatives to the Inca Trail, professional and caring staff.

River Explorers, C Garcilaso 210, int 128, T260926 or T984 909249, www.river explorers.com. An adventure company offering mountain biking, trekking and rafting trips (on the Apurímac, Urubamba and Tambopata). Experienced and qualified guides with environmental awareness.

Terra Explorer Peru, T237352, www.terra explorerperu.com. Offers a wide range of trips from high-end rafting in the Sacred Valley and expeditions in the Colca and Cotahuasi canyons, trekking the Inca Trail and others, mountain biking, kayaking (including on Lake Titicaca) and jungle trips. All guides are bilingual.

Cultural tours
Milla Tourism, Av Pardo 689 and Portal Comercio 195 on the plaza, T231710, www.milla turismo.com. Mon-Fri 0800-1300, 1500-1900, Sat 0800-1300. Mystical tours to Cuzco's Inca ceremonial sites such as Pumamarca and The Temple of the Moon. Guide speaks only basic English. They also arrange cultural and environmental lectures and courses. **Mystic Inca Trail**, Unidad Vecinal de Santiago, bloque 9, dpto 301, T221358, ivanndp@terra.com.pe. Specialize in tours of sacred Inca sites and study of Andean spirituality. This takes 10 days but it is possible to have shorter 'experiences'.

Shamans and drug experiences
San Pedro and Ayahuasca have been used since before Inca times, mostly as a sacred healing experience. If you choose to experience these incredible healing/teaching plants, only do so under the guidance of a reputable agency or shaman and always have a friend with you who is not partaking. If the medicine is not prepared correctly, it can be highly toxic and, in rare cases, severely dangerous. Never buy from someone who is not recommended, never buy off the streets and never try to prepare the plants yourself. **Another Planet**, Tandapata y Pasñapacana 148, San Blas, T241168, or T974 790411, www.anotherplanetperu.net. Run by Lesley Myburgh, who operates mystical and adventure tours in and around Cuzco, and is an expert in San Pedro cactus preparation. She arranges San Pedro sessions for healing in the garden of her house outside Cuzco.

Tours meet at **La Casa de la Gringa**, see Sleeping, above.
Eleana Molina, T984 751791, misticanativa@ yahoo.com. For Ayahuasca ceremonies.

Paragliding and ballooning
Globos de los Andes, Av de la Cultura 220, suite 36, T232352, www.globosperu.com. Hot-air ballooning in the Sacred Valley and expeditions with balloons and 4WD lasting several days.

Private guides
As most of the sights do not have any information or signs in English, a good guide can really improve your visit. Either arrange this before you set out or contract one at the sight you are visiting. A tip is expected at the end of the tour. Tours of the city or Sacred Valley cost US$50 for half-day, US$65 full day; a guide to Machu Picchu charges US$80 per day. A list of official guides is held by **Agotur Cuzco**, C Heladeros 157, Of 34-F, p 3, T233457, www.agoturcusco.org.pe. **South American Explorers** has a list and contact details for recommended local guides. See also www.leaplocal.org.

Transport

Cuzco p24, maps p26 and p31
Air
The airport is at Quispiquilla, near the bus terminal, 1.6 km from centre, airport information T222611/ 601. **Note** Check in 2 hrs before flight. Reconfirm 48 hrs before your flight. Flights may be delayed or cancelled during the wet season, or may leave early if the weather is bad. To **Lima**, 55 mins, daily flights with **Taca, Star Perú, LAN** and **Peruvian Airlines**. To **Arequipa**, 30 mins daily with **LAN**. To **Puerto Maldonado**, 30 mins, with **LAN** and **Star Perú**. To/from **La Paz, Aero Sur** Thu and Sun. Taxi to and from the airport costs US$2-3.50 (US$7.25 from the official taxi desk). Colectivos cost US$0.30 from Plaza San Francisco or outside the airport car park. Many

representatives of hotels and travel agencies operate at the airport, with transport to the hotel with which they are associated. Take your time to choose your hotel, at the price you can afford. Also in baggage retrieval are mobile phone rentals, ATMs, LAC Dollar money exchange, an Oxyshot oxygen sales stand and an **i perú** office. There are phone booths, restaurant, cafeteria and a Tourist Protection Bureau desk.

Bus

Long distance Terminal on Av Vallejo Santoni, block 2 (Prolongación Pachacútec), colectivo from centre US$0.30, taxi US$1. Platform tax US$0.35. Buses to **Lima** (20-24 hrs) go via **Abancay**, 195 km, 5 hrs (longer in the rainy season), and **Nazca**, on the Panamerican Highway. This route is paved but floods in the wet season often damage large sections of the highway. If prone to travel sickness, be prepared on the road to Abancay, there are many, many curves, but the scenery is magnificent. At Abancay, the road forks, the other branch going to **Andahuaylas**, a further 138 km, 10-11 hrs from Cuzco, and **Ayacucho**, another 261 km, 20 hrs from Cuzco. On both routes at night, take a blanket or sleeping bag to ward off the cold. All buses leave daily from the Terminal Terrestre. **Molina**, who also have an office on Av Pachacútec, just past the railway station, have buses on both routes. They run 3 services a day to Lima via Abancay and Nazca, and one, at 1900, to Abancay and Andahuaylas. **Cruz del Sur**'s service to Lima via Abancay leaves at 0730 and 1400, while their more comfortable services depart at 1500 and 1600. **San Jerónimo** and **Los Chankas** have buses to Abancay, Andahuaylas and Ayacucho at 1830. **Turismo Ampay** and **Turismo Abancay** go 3 times a day to Abancay, and **Expreso Huamanga** once. **Bredde** has 5 buses a day to Abancay. Fares: Abancay US$10, Andahuaylas US$14, Nazca US28.50-$46,

Lima also US$28.50-46; also US$49-57 (*Cruz del Sur Cruzero* and *VIP* classes). In Cuzco you may be told that there are no buses in the day from Abancay to Andahuaylas; this is not so as **Señor de Huanca** does so. If you leave Cuzco before 0800, with luck you'll make the connection at 1300 – worth it for the scenery. **Ormeño** has a service from Cuzco to Lima via Arequipa which takes longer (22 hrs), but is a more comfortable journey.

To Lake Titicaca and Bolivia: To **Juliaca**, 344 km, 5-6 hrs, US$5-12. The road is fully paved, but after heavy rain buses may not run. To **Puno**, via Juliaca, US$5-12; direct, US$8.50 (*bus cama* US$12), 6 hrs. Tourist service with 5 stops, **First Class** and **Inka Express** (Av La Paz C-32, Urb El Ovalo, Wanchac, T247887, www.inkaexpress.com), calling at Andahuaylillas church, Raqchi, La Raya, Sicuani and Pucará, US$30, lunch but not entrance tickets included. **Note** It is safest to travel by day on the Juliaca-Puno-Cuzco route.

To the **Sacred Valley**: To **Pisac**, 32 km, 1 hr, US$0.85, from C Puputi on the outskirts of the city, near the Clorindo Matto de Turner school and Av de la Cultura. Colectivos, minibuses and buses leave whenever they are full, between 0600 and 1600. Buses returning from Pisac are often full. The last one back leaves around 2000. Taxis charge about US$20 for the round trip. To Pisac, **Calca** (18 km beyond Pisac) and **Urubamba** a further 22 km, buses leave from Av Tullumayo 800 block, Wanchac, US$1. Combis and colectivos leave from 300 block of Av Grau, 1 block before crossing the bridge, for **Chinchero**, 23 km, 45 mins, US$0.75; and for **Urubamba** a further 25 km, 45 mins, US$0.75 (or US$1.80 Cuzco-Urubamba direct, US$1.80 for a seat in a colectivo taxi). To **Ollantaytambo** from Av Grau, 0745, 1945, US$2.85, or catch a bus to Urubamba. Direct taxi-colectivo service to Ollantaytambo from C Pavitos, leaves when full, US$3.60. Tours can be arranged to Chinchero, Urubamba and Ollantaytambo with a Cuzco travel agency. To Chinchero, US$6 pp; a taxi costs US$25 round-trip. Usually only day tours are organized for visits to the valley, US$20-25. Using public transport and staying overnight in Urubamba, Ollantaytambo or Pisac allows more time to see the ruins and markets.

Taxi
In Cuzco they are cheap and recommended when arriving by air, train or bus. They have fixed prices: in the centre US$1.20 in town (50% more after 2100 or 2200). In town it is advisable to take municipality-authorized taxis that have a sticker with a number on the window and a chequerboard pattern on the side. Safer still are licensed taxis, which have a sign with the company's name on the roof, not just a sticker in the window. These taxis are summoned by phone and are more expensive (**Aló Cusco** T222222, **Ocarina** T247080). Trips to **Sacsayhuaman** US$10; ruins of **Tambo Machay** US$15-20 (3-4 people); day trip US$50-85.

Train
To Juliaca and Puno, **Perú Rail** trains leave from the Av Sol station, Estación Wanchac, T238722. When arriving in Cuzco, a tourist bus meets the train to take visitors to hotels whose touts offer rooms. Machu Picchu trains leave from Estación San Pedro, opposite the San Pedro market.
   The train to **Juliaca/Puno** leaves at 0800, Mon, Wed, Fri and Sat, arriving at Puno at 1800, sit on the left for views (no Fri train Nov-Mar). The train makes a stop to view the scenery at La Raya. Always check whether the train is running, especially in the rainy season, when services may be cancelled. Only one class, *Andean Explorer*, US$220. The ticket office at Wanchac station is open Mon-Fri 0700-1700, Sat, Sun and holidays 0700-1200. The **Perú Rail** office at

Portal de Carnes 214 is open Mon-Fri 1000-2200, Sat, Sun and holidays 1400-2300 (take you passport or a copy when buying tickets). Buy tickets on www.perurail.com, or through a travel agent. Meals are served on the train. To **Ollantaytambo** and **Machu Picchu**, see page 68.

see page 68.

🛈 Directory

Cuzco *p24, maps p26 and p31*
Airline offices Aero Sur, Av Sol 948, CC Cusco Sol Plaza, of 120, T254691, www.aerosur.com. **LAN**, Av Sol 627-B, T225552. **Peruvian Airlines**, C del Medio 117, T254890. **Star Perú**, Av Sol 679 of 1, T262768. **Taca**, Av Sol 602-B, T249921. **Banks** Most of the banks are on Av Sol, and all have ATMs from which you can withdraw dollars or soles. **BCP**, Av Sol 189. **Interbank**, Av Sol y Puluchapata. Next door is **Banco Continental**. **BSCH**, Av Sol 459. **Scotiabank**, Maruri y Arequipa. There are ATMs around the Plaza de Armas, in San Blas and on Av La Cultura. Many travel agencies and *casas de cambio* (eg on Portal de Comercio, Plaza de Armas, and Av Sol) change dollars; some of them change TCs as well, but charge 4-5% commission. **LAC Dollar**, Av Sol 150, T257762, Mon-Sat 0900-2000, with delivery service to central hotels, cash and TCs. The street changers hang around Av Sol, blocks 2-3, every day; they will also change TCs. In banks and on the street check the notes. Dollars are accepted at many restaurants and at the airport. **Consulates** Belgium, Av Sol 954, T224322. **France**, Jorge Escobar, C Michaela Bastidas 101, p4, T233610. **Germany**, Sra Maria-Sophia Júrgens de Hermoza, San Agustín 307, T235459, acupari@terra.com.pe, open Mon-Fri, 1000-1200, appointments may be made by phone, also book exchange. **Ireland**, Charlie Donovan, Santa Catalina Ancha 360 (Rosie O'Grady's), T243514. **Italy**, Sr Fedos Rubatto, Av Garcilaso 700, T224398. Mon-Fri 0900-1200, 1500-1700. **Netherlands**, Sra Marcela Alarco, Av Pardo 827, T241897,

marcela_alarco@yahoo.com, Mon-Fri 0900-1500. **Spain**, Sra Juana María Lambarri, Av Pardo 1041, T984 650106. **Switzerland**, Av Regional 222, T243533. **UK**, Barry Walker, Av Pardo 895, T239974, bwalker@amauta.rcp. net.pe. **US Agent**, Dra Olga Villagarcía, Av Pardo 845, T231474, CoresES@state.gov.

Internet You can't walk for 5 mins in Cuzco without running into an internet café, and new places are opening all the time. Most have similar rates, around US$0.50 per hr, although if you look hard enough there are cheaper places. The main difference between cafés is the speed of internet connection and the facilities on offer. The better places have scanners, webcams and CD burners, staff in these establishments can be very knowledgeable. **Language schools** Academia Latinoamericana de Español, Plaza Limacpampa 565, T243364, www.latino schools.com. The same company also has schools in Ecuador (Quito) and in Bolivia (Sucre). They can arrange courses that include any combination of these locations using identical teaching methods and materials. Professionally run with experienced staff. Many activities per week, including dance lessons and excursions to sites of historical and cultural interest. Good homestays. Private classes US$170 for 20 hrs, groups, with a maximum of 4 students US$125, again for 20 hrs. **Acupari**, the German-Peruvian Cultural Association, San Agustín 307, T242970, www.acupari.com. Spanish classes are run here. **Amauta Spanish School**, Suecia 480, T262345, www.amautaspanish. com. Spanish classes, one-to-one or in small groups, also Quechua classes and workshops in Peruvian cuisine, dance and music, US$10.50 per hr one-to-one, group tuition (2-6 people), US$98 for 20 hrs. They have pleasant accommodation on the same street, as well as a free internet café for students, and can arrange excursions and help find voluntary work. They also have a school in Urubamba and can arrange courses in

Tambopata, Lima and Argentina. **Amigos Spanish School**, Zaguán del Cielo B-23, T/F242292, www.spanish cusco.com. Certified, experienced teachers, friendly atmosphere. All profits support a foundation for disadvantaged children. Private lessons for US$8 per hr, US$108 for 20 hrs of classes in a small group. Comfortable homestays and free activities available, including a 'real city tour' through Cuzco's poor areas. **Cusco Spanish School**, Garcilaso 265, of 6, p 2, T226928, www.cuscospanish school.com. US$175 for 20 hrs private classes, cheaper in groups. School offers homestays, optional activities including dance and music classes, cookery courses, ceramics, Quechua, hiking and volunteer programmes. They also offer courses on an *hacienda* at Cusipata in the Vilcanota valley, east of Cuzco. **Excel**, Cruz Verde 336, T235298, www.excel-spanishlanguageprograms-peru.org. Very professional, US$7 per hr for private one-to-one lessons. US$229 for 20 hrs with 2 people, or US$277 with homestay, one-on-one for 20 hrs. **Fairplay Spanish School**, Pasaje Zavaleta C-5, Wanchac, T984 789252, www.fair play-peru.org. This relatively new NGO teaches Peruvians who wouldn't normally have the opportunity (Peruvian single mothers, for example) to become Spanish teachers themselves over several months of training. The agency then acts as an agent, allowing these same teachers to find work with visiting students. Classes with these teachers cost US$4.50 or US$6 per hr, of which 33% is reinvested in the NGO, the rest going direct to the teachers. Can also arrange volunteer work and homestay programmes. **La Casona de la Esquina**, Purgatorio 395, corner with Huaynapata, T235830. US$5 per hr for one-to-one classes. Recommended. **Mundo Verde**, Coviduc H-14 San Sebastián, T274574, www.mundoverde spanish.com. Spanish lessons with the option to study in the rainforest and the possibility of working on environmental and social projects while studying. Some of your money goes towards developing sustainable farming practices in the area. US$250 for 20 hrs tuition with homestay. **San Blas Spanish School**, Carmen Bajo 224, T247898, www.spanish schoolperu.com. Groups, with 4 clients maximum, US$90 for 20 hrs tuition (US$130 one-to-one). **Massage and therapies** Casa de la Serenidad, Santa María P-8, San Sebastián, T792224, www.shamanspirit.net. A shamanic therapy centre run by a Swiss-American healer and Reiki Master who uses medicinal 'power' plants. It also has bed and breakfast and has received very good reports. **Healing Hands**, based at *Loki Hostel*, faery amanita@hotmail.com. Angela is a Reiki, Shiatsu and CranioSacral Therapist. Very relaxing and recommended. **Medical services** Clinics: Hospital Regional, Av de la Cultura, T227661, emergencies 223691. Clínica Pardo, Av de la Cultura 710, T240387, www.clinica pardo.com. 24 hrs daily, trained

bilingual personnel, complete medical assistance coverage with international insurance companies, highly regarded. **Motorcycle hire** Perú Mototours, Saphi 578, T232742, www.perumoto tours. com. Helpful, good prices and machines. **Post offices** Av Sol, block 5, Mon-Sat 0730-2000; Sun and holidays 0800-1400. Stamps and postcards available. *Poste restante* is free and helpful. **Telephones** Phone offices around town. **Telefónica**, Av Sol 386, for telephone and fax, open Mon-Sat 0700-2300, Sun and holidays 0700-1800. International calls by pay phone or go through the operator (long wait possible), deposit required. **Useful addresses** Migraciones, Av Sol s/n, block 6 close to post office, T222741, Mon-Fri 0800-1300. **ISIC-Intej office**, Portal de Panes 123, of 107 (CC Los Ruiseñores), T256367, cusco@intej.org. Issues international student cards.

Sacred Valley of the Incas

The Río Urubamba cuts its way through fields and rocky gorges beneath the high peaks of the Cordillera. Brown hills, covered in wheat fields, separate Cuzco from this beautiful high valley, which stretches from Sicuani (on the railway to Puno) to the gorge of Torontoi, 600 m lower, to the northwest of Cuzco. Upstream from Pisac, the river is usually called the Vilcanota; downstream it is the Urubamba, and their valleys are collectively known by as the Sacred Valley of the Incas.

The name conjures up images of ancient rulers and their god-like status, with the landscape itself as their temple. And so it was, but the Incas also built their own tribute to this dramatic land in monuments such as Machu Picchu, Ollantaytambo, Pisac and countless others. For the tourist, the famous sights are now within easy reach of Cuzco, but the demand for adventure, to see lost cities in a less 21st-century context, means that there is ample scope for exploring. But if archaeology is not your thing, there are markets to enjoy, birds to watch, trails for mountain-biking and a whole range of hotels to relax in. The best time to visit is April to May or October to November. The high season is June-September, but the rainy season, from December to March, is cheaper and pleasant enough.

Pisac → *Phone code: 084.*

Pisac, 30 km north of Cuzco, has a traditional Sunday morning **market**, at which local people sell their produce in exchange for essential goods. It is also a major draw for tourists who arrive after 0800 until 1700. Pisac has other, somewhat less crowded but more commercial markets on Tuesday and Thursday morning. Each Sunday at 1100 there is a Quechua mass. On the plaza are the church and a small interesting **Museo Folklórico**. The **Museo Comunitario Pisac** ① *Av Amazonas y Retamayoc K'asa, museopisac@ gmail.com, daily 1000-1700, free but donations welcome* has a display of village life, created by the people of Pisac. There are many souvenir shops on Bolognesi. Local fiesta: 15 July.

High above the town on the mountainside is a superb **Inca fortress** ① *0700-1730, guides charge about US$5, you must show your BTC multi-site ticket to enter.* The walk up to the ruins begins from the plaza (but see below), past the Centro de Salud and a control post. The path goes through working terraces, giving the ruins a context. The first group of buildings is Pisaqa, with a fine curving wall. Climb then to the central part of the ruins, the Intihuatana group of temples and rock outcrops in the most magnificent Inca masonry. Here are the Reloj Solar ('Hitching Post of the Sun') – now closed because thieves stole a piece from it, palaces of the moon and stars, solstice markers, baths and water channels. From Intihuatana, a path leads around the hillside through a tunnel to Q'Allaqasa, the military area. Across the valley at this point, a large area of Inca tombs in holes in the hillside can be seen. The end of the site is Kanchiracay, where the agricultural workers were housed. Road transport approaches from this end. The descent takes 30 minutes. At dusk you will hear, if not see, the *pisaca* (partridges), after which the place is named. Even if going by car, do not rush as there is a lot to see and a lot of walking to do. Road transport approaches from the Kanchiracay end. The drive up from town takes about 20 minutes. Walking up, although tiring, is recommended for the views and location. It's at least one hour uphill all the way. The descent takes 30 minutes on foot. Horses are available for US$5 per person. Combis charge US$0.75 per person and taxis US$4 one way up to the ruins from near the bridge. Then you can walk back down (if you want the taxi to take you back down negotiate a fare).

Pisac to Urubamba

Calca, 2900 m, is 18 km beyond Pisac. There are basic hotels and eating places and buses stop on the other side of the divided plaza. *Fiesta de la Vírgen Asunta* 15-16 August. The ruins of a small Inca town, **Huchuy Cuzco** ① *US$7.15 for trek and entry*, are dramatically located on a flat esplanade almost 600 m above Calca, from where a road has been built to the ruins. Alternatively, a steep trail goes to the site from behind the village of Lamay, across the river. A magnificent one- or two-day trek leads to Huchuy Cuzco from Tambo Machay, the route once taken by the Inca from his capital to his country estate.

The **Valle de Lares** is beautiful for walking and cycling, with its magnificent mountains, lakes and small villages. You start near an old hacienda in Huarán (2830 m), cross two passes over 4000 m and end at the hot springs near Lares. From this village, transport runs back to Calca. Alternatively, you can add an extra day and continue to Ollantaytambo. Several agencies in Cuzco offer trekking and biking tours to the region and some offer this trek as an alternative Inca Trail.

About 3 km east of Urubamba, **Yucay** has two grassy plazas divided by the restored colonial church of Santiago Apóstol, with its oil paintings and fine altars. On the opposite side from Plaza Manco II is the adobe palace built for Sayri Túpac (Manco's son) when he emerged from Vilcabamba in 1558. In Yucay monks sell milk, ham and eggs from their farm on the hillside.

Urubamba → *Phone code: 084. Altitude: 2863 m.*

Like many places along the valley, Urubamba is in a fine setting with snow-capped peaks in view. Calle Berriózabal, on the west edge of town, is lined with pisonay trees. The large market square is one block west of the main plaza. The main road skirts the town and the bridge for the road to Chinchero is just to the east of town. Visit **Seminario-Bejar Ceramic Studio** ① *Berriózabal 111, T201002, www.ceramicaseminario.com.* Pablo Seminario and his workshop have investigated and use pre-Columbian techniques and designs, highly recommended. ATMs on the plaza and at the Pecsa service station. *Locutorios* in the centre. For local festivals, May and June are the harvest months, with many processions following ancient schedules. Urubamba's main festival, *El Señor de Torrechayoc*, occupies the first week of June.

About 6 km west of Urubamba is **Tarabamba**, where a bridge crosses the Río Urubamba. Turn right after the bridge to **Pichingoto**, a tumbled-down village built under an overhanging cliff. Also, just over the bridge and before the town to the left of a small, walled cemetery is a salt stream. Follow the footpath beside the stream to Salineras, a small village below which are a mass of terraced Inca salt pans which are still in operation (entry US$1.80); there are over 5000. The walk to the salt pans takes about 30 minutes. Take water as this side of the valley can be very hot and dry.

The Sacred Valley

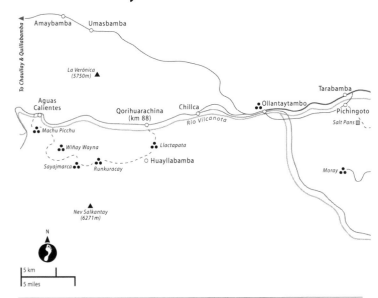

Chinchero and Moray

Chinchero (3762 m) ⓘ *site 0700-1730, on the BTC combined entrance ticket (see page 25)*, is just off a direct road to Urubamba. It has an attractive church built on an Inca temple. The church has been restored to reveal in all their glory the interior paintings. The ceiling, beams and walls are covered in beautiful floral and religious designs. The church is open on Sunday for mass and at festivals; ask in the tourist office in Cuzco for other times. Recent excavations there have revealed many Inca walls and terraces. The food market and the handicraft market are separate. The former is held every day, on your left as you come into town. The latter, on Sunday only, is up by the church, small, but attractive. On any day but Sunday there are few tourists. Fiesta, day of the Virgin, on 8 September.

At Moray, there are three 'colosseums', used by the Incas, according to some theories, as a sort of open-air crop nursery, known locally as the laboratory of the Incas. The great depressions contain no ruined buildings, but are lined with fine terracing. Each level is said to have its own microclimate. It is a very atmospheric place which, many claim, has mystical power, and the scenery is absolutely stunning (entry US$3.60, or by BTC). The most interesting way to get to Moray is from Urubamba via the Pichingoto bridge over the Río Urubamba. The climb up from the bridge is fairly steep but easy. The path passes by the spectacular **salt pans**, still in production after thousands of years, taking 1½-2 hours to the top. The village of Maras is about 45 minutes further on, then it's 9 km by road or 5 km through the fields to Moray. Tour companies in Cuzco offer cycle trips to Moray. There are no hotels at all in the area, so take care not to be stranded. (See Transport, for further details on how to get there.)

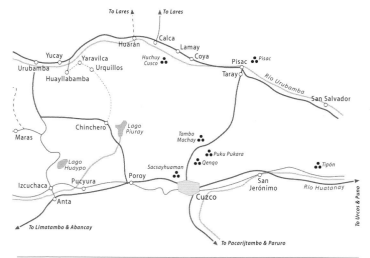

Ollantaytambo → *Phone code: 084. Altitude: 2800 m.*
ⓘ *Inca ruins open 0700-1730. If possible arrive very early, 0700, before the tourists. Admission is by BTC visitor's ticket, which can be bought at the site. Guides at the entrance.*
The Inca town, or *Llacta*, on which the present-day town is based is clearly seen in the fine example of Inca *canchas* (blocks), which are almost entirely intact and still occupied behind the main plaza. Entering Ollantaytambo from Pisac, the road is built along the long wall of 100 niches. Note the inclination of the wall: it leans towards the road. Since it was the Inca's practice to build with the walls leaning towards the interiors of the buildings, it has been deduced that the road, much narrower then, was built inside a succession of buildings. The road out of the plaza leads across a bridge, down to the colonial church with its enclosed *recinto*. Beyond is Plaza Araccama (and car park) with the entrance to the archaeological site.

The so-called **Baño de la Ñusta** (bath of the princess) is of grey granite, and is in a small area between the town and the temple fortress. Some 200 m behind the Baño de la Ñusta along the face of the mountain are some small ruins known as Inca Misanca, believed to have been a small temple or observatory. A series of steps, seats and niches have been carved out of the cliff. There is a complete irrigation system, including a canal at shoulder level, some 6 ins deep, cut out of the sheer rock face. The flights of terraces leading up above the town are superb, and so are the curving terraces following the contours of the rocks overlooking the Urubamba. These terraces were successfully defended by Manco Incas warriors against Hernando Pizarro in 1536. Manco Inca built the wall above the site and another wall closing the Yucay valley against attack from Cuzco. These are visible on either side of the valley.

The temple itself was started by Pachacútec, using Colla Indians from Lake Titicaca – hence the similarities of the monoliths facing the central platform with the Tiahuanaco remains. The massive, highly finished granite blocks at the top are worth the climb to see. The Colla are said to have deserted halfway through the work, which explains the many unfinished blocks lying about the site.

El Museo Catcco ⓘ *1 block from plaza in the Casa Horno, T084-204024, 0900-1900, US$1.50 requested as donation.* The museum has good displays of textiles, findings from local ruins, ethnographic and archaeological information. Tourist information and details of heritage trails are available in the museum. The **Bio Museo** ⓘ *K'uychipunku y Calle La Convención, T204181, T984 962607, www.biomuseo.org, Tue-Sun 0930-2030, US$1.80 requested as a donation,* houses a comprehensive collection of native herbs, potatoes and grains and holds workshops and evening storytelling sessions.

On the west side of the main ruins, a two-dimensional 'pyramid' has been identified in the layout of the fields and walls of the valley. A fine 750 m wall aligns with the rays of the winter solstice on 21 June. It can be appreciated from a high point about 3.5 km from Ollantaytambo.

Sacred Valley of the Incas listings

For Sleeping and Eating price codes and other relevant information, see pages 10-14.

For Sleeping and Eating price codes and other relevant information, see pages 10-14.

⊖ Sleeping

Pisac *p55*

\$\$\$ Royal Inka Pisac, Carretera Ruinas Km 1.5, T267236, www.royalinkahotel.com/hpisac.html. Including breakfast, converted hacienda with olympic-size swimming pool (US\$3.50 per day), sauna and jacuzzi for guests only, very pleasant, provides guides. This chain also has **Royal Inkas I** and **II** in Cuzco.

\$\$ Hostal Varayoc, Mcal Castilla 380, T223638, luzpaz3@hotmail.com. Renovated hotel around a colonial courtyard with working bread oven. Décor is smart and bathrooms are modern.

\$\$ Paz y Luz, T203204, www.pazyluzperu.com. 10-15 mins walk from Pisac Plaza, close to the river. American-owned, pleasant garden, nicely designed rooms, breakfast included. Diane Dunn offers healing from many traditions (including Andean), sacred tours, workshops and gatherings. Recommended.

\$\$ Pisac Inn, at the corner of Pardo on the Plaza, Casilla Postal 1179, Cuzco, T203062, www.pisacinn.com. Bright and charming local decor, pleasant atmosphere, private and shared bathrooms, hot water, sauna and massage. Good breakfast, the **Cuchara de Palo** restaurant serves meals using local ingredients, plus pizza and pasta, café.

\$ Res Beho, Intihuatana 642, T203001. Ask for room in main building, good breakfast, owner's son will act as guide to ruins at weekend.

Pisac to Urubamba *p55*
Yucay

\$\$\$-\$\$\$ Sonesta Posadas del Inca Sacred Valley, Plaza Manco II de Yucay 123, T201107, www.sonesta.com. Converted 300-year-old monastery, it is like a little village with plazas, chapel, 69 comfortable, heated rooms, price includes buffet breakfast. Lots of activities can be arranged, canoeing, horse riding, mountain biking, etc. **Inkafe** restaurant is open to all, serving Peruvian, fusion and traditional cuisine with a US\$15 buffet.

\$\$\$ La Casona de Yucay, Plaza Manco II 104, T201116, www.hotelcasonayucay.com. This colonial house was where Simón Bolívar stayed during his liberation campaign in 1824. With breakfast, heating, 2 patios and gardens, **Don Manuel** restaurant and bar.

\$\$ The Green House, Km 60.2 Huaran, T984 770130, www.thegreenhouseperu.com. A charming, Wi-Fi-free retreat, only 4 rooms, comfortable lounge, restaurant, small kitchen for guests, beautiful garden, restricted internet. Information on walks and day trips in the area. Warmly recommended.

\$\$ Hostal Y'Llary, on Plaza Manco II 107, T201112, www.hostalyllary.com. Including breakfast, hot water, parking.

Urubamba *p56*

\$\$\$\$ Río Sagrado (Orient Express), Km 76 Carretera Cuzco–Ollantaytambo, T201631, www.riosagrado.com. 4 km from Urubamba, set in beautiful gardens overlooking the river with fine views. Rooms and villas, **Mayu Wilka** spa, restaurant and bar, offers various packages.

\$\$\$\$ Sol y Luna, Fundo Huincho, west of town, T201620, www.hotelsolyluna.com. Nice bungalows and brand-new suites set off the main road in lovely gardens, pool, excellent gourmet restaurant, wine tastings, spa, handicrafts shop. Also has **Wayra** lounge bar and dining room, open to non-guests, for freshly-cooked, informal lunches, and arranges adventure and cultural activities and traditional tours. Profits go to Sol y Luna educational association, www.colegiosolyluna.com.

\$\$\$\$ Tambo del Inka, Av Ferrocarril s/n, T581777, www.luxurycollection.com/vallesagrado. A resort and spa on the edge of town, in gardens by the river. Completely remodelled with a variety of rooms and suites, fitness centre, swimming pools, **Hawa** restaurant, bar, business facilities and lots of activities arranged.

$$$$-$$$ Casa Andina Private Collection Sacred Valley, paradero 5, Yanahuara, between Urubamba and Ollantaytambo, T984 765501, www.casa-andina.com. In its own 3-ha estate, with all the facilities associated with this chain, plus 'Sacred Spa', gym, internet and planetarium, good restaurant, adventure options.

$$ Posada Las Tres Marías, Zavala 307, T201006, www.posadatresmarias.com. A little way from the centre, quiet. Comfortable, hot water, no TV, lovely garden and shady terrace, breakfast included (can be early). Recommended.

$ Hospedaje Los Jardines, Jr Convención 459, T201331, www.hospedajelosjardines. blogspot.com. Attractive guesthouse with comfortable rooms, hot water, non-smoking, delicious breakfast US$3.25 extra (vegans catered for), safe, lovely garden, laundry. Discounts for long stays. **Sacred Valley Mountain Bike Tours** also based here.

$ Hostal Buganvilla, Jr Convención 280, T205102, 984 618900. Sizable rooms with hot water, TV, breakfast on request, quiet.

$ Hostal Urubamba, Bolognesi 605, T201062. Basic, pleasant, cold water, cheaper without bath.

$ pp Las Chullpas, 3 km from town, T201568, www.uhupi.com/chullpas. Very peaceful, includes excellent breakfast, vegetarian meals, English and German spoken, Spanish classes, natural medicine, treks, riding, mountain biking, camping US$3 with hot shower. Mototaxi from town US$0.85, taxi (ask for Querocancha) US$2.

Chinchero p57

$$ La Casa de Barro, T306031 www.lacasa de barro.com. Modern hotel, price includes American breakfast, with hot water, bar, restaurant, tours arranged.

Ollantaytambo p58

$$$ Hostal Sauce, C Ventiderio 248, T204044, www. hostalsauce.com.pe. Smart, simple décor and views of the ruins from some rooms.

$$$ Ñustayoc Mountain Lodge and Resort, about 5 km west of Ollantaytambo, just before Chillca and the start of the Inca Trail, T01-275 0706, www.nustayoclodge. com. Large lodge in a wonderful location with great views of the Verónica massif and other peaks. Lovely flower-filled garden and grounds, nicely decorated, spacious rooms, includes continental breakfast.

$$$ Pakaritampu, C Ferrocarril s/n, T204020, www.pakaritampu.com. Includes breakfast, modern, TV room, restaurant and bar, internet service for guests, laundry, safe and room service. Adventure sports can be arranged. Lunch and dinner are extra. Excellent quality and service.

$$$-$$ Apu Lodge, Calle Lari, T797162, www.apu lodge.com. On the edge of town, great views of the ruins and surrounding mountains. Run by Scot Louise Norton and husband Arturo, good service, can help organize tours and treks. They work with Leap Local (www.leaplocal.org) guides project.

$$$-$$ El Albergue Ollantaytambo, within the railway station gates, T204014, www.elalbergue.com. Owned by North American artist Wendy Weeks. Price includes breakfast; also has **Café Mayu** on the station and a good restaurant. Characterful rooms, some with safe, Wi-Fi, lovely gardens, great showers and a eucalyptus steam sauna. Books for sale and exchange, also handicrafts. Private transport can be arranged to nearby attractions, also mountain-biking, rafting and taxi transfers to the airport. Recommended.

$$ Hostal Iskay II, Patacalle s/n, T204004, www.hostaliskay.com. In the Inca town. Car access is difficult. Only 6 rooms, price includes buffet breakfast, hot water, internet, Wi-Fi, free tea and coffee, use of kitchen. Good reports.

$$ Hostal K'uychipunku, K'uychipunku 6, T204175, www.kuychipunku.com. Close to

Plaza Araccama, hot water, breakfast included, modern, some rooms with view, courtyard, internet and Wi-Fi.

$$ Hostal Munay Tika, Av Ferrocarril 118, T204111, www.munaytika.com. Price includes breakfast, dinner served by arrangement. To use the sauna costs US$5 with prior notice, also has a nice garden, good.

$$ Hotel Sol Ollantay, C Ventiderio s/n by the brigde between the 2 plazas, T204130, www.sol-ollantay.com. Tastefullly renovated in 2009. Good views from most rooms. With breakfast, hot water.

$$-$ Don Ascencio B&B, Av Ferrocarril s/n, T204178, garitho@hotmail.com. New in 2010, with breakfast, TV, heaters if needed. Beside it is **Orishas** bar/restaurant, **$$**, with Wi-Fi, a bit more upmarket than average, good café.

$$-$ KB Tambo, between the main plaza and the ruins, T204091, www.kbtambo.com. Spacious, comfortable rooms, suites, garden view or standard, hot water, Wi-Fi, flower-filled garden, good restaurant (**$$**), breakfast extra. Reserve in advance. Also offers adventure tours.

$$-$ Las Orquídeas, near the start of the road to the station, T204032, www.hostal lasorquideasollantaytambo.com. Price includes breakfast, hot water, Wi-Fi, fairly small but nice rooms, flower-filled patio.

$ pp Hostal Chaska Wasi, Calle del Medio (also C Taypi) north of the plaza, T204045, www.hostalchaskawasi. com. Cheaper with shared bath, with continental breakfast, rooms for up to 4 sharing. A B&B snuggled away in the small alleys behind the plaza, bar and terrace, lunch and dinner on request, simple, use of small kitchen, internet, laundry service. Owner Katy is very friendly.

$ Hostal Ollanta, south side of the plaza, T204116. Basic but in a great location. All rooms with shared bath.

$ pp Hostal Tambo, C Horno, north of the plaza, T773262 or 984 489094, paula1_79@ hotmail.com. Cheaper for groups, breakfast extra. Once past the brown door you emerge into a garden full of fruit trees and flowers. Small, rooms for up to 3 people, basic, shared bath, hot water.

Camping

Restaurant Huatucay, at the edge of the Inca town, between Patacalle and the road to Patacancha, has camping for US$3.60 pp. There are toilets, a minimarket and the restaurant serves typical food.

Eating

Pisac p55

$$-$ Miski Mijuna Wasi, on the Plaza de Armas, T203266. Serves tasty local food, typical and Novo Andino, also international dishes. Has a *pastelería* also.

$$-$ Mullu, Plaza de Armas 352 and Mcal Castilla 375, T208182. Open Tue-Sun 0900-1900. Café/restaurant related to the Mullu store in Cuzco, also has a gallery promoting local artists.

$ Doña Clorinda, on the plaza opposite the church. Tasty food, including vegetarian.

$ Valle Sagrado, Av Amazonas 116 (the main street where buses go towards Urubamba). Good quality, generous portions and a lunchtime buffet that includes vegetarian options. Go early before the tour groups arrive.

Bakery, Mcal Castilla 372. Sells excellent cheese and onion *empanadas* for US$0.25, suitable for vegetarians, and good wholemeal bread.

Blue Llama Café, corner of the plaza opposite Pisac Inn, T203135, www.bluellama cafe.com. Cute, colourful café with a huge range of teas, good coffee, breakfasts and daily menus.

Ulrike's Café, Plaza de Armas 828, T203195, ulrikescafe@terra.com.pe. Has possibly the best apple crumble with ice cream, excellent coffee, smoothies and a wide range of international dishes. Good value 3-course daily *menú*. A good place to chill out.

Urubamba *p56*

$$$ Tunupa, on road from Urubamba to Ollantaytambo, on riverbank, zappa@terra.com.pe. Same owners as Tunupa in Cuzco, colonial-style hacienda, excellent food and surroundings, pre-Columbian and colonial art exhibitions, buffet lunch 1200-1500, US$15, dinner 1800-2030.

$$$-$$ El Huacatay, Arica 620, T201790, http://elhuacatay.com. Open Mon-Sat. A small restaurant with a reputation for fine, creative fusion cuisine (local, Mediterranean, Asian).

$$ El Fogón, Parque Pintacha, T201534. Peruvian food. Recommended.

$$ El Maizal, on the main road, before the bridge, T201454. Country-style restaurant, buffet service with a variety of Novo Andino and international choices, beautiful gardens, open daytime only. Recommended.

$ La Chepita, Av 1 de Mayo, M6, in a small plaza. The place to go on Sun for regional food in the biggest portions you have ever seen. Get 1 plate between 2.

$ Pizza Wasi, Av Mcal Castilla 857, T434751 for delivery. Good pizzas and pastas. Mulled wine served in a small restaurant with nice decor, good value. Has another branch on Plaza Araccama in Ollantaytambo.

Café Plaza, Bolívar 440, on the plaza. Serves breakfasts, meals, desserts, teas and coffee and has a pottery shop next door.

Ollantaytambo *p58*

There are restaurants all over town offering menú turístico, pizzas, pastas, snacks, juices and hot drinks.

$$ Blue Puppy, C Horno at the plaza, T630464. Restaurant and lounge open for breakfast, lunch and dinner, serving Tex-Mex, local dishes, pizzas, soups, salads, and desserts. Also has a bar, sports and DVDs on the screen, new in 2010.

$$ Heart's Café, on Plaza de Armas, T204078, www.livingheartperu.org. Open 0700-2100. Mainly wholefood restaurant serving international and Peruvian dishes, including vegetarian, box lunch and takeaway available, good coffee. All profits to education and self-help projects in the Sacred Valley. Deservedly popular and recommended.

$$ Il Cappuccino and **Kusicoyllor**, Plaza Araccama. Good coffee and continental and American breakfasts. Also serves *menú turístico*, lunch and dinner, desserts, juices and light meals.

$$ Mayupata, Jr Convención s/n, across bridge on the way to the ruins, on the left, T204083. International choices and a selection of Peruvian dishes, desserts, sandwiches and coffee, opens 0600 for breakfast, and serves lunch and dinner. Bar has fireplace; river view, relaxing atmosphere.

$$-$ Alcázar Café, C del Medio, 50 m from Plaza, T204034. Vegetarian, but also offers meat and fish, and pasta. Arranges excursions to Andean communities.

$ La Ñusta, Plaza de Armas corner of Chaupi Calle, ask here about their *hospedaje*. Popular, good food, snacks, soups, salads and juices available.

Calicanto, on the righthand side just before the bridge leading to Plaza Araccama. For coffees and light meals, etc, overlooking the river that divides the town.

Inca's Park, Plaza de Armas. Central café which also has *hospedaje*, **$** with bath and hot water. Meals are not included in the lodging price.

⊛ Festivals and events

Ollantaytambo *p58*

On the Sun following Inti Raymi, there is a colourful festival, the **Ollanta-Raymi**. **6 Jan**: the **Bajada de Reyes Magos** (the Magi), with dancing, a bull fight, local food and a fair. **End-May/early-Jun**: 50 days after Easter, **Fiesta del Señor de Choquekillca**, patron saint of Ollantaytambo, with several days of dancing, weddings, processions, masses, feasting and drinking. **29 Oct**: the town's anniversary, with lots of dancing in traditional costume and many local delicacies for sale.

Urubamba p56

Agrotourism Chichubamba, Casa de ProPerú, Jr Rejachayoc, T201562, www.agro tourismsacredvalley.com. A community tourism project which lets visitors take part in a number of traditional activities (culinary, horticulture, textiles, ceramics, beekeeping, etc, US$3 pp, cheaper for groups), hiking US$10, lodging **$** pp and local meals. 20 mins' walk from Urubamba; follow the signs.

Horse riding Perol Chico, 5 km from Urubamba at Km 77, T084-974 798890/974 780020, www.perolchico.com. Dutch/Peruvian owned and operated, 1- to 14-day trips, good horses, riding is Peruvian Paso style.

Trekking Haku Trek, contact Javier Saldívar, T984 613001 (mob). Cooperative tourism project in the Chicón valley (the mountain valley above Urubamba), run by residents of the community, 1- and 2-day hiking trips based at a simple eco-lodge; profits are used to fund reforestation of the area.

Urubamba p56

Bus Terminal, west of town on the main road, about 3 km from centre. From Urubamba to **Calca**, **Pisac** (US$1, 1 hr) and **Cuzco**, about 2 hrs, US$1.80; also buses to Cuzco via Chinchero, same fare. Combis run to **Ollantaytambo**, 45 mins, US$0.50.

Chinchero and Moray p57

Road There is a paved road from the main road between Chinchero and Urubamba to the village of Maras and from there an unmade road in good condition leads to Moray, 9 km. Ask in Maras for the best route to walk, other than on the main road. Any bus between Urubamba and Cuzco via Chinchero passes the clearly marked turning to Maras. From the junction taxi colectivos charge US$1.50 pp to Maras, or you can walk (30 mins). There is public transport from Chinchero to Maras;

it stops running between 1700 and 1800. Taxi to Moray, 1-hr wait then take you to the salt pans, from where you can walk back to the Urubamba-Ollantaytambo road, US$20.

Ollantaytambo p58

Bus Colectivos leave all day for Urubamba and Cuzco from 1 block east of the main plaza. Direct bus Ollantaytambo to **Cuzco** at 0715 and 1945, US$2.85. Direct taxi colectivo service from C Pavitos, Cuzco, leaves when full US$3.60 to Ollantaytambo. Minibuses and taxis leave the small Terminal de Transportes just up from Ollantaytambo station (10-15 mins walk from the plaza) at train times for Urubamba and Cuzco, US$3.60 shared to either place, but they may try to charge US$24 as a private service only. Say you'll go to the colectivo terminal and they may reduce the price. Transfers and tours with **Aló K'antuyoc**, at the hostel of that name on Av Ferrocarril, T204147, kantuyoc@ hotmail.com. See also under trains to and from Machu Picchu, page 68. There are colectivos and mototaxis at the Plaza for the station when trains are due.You won't be allowed on the station unless you have previously bought a ticket (and it is best to buy tickets in Cuzco).

Pisac p55

Banks ATM on the plaza next to **Ulrike's Café**, sometimes hard to find behind the market stalls. Also money excange at the **Blue Llama Café**.

Ollantaytambo p58

Banks ATM at C Ventiderio 248, between the Plaza and Av Ferrocarril, and at Hostal Sauce. **Globalnet** on north side of Plaza. **Internet and telephone** Several places in town. **Medical services** Hampi Traveller's Clinic, Plaza de Armas, www.hampiland.com. Has ambulance and evacuation service and professional medical care.

Machu Picchu and the Inca trails

There is a tremendous feeling of awe on first witnessing Machu Picchu. The ancient citadel (42 km from Ollantaytambo by rail) straddles the saddle of a high mountain (2380 m) with steep terraced slopes falling away to the fast-flowing Urubamba river snaking its hairpin course far below in the valley floor. Towering overhead is Huayna Picchu, and green jungle peaks provide the backdrop for the whole majestic scene. Machu Picchu is a complete Inca city. For centuries it was buried in jungle, until Hiram Bingham stumbled upon it in 1911. It was then explored by an archaeological expedition sent by Yale University. The ruins – staircases, terraces, temples, palaces, towers, fountains and the famous Intihuatana (the so-called 'Hitching Post of the Sun') – require at least a day. Take time to appreciate not only the masonry, but also the selection of large rocks for foundations, the use of water in the channels below the Temple of the Sun and the surrounding mountains.

Ins and outs

Entrance to Machu Picchu The site is open from 0600 to 1730. Entrance fee is 126 soles, 64 for Peruvians, 63 with ISIC card (US$45 and 22 approximately). Tickets must be bought in soles, in advance from **Ministerio de Cultura** in Aguas Calientes ① *Av Pachacútec cuadra 1, 0500-2200 (also i perú here, of 4, T211104, iperumachupicchu@prom peru.gob.pe, daily 0900-1300, 1400-2000)*, Cuzco (see page 26), www.drc-cusco.gob.pe, or online, http://boletajevirtual.drc-cusco.gob.pe or www.machupicchu.gob.pe (online tickets can be paid for by Visa card, or at any branch of Banco de la Nación). You can deposit your luggage at the entrance for US$1. Guides are available at the site, they are often very knowledgeable and worthwhile. The official price for a guide is US$80 for a full tour for 1-10 people. Site wardens are also informative, in Spanish only. A guarded gate by the river in Aguas Calientes opens only at 0530, so it is not possible to walk up to the ruins to be there before the first buses. After 1530 the ruins are quieter, but note that the last bus down from the ruins leaves at 1730. Monday and Friday are bad days in high season because there is usually a crowd of people on guided tours who are going or have been to Pisac market on Sunday. The hotel is located next to the entrance, with a self-service restaurant. Take your own food and drink if you don't want to pay hotel prices, and take plenty of drinking water. Note that food is not officially allowed into the site and drink can only be carried in canteens/water bottles. In the dry season sandflies can be a problem, so take insect repellent and wear long clothes.

Around the site

Huayna Picchu, the mountain overlooking the site (on which there are also ruins), has steps to the top for a superlative view of the whole site, but it is not for those who are afraid of heights and you shouldn't leave the path. The climb takes up to 90 minutes but the steps are dangerous after bad weather. Visitors are given access to the main path at 0700 and 1000 daily, latest return time 1500 (maximum 200 people per departure). Check with the Ministerio de Cultura in Aguas Calientes or Cuzco for current departure times and to sign up for a place. The other trail to Huayna Picchu, down near the Urubamba, is via the Temple of the Moon, in two caves, one above the other, with superb Inca niches inside. For the trail to the Temple of the Moon: from the path to Huayna Picchu, take the marked trail to the left. It is in good shape, although it descends further than you think it should. After the Temple you may proceed to Huayna Picchu, but this path is overgrown, slippery in the wet and has a crooked ladder on an exposed part about 10 minutes before reaching the top (not for the faint-hearted). It is safer to return to the main trail to Huayna Picchu, although this adds about 30 minutes to the climb. The round trip takes about four hours. Before doing any trekking around Machu Picchu, check with an official which paths may be used, or which are one-way.

   The famous Inca bridge is about 45 minutes along a well-marked trail south of the Royal Sector. The bridge (on which you cannot walk) is spectacularly sited, carved into a vertiginous cliff-face. East of the Royal Sector is the path leading up to **Intipunku** on the Inca Trail (45 minutes, fine views).

Aguas Calientes

Those with more time should spend the night at Aguas Calientes and visit the ruins early in the morning, when fewer people are around. Most hotels and restaurants are near the railway station, on the plaza, or on Avenida Pachacútec, which leads from the plaza to the **thermal baths** ① *0500-2030, US$3.15, 10 mins walk from the town* (a communal pool, smelling of sulphur) good bar for cocktails in the pool. You can rent towels and bathing costumes (US$3) at several places on the road to the baths; basic toilets and changing facilities and showers for washing *before* entering the baths; take soap and shampoo, and keep an eye on valuables. The **Museo Manuel Chávez Ballon** ① *Carretera Hiram Bingham, Wed-Sun 0900-1600, US$7*, displays objects found at Machu Picchu.

Machu Picchu listings

For Sleeping and Eating price codes and other relevant information, see pages 10-14.

⊙ Sleeping

Machu Picchu *p64*
$$$$ Machu Picchu Sanctuary Lodge, reservations as for the *Hotel Monasterio* in Cuzco, which is under the same management (Peru Orient Express Hotels), T084-984 816956, www.sanctuarylodge.net. Comfortable, good service, helpful staff, food well-cooked and presented. Electricity and water 24 hrs a day, prices are all-inclusive, restaurant for residents only in the evening, but the buffet lunch is open to all. Usually fully booked well in advance, try Sun night as other tourists find Pisac market a greater attraction.

Aguas Calientes *p66*
$$$$ Inkaterra Machu Picchu Pueblo, Km 104, 5 mins walk along the railway from town, T211122. Reservations: C Andalucía 174, Miraflores, Lima, T01-610 0400; in Cuzco at Plaza las Nazarenas 113 p2, T234010, www.inkaterra.com. Beautiful colonial-style bungalows in village compound surrounded by cloud forest, lovely gardens with a lot of steps between the public areas and rooms, pool, restaurant, also campsite with hot showers at good rates, offer tours to Machu Picchu, several guided walks on and off the property, great buffet breakfasts included

in price. Also has the Café Inkaterra by the railway line. Recommended.
$$$$ Sumaq Machu Picchu, Av Hermanos Ayar Mz 1, Lote 3, T211059, www.sumaq hotelperu.com. New 5-star on the edge of town, between railway and road to Machu Picchu. Suites and luxury rooms with Wi-Fi, heating, cable TV, etc, restaurant and bar, spa.
$$$ Gringo Bill's (**Hostal Q'oñi Unu**), Colla Raymi 104, T211046, www.gringobills. com (in Cuzco Av El Sol 520, T223663). With breakfast, hot water, laundry, money exchange, luggage stored, good beds, good restaurant, breakfast from 0530, packed lunch available. Views of the plaza are now oscured by the monstrous new municipal building.
$$$ La Cabaña, Av Pachacútec M20-3, T211048, www.lacabanamachupicchu.com. With breakfast, hot water, café, laundry service, helpful, popular with groups.
$$$ Presidente, at the old station, T211034, www.hostalpresidente.com. Adjoining Hostal Machu Picchu, see below, more upmarket but little difference, rooms without river view cheaper, price includes breakfast.
$$$ Rupa Wasi, Huanacaure 180, T211101, www.rupawasi.net. Charming 'eco-lodge' up a small alley off Collasuyo, laid back, comfortable, great views from the balconies, purified water available, organic garden, good breakfasts, half-board available, excellent restaurant, **The Tree House**, and cookery classes.

$$ Hostal Machu Picchu, at the old station, T211065, sierrandina@gmail.com. Functional, quiet, Wilber, the owner's son, has travel information, hot water, nice balcony over the Urubamba, grocery store, price includes breakfast. Recommended.

$$ Hostal Pachakúteq, up the hill beyond *Hostal La Cabaña*, T211061. Hot water, good breakfast, quiet, family-run. Recommended.

$$ Hostal Wiracocha Inn, C Wiracocha, T211088, www.wiracochainn.com. Hot water, breakfast included, small garden, helpful, popular with groups, also has higher-priced suites.

$ pp Hostal Los Caminantes, Av Imperio de los Incas 140, by the railway just beyond the old station, T211083. With bath and hot water, breakfast extra, basic but clean.

$ Hostal Pirwa, C Túpac Inka Yupanki, www.pirwahostelscusco.com. With breakfast, TV, bath and luggage store, in the same group as in Cuzco, Lima and elsewhere.

$ Las Bromelias, Colla Raymi, T211145, just off Plaza before Gringo Bill's. Cheaper without bath, small, hot water.

$ Terrazas del Inca, C Wiracocha s/n, T211113, www.terrazasdelinca.com. Safety deposit box, continental breakfast included, kitchen use, helpful staff. Recommended.

Camping The only official campsite is in a field by the river, just below Puente Ruinas station, toilets, showers, US$3.50 pp. Do not leave your tent and belongings unattended.

🍴 Eating

Aguas Calientes *p66*
The old station and Av Pachútec are lined with eating places, many of them *pizzerías*. Tax is often added as an extra to the bill.

$$$ Café Inkaterra, on the railway, just below the Machu Picchu Pueblo Hotel. US$15 for a great lunch buffet with scenic views of the river.

$$ Indio Feliz, C Lloque Yupanqui, T211090. Great French cuisine, excellent value and service, set 3-course meal for US$10, good pisco sours in the new bar, great atmosphere. Highly recommended.

$$ Inka Wasi, Av Pachacútec. Very good choice, has an open fire, full Peruvian and international menu available.

$$ Inka's Pizza Pub, on the plaza. Good pizzas, also changes money.

$$ Pueblo Viejo, Av Pachacútec (near plaza). Good food in a spacious but warm environment. Price includes use of the salad bar.

$$ Toto's House, Av Imperio de los Incas, on the railway line. Same owners as Pueblo Viejo. Good value and quality *menú*, buffet from 1130-1500.

$ Discovery, Plaza de Armas, T211355. The best coffee and internet connection in Aguas Calientes. Several computers and Wi-Fi.

$ Govinda, Av Pachacútec y Túpac Inka Yupanki. Vegetarian restaurant with a cheap set lunch. Recommended.

$ Paraguachayoc, Av Pachacútec, at the top near the baths. Charming little restaurant with trout farm where you can catch your own dinner. US$5 for a whole trout with chips and drink.

🍸 Bars and clubs

Aguas Calientes *p66*
Waisicha Pub, C Lloque Yupanqui. For good music and atmosphere.

🥾 Activities and tours

Aguas Calientes *p66*
Peru Sightseeing, www.perusightseeing. com. The only agency in Aguas Calientes, guided trips to Machu Picchu with audio tours as well as local guides, 2 or 3 day packages, or just the Machu Picchu tour. Also half-day tours in the area to Mandor and the Machu Picchu musuem. Can make onward travel arrangements.

Machu Picchu *p64*

Bus Buses leave **Aguas Calientes** for Machu Picchu every 30 mins from 0630 until 1300, 25 mins. US$14 return, US$7 single, valid 48 hrs. The bus stop in Aguas Calientes is 50 m from the railway station, with the ticket office opposite. Tickets can also be bought in advance at **Consetur**, Sta Catalina Ancha, Cuzco, which saves queuing when you arrive in Aguas Calientes. Buses return from the ruins to Aguas 0700-0900 and 1200-1730. The walk up from Aguas Calientes follows an Inca path, but it is in poor condition and crosses the motor road (take care).

Train Three companies operate: **PerúRail** (Av Pachacútec, Wanchac Station, T581414, www.perurail.com) to Machu Picchu from Poroy, near Cuzco, from Urubamba and from Ollantaytambo. **Inca Rail** (Portal de Panes 105, Plaza de Armas, Cuzco, T233030, or Lima T613 5288, www.incarail.com) from Ollantaytambo to Machu Picchu. **Machu Picchu Train** (Av El Sol 576, Cuzco, T221199, www.machupicchutrain.com) also runs from Ollantaytambo. They go to Aguas Calientes (the official name of this station is 'Machu Picchu'). The station for the tourist trains at Aguas Calientes is on the outskirts of town, 200 m from the Pueblo Hotel and 50 m from where buses leave for Machu Picchu ruins. There is a paved road between Aguas Calientes and the start of the road up to the ruins. **Note** Services may be disrupted in the rainy season, especially Jan-Feb.

There are 4 classes of **PerúRail** tourist train: **Vistadome** (US$71 one-way from Poroy, US$43-60 from Ollantaytambo); **Expedition** (US$48 Poroy-Machu Picchu one-way, US$38-43 from Ollantaytambo); **Auto Vagón** (from the Hotel Tambo del Inka in Urubamba); and the luxurious **Hiram Bingham** service with meals, drinks and entertainment (US$641 return from Poroy).

Services from Poroy and Urubamba run once a day; those from Ollantaytambo 5 times a day each. Seats can be reserved even if you're not returning the same day. These trains have toilets, video, snacks and drinks for sale. You must have your original passport to travel on the trains to Machu Picchu. Tickets for all trains may be bought at Wanchac station and the sales office on Portal de Carnes, Plaza de Armas, in Cuzco, at travel agencies, or via PerúRail's website, www.perurail.com.

Inca Rail has 3 trains a day Ollantaytambo-Machu Picchu (*Yllari* at sunrise, *Waala* in the morning and *Tutayay* at sunset), US$60 one way executive class, US$110 one way 1st class. A/c and heating, snacks available.

Machu Picchu Train also has 3 trains a day Ollantaytambo–Machu Picchu (*The Lost City Traveller* at 0720, returning 1612, *Cuzco Imperial* 1148, returning 1915, and *Sunrise* at 1236, returning 1032). The Lost City Traveller fare is US$59. Journey time is 1 hr 25 mins. Coaches have been specially designed for the service.

Tourists may not travel on the local train to Machu Picchu, but there is a way to avoid the train altogether. Take a bus from Cuzco towards Quillabamba at 1900, US$6 (other buses in the day may not connect with onward transport). Get out at **Santa María** (about 7 hrs) where minibuses wait to go to **Santa Teresa**, 2 hrs, US$2.10. Your reach Santa Teresa by sunrise in time to buy breakfast. From Santa Teresa you have to cross the Río Urubamba. Cross the new bridge and walk 6 km to the Central Hidroeléctrica, a nice, flat road, or take a combi, US$10-15. From the Hidroeléctrica train station it's 40 mins on the local train to Aguas Calientes at 1520, US$8 for tourists, or you can walk along the railway in 2-3 hrs (at Km 114.5 is **$** pp **Hospedaje Mandor**, about 2 km from bridge to Machu Picchu). To return, at 0600 walk from Aguas Calientes to Santa Teresa to catch a bus at 1000 to Santa María, arrive at 1200. At 1300 take a bus back to Cuzco, arriving between 1900-2000. Or take the local train from Aguas Calientes to Santa Teresa at 1210, stay in a hostal, then take the 1000 bus to Santa María. If using this route, don't forget you can pre-book your ticket for Machu Picchu online or in Cuzco, if you don't want to buy it in Aguas Calientes.

Directory

Aguas Calientes *p66*
Banks Several ATMs in town, but they may run out of cash at weekends. **BCP** changes TCs. **Internet** Many internet shops, average price US$1 per hr; slow connection. **Medical services** Hampi Land, C Hermanos Ayar, Lote 6 Mz 10, T782641, www.hampiland.com. Professional, 24-hr medical care for tourists, with emergency rescue and ambulance services, pharmacy, oxygen. **Urgent Medical Center**, Av de Los Incas 119, T211005, 984 761314 (mob). Good care at affordable prices. **Post offices** Serpost agencies: just off the plaza, between the Centro Cultural Machu Picchu and Galería de Arte Tunupa. **Telephones** Office is on C Collasuyo and there are plenty of phone booths around town.

Inca trails

The most impressive way to reach Machu Picchu is via the centuries-old Inca Trail that winds its way from the Sacred Valley near Ollantaytambo, taking three to five days. The spectacular hike runs from Km 88, Qorihuayrachina (2299 m), a point immediately after the first tunnel 22 km beyond Ollantaytambo station. A sturdy suspension bridge has now been built over the Río Urubamba. Guided tours often start at Km 82, Piscacucho, reached by road. Rules for hiking the trail are detailed below. What makes this hike so special is the stunning combination of Inca ruins, unforgettable views, magnificent mountains, exotic vegetation and extraordinary ecological variety.

Ins and outs

Equipment The Inca Trail is rugged and steep, but the magnificent views compensate for any weariness which may be felt. It is cold at night, however, and weather conditions change rapidly, so it is important to take not only strong footwear, rain gear and warm clothing but also food, water, water purification for when you fill bottles from streams, insect repellent, a supply of plastic bags, coverings, a good sleeping bag, a torch/flashlight and a stove for preparing hot food and drink to ward off the cold at night. A stove using paraffin (kerosene) is preferable, as fuel can be bought in small quantities in markets. A tent is essential, but if you're hiring one in Cuzco, check carefully for leaks. Walkers who have not taken adequate equipment have died of exposure.

All the necessary equipment can be rented; see page 43 under Camping equipment and Activities and tours. Good maps of the Trail and area can be bought from **South American Explorers** in Lima or Cuzco. If you have any doubts about carrying your own pack, reasonably priced porters/guides are available. Carry a day-pack for your water, snacks, etc in case you walk faster than the porters and you have to wait for them to catch you up.

Tours Travel Agencies in Cuzco arrange transport to the start, equipment, food, etc, for an all-in price for all treks that lead to the Machu Picchu Historical Sanctuary. Prices vary from US$450 to US$540 per person for a four day/three night trek on the Classic Inca Trail. If the price is significantly lower, you should be concerned as the company will be cutting corners and may not be paying the environment the respect the regulations were designed to instil. All are subject to strict rules introduced in 2001 and must be licensed. Tour operators taking clients on any of the Inca Trails leading to the Machu Picchu Historical Sanctuary have to pay an annual fee. Groups of up to seven independent travellers who do not wish to use a tour operator are allowed to hike the trails if they contact an independent, licensed guide to accompany them, as long as they do not contact any other persons such as porters or cooks. There is a maximum of 500 visitors per day allowed on the Classic Inca Trail. Operators pay US$12 for each porter and other trail staff; porters are not be permitted to carry more than 20 kg. Littering is banned, as is carrying plastic water bottles (canteens only may be carried). Pets and pack animals are prohibited, but llamas are allowed as far as the first pass. Groups have to use approved campsites only.

Trail tickets On all hiking trails (Km 82 or Km 88 to Machu Picchu, Salkantay to Machu Picchu, and Km 82 or Km 88 to Machu Picchu via Km 104) adults must pay US$86, students and children under 15 US$43. On the Camino Real de los Inkas from Km 104 to

Wiñay-Wayna and Machu Picchu the fee is US$51 per adult, US$28 for students and children and Salkantay to Huayllabamba and Km 88, US$51. The Salkantay trek is subject to a trekking charge of US$45. All tickets must be bought at the Ministerio de Cultura office on Calle San Bernardo in Cuzco; tickets are only sold on presentation of a letter from a licensed tour operator on behalf of the visitor, including full passport details. Tickets are non-refundable and cannot be changed so make sure you provide accurate passport details to your tour operator. None is sold at the entrance to any of the routes. See page 45 on the need to reserve your place on the Trail in advance. You can save a bit of money by arranging your own transport back to Ollantaytambo in advance, either for the last day of your tour, or by staying an extra night in Aguas Calientes and taking the early morning train, then take a bus back to Cuzco. If you take your own tent and sleeping gear, some agencies give a discount. Make sure your return train ticket to Cuzco has your name on it (spelt absolutely correctly) for the tourist train, otherwise you have to pay for any changes.

The Trail is closed each February for cleaning and repair. The Annual Inca Trail Clean-up takes place usually in September. Many agencies and organizations are involved and volunteers should contact South American Explorers in Cuzco for full details of ways to help.

Advice Four days would make a comfortable trip (though much depends on the weather). Allow a further day to see Machu Picchu when you have recovered from the hike. You cannot take backpacks into Machu Picchu; leave them at ticket office, US$1. The first two days of the Trail involve the stiffest climbing, so do not attempt it if you're feeling unwell. Leave all your valuables in Cuzco and keep everything inside your tent, even your shoes. Security has, however, improved in recent years. Always take sufficient cash to tip porters and guides at the end (S/.50-100 each, but at your discretion). Avoid the July-August high season and check the conditions in the rainy season from November to April (note that this can vary). In the wet it is cloudy and the paths are very muddy and difficult. Also watch out for coral snakes in this area (black, red, yellow bands).

The Trail

The trek to the sacred site begins either at Km 82, **Piscacucho**, or at Km 88, **Qorihuayrachina**, at 2600 m. In order to reach Km 82 hikers are transported by their tour operator in a minibus on the road that goes to Quillabamba. From Piri onward the road follows the riverbank and ends at Km 82, where there is a bridge. The Inca Trail equipment, food, fuel and field personnel reach Km 82 (depending on the tour operator's logistics) for the Sernanp staff to weigh each bundle before the group arrives. When several groups are leaving on the same day, it is more convenient to arrive early. Km 88 can only be reached by train, subject to schedule and baggage limitations. The train goes slower than a bus, but you start your walk nearer to Llaqtapata and Huayllabamba. (See below for details of variations in starting points for the Inca Trail.)

The walk to **Huayllabamba**, following the Cusichaca River, needs about three hours and isn't too arduous. Beyond Huayllabamba, a popular camping spot for tour groups, there is a camping place about an hour ahead, at **Llulluchayoc** (3200 m). A punishing 1½ hour climb further is **Llulluchapampa**, an ideal meadow for camping. If you have the energy to reach this point, it will make the second day easier because the next stage, the ascent to the first pass, **Warmiwañuska** (Dead Woman's Pass) at 4200 m, is tough; 2½ hours.

Afterwards take the steep path downhill to the Pacamayo valley. Beware of slipping on the Inca steps after rain. Tour groups usually camp by a stream at the bottom (1½ hours from the first pass). It is no longer permitted to camp at **Runkuracay**, on the way up to the second pass (a much easier climb, 3850 m). Magnificent views near the summit in clear weather. A good overnight place is about 30 minutes past the Inca ruins at **Sayacmarca** (3500 m), about an hour on after the top of the second pass.

A gentle two-hour climb on a fine stone highway leads through an Inca tunnel to the third pass. Near the top there's a spectacular view of the entire Vilcabamba range. You descend to Inca ruins at **Phuyopatamarca** (3650 m), well worth a long visit, even camping overnight. There is a 'tourist bathroom' here where water can be collected (but purify it before drinking).

From there steps go downhill to the impressive ruins of **Wiñay-Wayna** (2700 m, entry US$5.75), with views of the recently cleared terraces of Intipata. Access is possible, but the trail is not easily visible. There is a basic hostel with bunk beds, **$** per person, showers and a small restaurant. There is a small campsite in front of the hostel. After Wiñay-Wayna there is no water and no camping till Machu Picchu. The path from this point goes more or less level through jungle until the steep staircase up to the **Intipunku** (two hours), where there's a magnificent view of Machu Picchu, especially at dawn, with the sun alternately in and out, clouds sometimes obscuring the ruins, sometimes leaving them clear.

Get to Machu Picchu as early as possible, preferably before 0830 for best views but in any case before the tourist trains in high season. **Note** Camping is not allowed at Intipunku; guards may confiscate your tent. You may only camp in the field by the river below Puente Ruinas station.

Alternative Inca trails

The **Camino Real de los Inkas** starts at Km 104, where a footbridge gives access to the ruins of Chachabamba and the trail which ascends, passing above the ruins of Choquesuysuy to connect with the main trail at Wiñay-Wayna. This first part is a steady, continuous ascent of three hours (take water) and the trail is narrow and exposed in parts. Many people recommend this short Inca Trail. Good hiking trails from Aguas Calientes (see page 66) have been opened along the left bank of the Urubamba, for day hikes crossing the bridge of the hydroelectric plant to Choquesuysuy. A three-night trek goes from Km 82 to Km 88, then along the Río Urubamba to Pacaymayo Bajo and Km 104, from where you take the Camino Real de los Inkas.

Two treks involve routes from **Salkantay**: one, known as the High Inca Trail joins the classic Trail at Huayllabamba, then proceeds as before on the main Trail through Wiñay Wayna to Machu Picchu. To get to Salkantay, you have to start the trek in Mollepata, northwest of Cuzco in the Apurímac valley. *Ampay* buses run from Arcopata on the Chinchero road, or you can take private transport to Mollepata (three hours from Cuzco). Salkantay to Machu Picchu this way takes three nights. The second Salkantay route, known as the **Santa Teresa Trek**, takes four days and crosses the 4500-m Huamantay Pass to reach the Santa Teresa valley, which you follow to its confluence with the Urubamba. The goal is the town of Santa Teresa from where you can go to La Hidroeléctrica station for the local train to Aguas Calientes (see page 68). On this trek, **Machu Picchu Lodge to Lodge** ① *Mountain Lodges of Peru, T084-243636 (in Lima T01-421 6952, in North America T1-510-525 8846, in Europe 43-664-434 3340), www.mountainlodgesofperu.com,* a series of lodges have been set up. Fully guided tours take 7 days, going from lodge to lodge, which are at Soraypampa (**Salkantay Lodge and Adventure Resort**), Huayraccmachay (**Wayra Lodge**), Collpapampa (**Colpa Lodge**) and Lucmabamba (**Lucma Lodge**). Contact **Mountain Lodges of Peru** for rates, departure dates and all other details.

There are other routes which approach the Inca trails to Machu Picchu, such as Km 77, Chillca, up the Sillque ravine in the Qente valley, which is commonly called the Lago Ancascocha route. A common starting point for this trek is the community of Huarocondo. You can end this trek either at Huayllabamba, where you join the Classic Inca Trail (for further walking), or at the railway line at Km 82 (for transport to the Sacred Valley). Then there is another access through the Millpo Valley in the Salkantay area. From the Vilcabamba mountain range, one can reach Machu Picchu by hiking down from Huancacalle to Chaulla by road, getting to Santa Teresa and walking to La Hidroeléctrica station. Tour operators which specialize in trekking can advise on these routes.

Inca Jungle Trail This is offered by several tour operators in Cuzco: on the first day you cycle downhill from Abra Málaga to Santa María (see Train, above, page 68), 4-5 hours of riding on the the main Quillabamba–Cuzco highway with speeding vehicles inattentive to cyclists on the road. It's best to pay for good bikes and back-up on this section. The second day is a hard seven-hour trek from Santa María to Santa Teresa. It involves crossing three adventurous bridges and bathing in the hot springs at Santa Teresa (US$1.65 entry). The third day is a six-hour trek from Santa Teresa to Aguas Calientes and the final day is a guided tour of Machu Picchu.

Choquequirao

① *Entry US$13.50, students US$6.75.*

Choquequirao is another 'lost city of the Incas', built on a ridge spur almost 1600 m above the Apurímac. Although only 30% has been uncovered, it is reckoned to be a larger site than Machu Picchu, but with fewer buildings. The main features of Choquequirao are the **Lower Plaza**, considered by most experts to be the focal point of the city. The **Upper Plaza**, reached by a huge set of steps or terraces, has what are possibly ritual baths. A beautiful set of slightly curved agricultural terraces run for over 300 m east-northeast of the Lower Plaza.

Usnu is a levelled hilltop platform, ringed with stones and giving awesome 360-degree views. The **Ridge Group**, still shrouded in vegetation, is a large collection of unrestored buildings some 50-100 m below the Usnu. The **Outlier Building**, isolated and surrounded on three sides by sheer drops of over 1.5 km into the Apurímac Canyon, possesses some of the finest stonework within Choquequirao. **Capuliyoc**, nearly 500 m below the Lower Plaza, is a great set of agricultural terraces, visible on the approach from the far side of the valley. One section of terraces is decorated with llamas in white stone.

There are three ways in to Choquequirao. None is a gentle stroll. The shortest way is from **Cachora**, a village on the south side of the Apurímac, reached by a side road from the Cuzco-Abancay highway, shortly after Saywite. It is four hours by bus from Cuzco to the turn-off, then a two-hour descent from the road to Cachora (from 3695 m to 2875 m). Guides (Celestino Peña is the official guide) and mules are available in Cachora. From the village you need a day to descend to the Río Apurímac then seven hours to climb up to Choquequirao. Allow 1-2 days at the site then return the way you came. This route is well-signed and in good condition, with excellent campsites and showers en route. Horses can be hired to carry your bags. The second and third routes take a minimum of eight days and require thorough preparation. You can start either at Huancacalle, or at Santa Teresa, between Machu Picchu and Chaullay. Both routes involve an incredible number of strenuous ascents and descents. You should be acclimatised for altitudes ranging from 2400 m to between 4600 and 5000 m and be prepared for extremes of temperature. In each case you end the trail at Cachora. It is possible to start either of these long hikes at Cachora, continuing even from Choquequirao to Espíritu Pampa.

Saywite ➔ *3 km from the main road at Km 49 from Abancay, 153 km from Cuzco, US$4, students US$2. Altitude: 3500 m.*

Beyond the town of Curahuasi, 126 km from Cuzco, is the large carved rock of Saywite. It is a UNESCO World Heritage Site. The principal monolith is said to represent the three regions of jungle, sierra and coast, with the associated animals and Inca sites of each. It is fenced in, but ask the guardian for a closer look. It was defaced, allegedly, when a cast was taken of it, breaking off many of the animals' heads. Six further archaeological areas fall away from the stone and its neighbouring group of buildings. The site is more easily reached from Abancay than Cuzco.

Choquequirao listings

For Sleeping and Eating price codes and other relevant information, see pages 10-14.

● Sleeping

Choquequirao *p73*

$$ pp **Los Tres Balcones**, Jr Abancay s/n, Cachora, www.choquequirau.com. Hostel designed as start and end-point for the trek to Choquequirao. Breakfast included, comfortable, hot showers, restaurant and pizza oven, camping. Shares information with the town's only internet café. They run a 5-day trek to Choquequirao, US$550, with camping gear (but not sleeping bag), all meals and lunch at the Hostel afterwards, entrance to the ruins, horses to carry luggage (US$650 including transport from Cuzco and bilingual tour guide).

$ pp **Casa de Salcantay**, Prolongación Salcantay s/n, T984 397336, www.salcantay. com. Price includes breakfast, dinner available if booked in advance. Dutch-run hostel with links to community projects, comfortable, small, Dutch, English, German spoken, can help with arranging independent treks, or organize treks with tour operator.

$ pp **La Casona de Ocampo**, San Martín 122, T237514, lacasonadeocampo@yahoo.es. Rooms with hot shower all day, free camping, owner Carlos Robles is knowledgeable.

● Transport

Choquequirao *p73*

From Cuzco take the first Abancay bus of the morning with **Bredde** at 0600, buy your ticket the night before to get a seat. Buses run from Abancay (Jr Prado Alto entre Huancavelica y Núñez) to **Cachora** at 0500 and 1400, return 0630 and 1100, 2 hrs, US$1.50. Cars run from the Curahuasi terminal on Av Arenas, Abancay, US$10 for whole vehicle. Trek from Cachora to Choquequirao.

Lake Titicaca

Straddling Peru's southern border with landlocked Bolivia are the deep, sapphire-blue waters of mystical Lake Titicaca, everyone's favourite school geography statistic. This gigantic inland sea covers up to 8500 sq km and is the highest navigable lake in the world, at an average 3810 m above sea level. Its shores and islands are home to the Aymara, Quechua and Uros peoples. Here you can wander through old traditional villages where Spanish is a second language and where ancient myths and beliefs are still held.

The main city on the lake is Puno, where chilled travellers gather to stock up on warm woollies to keep the cold at bay. The high-altitude town is the departure point for the islands, and is also well placed to visit the remarkable funeral towers of Sillustani. Even if you're feeling a bit ruined-out by this stage in your Peruvian odyssey, Sillustani is well worth the effort.

Puno and around → *Phone code: 051. Population: 100,170. Altitude: 3855 m.*

On the northwest shore of Lake Titicaca, Puno is capital of its department and Peru's folklore centre with a vast array of handicrafts, festivals and costumes and a rich tradition of music and dance. Puno gets bitterly cold at night: from June to August the temperature at night can fall to -25°C, but generally not below -5°C.

Ins and outs
Tourist offices: i perú ① *Jr Lima y Deústua, near Plaza de Armas, T365088, iperupuno@promperu. gob.pe, daily 0830-1930.* Helpful English-speaking staff, good information and maps. Municipal website: www.munipuno.gob.pe. **Dircetur** ① *Ayacucho 684, T364976, puno@mincetur.gob.pe*, with a desk at the Terminal Terrestre. **Indecopi**, the consumer protection bureau, has an office at ① *Jr Deústua 644, T363667,*

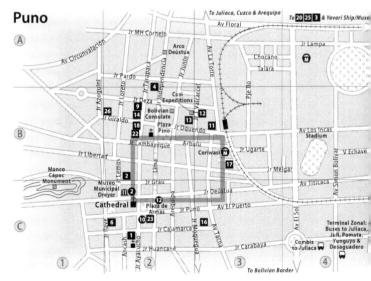

Sleeping 🛏
1 Balsa Inn *C2*
2 Casa Andina Plaza *B2*
3 Casa Andina Private Collection Puno *A4*
4 Casa Andina Tikarani *B2*
5 Colón Inn *Puno centre*
6 Conde de Lemos *C2*
7 El Buho *Puno centre*
8 Hacienda Puno *Puno centre*
9 Hosp Res Margarita *B2*
10 Hostal Europa *Puno centre*
11 Hostal Illampu *B3*
12 Hostal Imperial & Los Uros *B3*
13 Hostal Italia *B2*
14 Hostal Los Pinos *B2*
15 Hostal Pukara *Puno centre*
16 Hostal Rubi 'Los Portales' *C3*
17 Inka's Rest *B3*
18 Intiqa *B2*
19 Julio César *Puno centre*
20 Libertador Lago Titicaca *A4*
21 Plaza Mayor *Puno centre*
22 Posada Don Giorgio *B2*
23 Puno Plaza *C2*
24 Sillustani *Puno centre*
25 Sonesta Posadas del Inca *A4*
26 Tambo Real *B2*

Eating 🍴
1 Cafetería Mercedes *Puno centre*
2 Casa del Corregidor *C2*
3 Casa Grilli La Estancia *Puno centre*
4 Chifa Nan Hua *B2*
5 Don Piero *Puno centre*
6 Govinda *Puno centre*
7 IncAbar *Puno centre*
8 Internacional *Puno Centre*
9 La Hostería *Puno Centre*
10 La Plaza *C2*

jpilco@indecopi.gob.pe. **Tourist police** ① *Jr Deústua 558, T354764, daily 0600-2200. Report any scams, such as unscrupulous price changes, and beware touts (see page 83).*

Sights

The **Cathedral** ① *Mon-Fri 0800-1200, 1500-1800, Sat-Sun until 1900*, completed in 1657, has an impressive baroque exterior, but an austere interior. Across the street from the Cathedral is the **Balcony of the Conde de Lemos** ① *Deústua y Conde de Lemos, art gallery open Mon-Fri 0800-1600* where Peru's Viceroy stayed when he first arrived in the city. The **Museo Municipal Dreyer** ① *Conde de Lemos 289, Mon-Sat 1030-2200, Sun 1600-2200, US$5 includes 45-min guided tour,* has been combined with the private collection of Sr Carlos Dreyer. A short walk up Independencia leads to the **Arco Deústua**, a monument honouring those killed in the battles of Junín and Ayacucho. Nearby, is a mirador giving fine views over the town, the port and the lake beyond. The walk from Jr Cornejo following the Stations of the Cross up a nearby hill, with fine views of Lake Titicaca, has been recommended, but be careful and don't go alone (the same applies to any of the hills around Puno, eg Huajsapata).

Puno centre

Avenida Titicaca leads to the port from where boats go to the islands. From its intersection with Avenida Costanera towards the pier, one side of the road is lined with the kiosks of the **Artesanos Unificados de Puno**, selling crafts. Closer to the port are food kiosks. On the opposite side of the road is a shallow lake where you can hire pedal boats ① *US$0.70 pp for 20 mins*. At the pier are the ticket counters for transport to the islands. The **Malecón Bahía de los Incas**, a lovely promenade along the waterfront, extends to the north and south; it is a pleasant place for a stroll and for birdwatching. The *Yavari*, the oldest ship on Lake Titicaca ① *0815-1715, free but donations of US$6 welcome to help with maintenance costs*, is berthed near the entrance to the Sonesta Posada del Inca hotel and is you have to go through the hotel to get to it. Alternatively, a boat from the port costs US$2 return, with wait. The ship was built in England in 1862 and was shipped in kit form to Arica, then by rail to Tacna and by mule to Lake Titicaca. The journey took six years. The *Yavari* was launched on Christmas Day 1870. Project addresses: England: 61 Mexfield Rd,

11 Los Balcones de Puno *Puno Centre*
12 Mojsa *C2*
13 Pizzería/Trattoria El Buho *Puno centre*
14 Remembranzas *Puno Centre*
15 Ricos Pan *Puno centre*
16 Tradiciones del Lago *Puno centre*
17 Tulipans *Puno centre*
18 Ukukus *Puno centre*
19 Vida Natural *C3*

Bars & clubs 🎵
20 Pub Ekeko's *Puno Centre*

London SW15 2RG, T44-20-8874 0583, yavarilarken@talktalk .net. In Puno: T051-369329, yavariguldentops@hotmail.com. Visit www.yavari.org. Another old ship is the MN *Colla* ① *moored in Barrio Guaje, beyond the Hotel Sonesta Posada del Inka, T368156, daily 0800-1700*, built in Scotland and launched on the lake in 1892. Its museum is similar to the Yavari. Its restaurant serves Peruvian specialties, set menu US$7, buffet US$8, if they have dinner reservations they stay open in the evening. Berthed next to Colla is Hull (UK)-built MS *Ollanta*, which sailed the lake from 1926 to the 1970s.

Around Puno
Anybody interested in religious architecture should visit the villages along the western shore of Lake Titicaca. An Inca sundial can be seen near the village of **Chucuíto** (19 km), which has an interesting church, La Asunción, and houses with carved stone doorways. Visits to Chucuíto usually include the Templo de la Fertilidad, **Inca Uyo**, which boasts many phalli and other fertility symbols. The authenticity and original location of these objects is the subject of debate.

Juli, 80 km, has some fine examples of religious architecture. **San Pedro** on the plaza, is the only functioning church ① *open 0630-1130, 1400-1600, except Tue when only for mass at 0700 and Sun for mass at 0730, 1100 and 1800, free, but donations appreciated.* It contains a series of paintings of saints, with the Via Crucis scenes in the same frame, and gilt side altars above which some of the arches have baroque designs. **San Juan Letrán** ① *daily 0800-1600, US$1.20,* has two sets of 17th-century paintings of the lives of St John the Baptist and of St Teresa, contained in sumptuous gilded frames. San Juan is a museum. It also has intricate *mestizo* carving in pink stone. **Santa Cruz** is closed to visitors, but there is a view of the lake from the plaza in front. The fourth church, **La Asunción** ① *daily 0800-1630, US$1.20,* is also a museum. The nave is empty, but its walls are lined with colonial paintings with no labels. The original painting on the walls of the transept can be seen. Its fine bell tower was damaged by earthquake or lightning. Outside is an archway and atrium which date from the early 17th century. Needlework, other weavings, handicrafts and antiques are offered for sale in town. Near Juli is a small colony of flamingos. Many other birds can be seen from the road. Colectivo Puno-Juli US$1.20; return from Juli outside market at Ilave 349.

A further 20 km along the lake is **Pomata** (bus from Juli US$0.50, US$1.70 from Puno), whose red sandstone church of Santiago Apóstol ① *daily 0700-1200, 1330-1600, US$0.70, but if guardian is not there, leave money on the table* has a striking exterior and beautiful interior, with superb carving and paintings. At **Zepita**, near Desaguadero, the 18th-century Dominican church is also worth a visit.

Near Puno are the *chullpas* (pre-Columbian funeral towers) of **Sillustani** ① *32 km from Puno on an excellent road, US$1.90, take an organized tour; about 3-4 hrs, leave 1430, US$8.50-10, tours usually stop at a Colla house on the way, to see local products*, in a beautiful setting on a peninsula in Lake Umayo. John Hemming writes: "Most of the towers date from the period of Inca occupation in the 15th century, but they are burial towers of the Aymara-speaking Colla tribe. The engineering involved in their construction is more complex than anything the Incas built – it is defeating archaeologists' attempts to rebuild the tallest 'lizard' *chullpa*." There is a museum and handicraft sellers wait at the exit. Photography is best in the afternoon light, though this is when the wind is strongest. The scenery is barren, but impressive. There is a small community at the foot of the promontory.

Llachón → *Population: 1300.*

At the eastern end of the Península de Capachica, which encloses the northern side of the Bahía de Puno, the pretty farming villages of Llachón, Santa María and Ccotos have become a focus of community-based tourism. On Capachica there are currently six organizations, each with a dozen or more families and links to different tour operators in Puno, Cuzco or abroad. The scenery is very pretty, with sandy beaches, pre-Inca terracing, trees and flowers. The view of the sunset from the Auki Carus hill is reckoned to be better even than from Taquile. Visitors share in local activities and 70% of all produce served is from the residents' farms. Throughout the peninsula the dress of the local women is very colourful, with four-cornered hats called *monteros*, matching vests and colourful *polleras*. The peninsula is good for hiking, mountain biking and sailing; boats can be hired.

Puno and around listings

For Sleeping and Eating price codes and other relevant information, see pages 10-14.

☐ Sleeping

Puno *p76, map p76*

A number of luxury hotels are opening in and around the city. Prices vary according to season. Many touts try to persuade tourists to go to a hotel not of their own choosing. Be firm.

$$$$ Libertador Lago Titicaca, on Isla Esteves linked by a causeway 5 km northeast of Puno (taxi US$3), T367780, www.libertador.com.pe. A modern hotel, built on a Tiahuanaco-period site, spacious, good views, phone, bar, good restaurant, disco, good service, electricity and hot water all day, parking.

$$$$ Sonesta Posadas del Inca, Av Sesqui-centenario 610, Huaje, 5 km from Puno on the lakeshore, T364111, www.sonesta.com/ laketiticaca/. 62 rooms with heating, facilities for the disabled, friendly, local textile decorations, good views, *Inkafé* restaurant has an Andean menu, folklore shows.

$$$$-$$$ Casa Andina Private Collection Puno, Av Sesquicentenario 1970, T363992. This recommended chain's lakeshore luxury property. The group also has **$$$ Casa Andina Plaza**, Jr Grau 270, 1 block from plaza, T367520, includes breakfast, TV, heating, non-smoking rooms, safe, central. Business centre with internet, parking; and **$$$ Casa Andina Tikarani**, Independencia 185, T367803, similar to the **Plaza**, but further from the centre. Visit www.casa-andina.com.

$$$ Intiqa, Jr Tarapacá 272, T366900, www.intiqa hotel.com. New in 2009, built around a sunny courtyard with good restaurant. Stylish, rooms have heaters, phone, Wi-Fi, professional staff. Associated with **La Casa de Wiracocha**, at No 260, for select Peruvian handicrafts.

$$$ Plaza Mayor, Deústua 342, T366089, www.plazamayorhostal.com. Comfortable, well-appointed, good big beds, buffet breakfast included, hot water, laundry. Recommended.

$$$ Puno Plaza, Jr Puno 425, T351424, www.punoplaza.com. Tastefully decorated modern hotel overlooking the Plaza de Armas, includes buffet breakfast, very comfortable rooms, all with bathtub or jacuzzi, heater, safety box, internet in lobby, good restaurant.

$$$-$$ Hacienda Puno, Jr Deústua 297, T356109, www.lahaciendapuno.com. Refurbished colonial house, with buffet breakfast, hot water, TV, café, comfortable, internet. Recommended.

$$ Balsa Inn, Cajamarca 555, T363144, www.hotelbalsainn.com. With breakfast, hot water, TV, comfortable, safe, heating, very helpful.

$$ Colón Inn, Tacna 290, T351432, www.coloninn.com. Colonial style, good rooms with hot shower, price includes tax and buffet breakfast, Wi-Fi, internet, good service, safe, restaurant *Sol Naciente* and pizzería *Europa*, the Belgian manager Christian Nonis is well known, especially for his work on behalf of the people on Taquile island. Recommended.

$$ Conde de Lemos, Jr Puno 675, T369898, www.condelemosinn.com. Convenient, comfortable, colonial style, with breakfast, heating, washing machine, internet, Wi-Fi, elevator, wheel chair friendly, restaurant.

$$ El Buho, Lambayeque 142, T366122, www.peruhotelsguide.com/hotelbuho. Hot water, nice rooms with heaters, TV, restaurant, safe, discount for Footprint book owners, travel agency for trips and flights. Recommended.

$$ Hostal Imperial, Teodoro Valcarcel 145, T352386, www.hostalimperial.com. **$** in low season, basic but big rooms, good hot showers, safe, helpful, stores luggage, comfortable.

$$ Hostal Italia, Teodoro Valcarcel 122, T352521, www.hotelitaliaperu.com. 2 blocks from the station. With breakfast, cheaper in low season, good, safe, hot water, good food, small rooms, staff helpful.

$$ Hostal Pukara, Jr Libertad 328, T368448, pukara@terra.com.pe. Excellent, English spoken, central, quiet, free coca to drink in evening, breakfast.

$$ pp MN Yavari, Muelle del Hotel Sonesta Posada del Inka, T369329 (in Lima T01-255 7268), reservasyavari@gmail.com. B&B is available on board, 3 twin rooms with shared bath. Dinner served on request downstairs in the Victorian saloon, **$$**.

$$ Posada Don Giorgio, Tarapacá 238, T363648, www.posadadongiorgio.com. Breakfast, TV, hot water, large rooms, nicely decorated, comfortable.

$$ Sillustani, Tarapacá 305 y Lambayeque, T351881, www.sillustani.com. Price includes breakfast and taxes, hot water, cable TV, safety deposit, heaters, internet, well-established, popular, reservations advised.

$$ Tambo Real, Jr Santiago Giraldo 362, T366060, www.tamborealtitikaka.com. Good value, bright rooms, price includes breakfast, upgraded bathrooms in 2009, family-owned, helpful, Wi-Fi, computers for guests' use (20 mins free), tea and coffee in the lobby all day. Recommended.

$$-$ Hostal Rubi 'Los Portales', Jr Cajamarca 152-154, T353384, www.mancocapacinn.com/i_rubilodge_espanol.htm. Safe, breakfast US$2, hot water, TV, good, tours arranged. Recommended.

$ Hospedaje Residencial Margarita, Jr Tarapacá 130, T352820, www.hostal margaritapuno.com. Large building, family atmosphere, hot water most of the day, stores luggage, tours can be arranged. Recommended.

$ Hostal Europa, Alfonso Ugarte 112, near train station, T353026, heuropa@ terramail.com. Very popular, cheaper without bath, luggage may be stored (don't leave valuables in your room), hot water sometimes, garage space for motorcycles.

$ Hostal Illampu, Av La Torre 137-interior, T353284, www.illampu.3a2.com. Warm water, breakfast and TV extra, café, laundry, safe box (do not leave valuables in room), exchange money, arranges excursions (ask for Santiago).

$ Hostal Los Pinos, Tarapacá 182, T367398, hostalpinos@hotmail.com. Family run, breakfast US$2, hot showers, safe, luggage store, laundry facilities, helpful, cheap tours organized. Recommended.

$ pp Inka's Rest, Pasaje San Carlos 158, T368720, http://inkasresthostel.com. Includes breakfast, several apartments each with shared sitting area and shared bath, hot water, free internet, rooms a bit small, cooking and laundry facilities, a place to meet other travellers, reserve ahead.

$ Julio César, Av Tacna 336, T366026, www.juliocesarhoteles.com. Hot water, with breakfast, welcoming, some English spoken.

$ Los Uros, Teodoro Valcarcel 135, T352141, www.losuros.com. Cheaper without bath, cheaper in low season, hot water, breakfast available, quiet at back, good value, small charge to leave luggage, laundry, often full, changes TCs at a reasonable rate. Recommended.

$ pp The Point, Av Circunvalación Norte 278, Huajsapata, T351427, www.thepointhostels. com. Party hostel 3 long blocks from main plaza, with the regular facilities such as dorms for 3 to 12 people, twin rooms, hot water, **The Pointless Bar**, travel centre, free internet, kitchen, restaurant.

Around Puno: Chucuíto *p78*

$$$$ Titilaka Lodge, Comunidad de Huencalla s/n, on a private peninsula near Chucuíto, T01-700 5111 (Lima), www.titilaka. com. Opened in 2008, luxury boutique hotel offering all-inclusive packages in an exclusive environment on the edge of the lake. Plenty of activities available.

$ pp Albergue Juvenil Las Cabañas, Jr Tarapacá 538, T369494, 951-751196, www.chucuito.com. Great wee cottages, meals, will collect you from Puno if you phone in advance. Highly recommended.

$ pp Sra Nely Durán Saraza, Chucuíto Occopampa, T951 586240 (mob). 2 nice rooms, one with lake view, shared bath, hot water, breakfast and dinner available, very welcoming and interesting.

Llachón *p79*

Families offer accommodation on a rotational basis and, as the community presidents change each year, the standard of facilites changes from year-to-year and family-to family. All hosts can arrange boat transport to Amantaní. Among those who offer lodging (**$** per bed, meals extra) are: Tomás Cahui Coila, **Centro Turístico Santa María Llachón**, T951 923595, www.explore titicaca.com; **Primo Flores**, Santa María, T951 821392/951 680040/951 410901, primopuno@hotmail.com; **Valentín Quispe**, T051-951 821392 (mob), llachon@yahoo.com. But do recognize that there are other families who accept guests.

❷ Eating

Puno *p76, map p76*

$$ IncAbar, Lima 348, T368031. Open for breakfast, lunch and dinner, interesting dishes in creative sauces, fish, pastas, curries, café and couch bar, nice decor.

$$ Internacional, Moquegua 201, T352502. Very popular, excellent trout, good pizzas, service variable.

$$ La Hostería, Lima 501, T365406. Good set meal and à la carte dishes including local fare like alpaca and cuy, pizza, also breakfast, music in the evening.

$$ La Plaza, Puno 425, Plaza de Armas. Good food, international dishes and *comida nueva andina*, good service.

$$ Los Balcones de Puno, Jr Libertad 345, T365300. Peruvian and international food, daily folklore show 1900-2100.

$$ Mojsa, Lima 635 p 2, Plaza de Armas. Good international and *novo andino* dishes, also has an arts and crafts shop. Recommended.

$$ Tradiciones del Lago, Lima 418, T368140, www.tradicionesdelago.com. Buffet, à la carte and a big selection of Peruvian food.

$$ Tulipans, Lima 394, T351796. Sandwiches, juices and a lunchtime menu are its staples. One of the few places in Puno with outdoor seating in a pleasant colonial courtyard, a good option for lunch.

$$-$ Don Piero, Lima 360. Huge meals, live music, try their 'pollo coca-cola' (chicken in a sweet and sour sauce), slow service, popular, tax extra.

$$-$ Pizzería/Trattoria El Buho, Lima 349 and at Jr Libertad 386, T356223. Excellent pizza, lively atmosphere, open 1800 onwards, pizzas US$2.35-3.

$ Casa Grilll La Estancia, Libertad 137, T51-365469 . Salad bar, huge steaks, grilled meat and peruvian food. Very popular with locals for huge lunches and a few beers.

$ Chifa Nan Hua, Arequipa 378. Tasty Chinese, big portions.

$ Govinda, Deústua 312. Cheap vegetarian lunch menus, closes at 2000.

$ Remembranzas, Jr Moquegua 200. Pizzas as well as local food. Open 0630-2200.

$ Ukukus, Libertad 216 and Pje Grau 172, T367373, 369504. Good combination of Andean and novo andino cuisine as well as pizzas and some Chinese chifa style.

$ Vida Natural, Tacna 141. Breakfast, salads, fruits, also vegetarian meals midday and evening.

Cafés

Cafetería Mercedes, Jr Arequipa 144. Good menú US$1.50, bread, cakes, snacks, juices.

Casa del Corregidor, Deústua 576, aptdo 2, T365603. In restored 17th-century building, sandwiches, good snacks, coffee, good music, great atmosphere, nice surroundings with patio. Also has a Fair Trade store offering products directly from the producers.

Ricos Pan, Jr Lima 424. Café and bakery, great cakes, excellent coffees, juices and pastries, breakfasts and other dishes, Mon-Sat 0600-2300. Branches at Arequipa cuadra 3 and Moquegua 330.

🎵 Bars and clubs

Puno *p76, map p76*
Dómino, Libertad 443. "Megadisco", happy hour 2000-2130 Mon-Thu, good.
Positive, Jr Lima 382. Drinks, large screen TV, modern music, occasional heavy metal rock groups.
Pub Ekeko's, Lima 355. Live music every night, happy hour 2000-2200.

⊕ Festivals and events

Puno *p76, map p76*
Feb: at the **Fiesta de la Virgen de la Candelaria**, 1st 2 weeks in **Feb**, bands and dancers from all the local towns compete in a *Diablada*, or Devil Dance. The festivities are better at night on the streets than the official functions in the stadium. Check the dates in advance as Candelaria may be moved if pre-Lentern carnival coincides with it. A candlelight procession through darkened streets takes place on **Good Friday**. **3 May**: Festividad de las Cruces, celebrated with masses, a procession and the Alasita festival of miniatures. **29 Jun**: colourful festival of **San Pedro**, with a procession at Zepita (see page 78). **4-5 Nov**: pageant dedicated to the founding of Puno and the emergence of Manco Cápac and Mama Ocllo from the waters of Lake Titicaca.

⊙ Shopping

Puno *p76, map p76*
Markets Puno is the best place in Peru to buy alpaca wool articles, bargaining is appropriate. Along the avenue leading to the port is the large **Mercado Artesanal Asociación de Artesanos Unificados**, daily 0900-1800. Closer to the centre are **Mercado Coriwasi**, Ugarte 150, daily 0800-2100 and

Central Integral de Artesanos del Perú (CIAP), Jr Deústua 576, Mon-Sat 1000-1800. The **Mercado Central**, in the blocks bound by Arbulú, Arequipa, Oquendo and Tacna has all kinds of food, including good cheeses as well as a few crafts. Beware pickpockets in the market. You will be hassled on the street and outside restaurants to buy woollen goods, so take care.

⛰ Activities and tours

Puno *p76, map p76*
Watch out for unofficial tour sellers, *jalagringos*, who offer hotels and tours at varying rates, depending on how wealthy you look. They are everywhere: train station, bus offices, airport and hotels. Ask to see their guide's ID card. Only use agencies with named premises, compare prices and only hand over money at the office, never on the street or in a hotel.

Agencies organize trips to the Uros floating islands (see page 86) and the islands of Taquile and Amantaní, as well as to Sillustani, and other places. Make sure that you settle all details before embarking on the tour. We have received good reports on the following:
All Ways Travel, Casa del Corregidor, Deústua 576, p 2, T353979, and at Tacna 285, of 104-2042, T355552, www.titicacaperu. com. Very helpful, kind and reliable, speak German, French, English and Italian. They offer a unique cultural tour to the islands of Anapia and Yuspique in Lake Wiñaymarka, beyond the straits of Tiquina, "The Treasure of Wiñaymarka", departures Thu and Sun.
Cusi Expeditions, Jr T Varcarcel 164, T369072, reservascusi@terra.com.pe. They own most of the boats which operate the standard tours of the Islands. You will very likely end up on a Cusi tour so it's best to buy from them directly to get the best price and the most accurate information.
Edgar Adventures, Jr Lima 328, T353444, www.edgaradventures.com. English, German

and French spoken, very helpful and knowledgeable. Constantly exploring new areas, lots of off-the-beaten-track tours, eg kayaking tour of Llachón. Community-minded, promote responsible tourism. Consistently recommended.

Käfer Viajes, Arequipa 179, T354742, www.kafer-titicaca.com. Efficient and helpful.

Kontiki Tours, Jr Melgar 188. T355887, www.kontikiperu.com. Receptive tour agency specializing in special interest excursions.

Nayra Travel, Jr Lima 419, of 105, T337934, www.nayratravel.com. Small agency run by Lilian Cotrado and her helpful staff, traditional local tours and a variety of options in Llachón. Can organize off-the-beaten track excursions for a minimum of 2 people. Recommended.

Peru Up to Date, Arequipa 340, T951 921549, www.peruuptodate.com. New, offers tours in the Puno and Titicaca area.

Pirámide Tours, Jr Rosendo Huirse 130, T366107, www.titikakalake.com. Out of the ordinary and classic tours, flexible, personalized service, modern fast launches, very helpful, works only via internet, overseas clients.

Titikaka Explorers, Jr Puno 633 of 207, T368903, www.titikaka-explorer.com. Good service, helpful.

⊖ Transport

Puno p76, map p76

Air The airport is at Juliaca, 1 hr away from Puno. It is small but well organized. Flights to/from **Lima**, 2¼ hrs, 3 a day with **LAN** (T322228 or airport T324448) via **Arequipa** (30 mins), **Cuzco** and direct, **StarPerú** (T326570) once a day via Arequipa, and **TACA**, T0800-1-(TACA)8222. Minibus 1-B on Núñez, US$0.15; from airport to town they take you to your hotel. Beware overcharging for transport from Juliaca airport. If you have little luggage, combis stop just outside the airport parking area. Taxi from Plaza Bolognesi, US$1.75; taxi from airport US$3.50, or US$2 from outside airport gates. Airport transfers from **Puno** US$3.40 pp with

Camtur, Jr Tacna 336, of 104, T951 967652 and **Rossy Tours**, Jr Tacna 308, T366709, www.rossytours.tk. Many Puno hotels offer an airport transfer. Taxi to the airport US$17-20. If taking regular public transport to Juliaca and a taxi to the airport from there, allow extra time as the combis might drive around looking for passengers before leaving Puno.

Bus All long-distance buses, except some Cuzco services and buses to La Paz (see below), leave from the Terminal Terrestre, which is at 1 de Mayo 703 y Victoria, by the lake, T364733. It has a tourist office, snack bars and toilets. Platform tax US$0.35. Small buses and colectivos for Juliaca, Ilave and towns on the lake shore between Puno and Desaguadero, including Yunguyo, leave from Av Bolívar between Jrs Carabaya and Palma. To **Juliaca**, 44 km, 45 mins, bus US$0.70, combi US$1.

To **Cuzco**: the road Puno-Juliaca-Cuzco is now fully paved and in good condition. Bus services are consequently an acceptable alternative to the train; 388 km, 5-7 hrs. There are 3 levels of service: regular via Juliaca, US$5-7, 7 hrs; direct, without stopping in Juliaca, with **Tour Perú**, Jr Tacna, T352991, www.tourperu. com.pe, at 0800, US$8.50 and 2130 (bus cama US$10), 6 hrs; tourist service with 5 stops (Pukará, Sicuani for lunch, La Raya, Raqchi and Andahuayllillas), leave at 0730, US$30 plus museum entry fees (US$7), includes lunch, 10 hrs, with **Inka Express**, Jr Tacna 346 and at the Terminal Terrestre, T365654, www.inka express.com (leaves from the Terminal and may pick up from hotel on request), **First Class**, Tacna 280-300, T364640, firstclass@terra.com.pe, or **Turismo Mer**, Jr Tacna 336, T367223, www.turismomer.com. In high season, reserve 2 days ahead. **Note** It is advisable to travel by day, for safety as well as for the views. If you wish to travel by bus and cannot go direct, it is no problem to take separate buses to Juliaca, then to Sicuani, then to Cuzco.

Boats on Lake Titicaca Boats to the islands leave from the terminal in the harbour (see map); *trici-taxi* from centre, US$1.

Taxi 3-wheel 'Trici-Taxis', cost about US$0.20 per km and are the best way to get around.

Trains The railway runs from Puno to Juliaca (44 km), where it divides, to Cuzco (381 km) and Arequipa (279 km; no passenger service). To **Cuzco** *Andean Explorer*, US$220 (no other class) Mon, Wed, Fri and Sat at 0800, arriving in Cuzco at about 1800 (no Fri train Nov-Mar); try to sit on the right hand side for the views. The train stops at La Raya, the highest pass on the line; 210 km from Puno, at 4321 m (local market; toilets US$0.20). Up on the heights breathing may be a little difficult, but the descent along the Río Vilcanota is rapid. The ticket office is open 0700-1700 Mon-Fri, 0700-1200 Sat, Sun and holidays; in high season buy several days in advance, passport required. The station is well guarded by police and sealed off to those without tickets. At 38 km beyond La Raya pass is **Sicuani**, an important agricultural centre. Excellent items of llama and alpaca wool and skins are sold on the railway station and at the Sunday morning market. Around Plaza Libertad there are several hat shops.

Llachón *p79*
Boats Only 1 weekly public boat from Llachón to Puno, Fri 0900, returning to Llachón Sat 1000, US$1.20, 3½ hrs. The daily 0800 boat to Amantantí may drop you off at Colata (at the tip of the peninsula), a 1 hr walk from Llachón, confirm details in advance. Returning to Puno, you can try to flag down the boat from Amantaní which passes Colata between 0830 and 0930. In Santa María (Llachón), boats can be hired for trips to Amantaní (40 mins) and Taquile (50 mins), US$20 return, minimum 10 passengers.

Combis run daily from Bellavista market (known as El Contrabando) in Puno to **Capachica**, from 0700 to 1600, 1½ hrs, US$1.35, where you get another *combi* or bus to **Llachón**, leave when full, 30 mins, US$0.70.

Puno *p76, map p76*
Airline offices LAN, Tacna y Libertad, T367227. **Star Perú**, Melgar 106, T364615.
Banks BCP, Lima 510. **Banco Continental**, Lima 411. **Interbank**, Lima 444. **Scotiabank**, Lima y Deústua. For cash go to the *cambios*, the travel agencies or the better hotels. Best rates with money changers on Jr Lima, many on 400 block, and on Tacna near the market, eg Arbulu y Tacna. Check your Peruvian soles carefully. Rates for bolivianos are sometimes better in Puno than in Yunguyo; check with other travellers. **Consulates** Bolivia, Jr Arequipa 136, T351251, consular visas take about 48 hrs, Mon-Fri 0830-1400.
Internet and telephones There are offices everywhere in the centre, upstairs and down. Average price US$0.30-0.45 per hr. Particularly good is **Choz@net**, Lima 339, p 2, fast computers and a small snack bar. **Post offices** Jr Moquegua 268, Mon-Sat 0800-2000. **Useful addresses**
Immigration: Ayacucho 280, T357103, Mon-Fri 0800-1300, 1500-1700.

The islands

The Uros
ⓘ *US$1.70 entry.*

The people of Uros or the 'floating islands' in Puno Bay fish, hunt birds and live off the lake plants, most important of which are the reeds they use for their boats, houses and the very foundations of their islands. Visitors to the floating islands encounter more women than men. These women wait every day for the tour boats to sell their handicrafts. The few men one does see might be building or repairing boats or fixing their nets. The rest are out on the lake, hunting and fishing. The Uros cannot live from tourism alone and it is better to buy handicrafts or pay for services than just to tip. They glean extra income from tourists offering overnight accommodation in reed houses, selling meals and providing Uro guides for two-hour tours, US$3.40. Organized tour parties are usually given a boat building demonstration and the chance to take a short trip in a reed boat (US$0.70 pp). Some islanders will also greet boat loads of tourists with a song and will pose for photos. The islanders, who are very friendly, appreciate gifts of pens, paper, etc for their two schools. This form of tourism on the Uros Islands is now well-established and, whether it has done irreparable harm or will ultimately prove beneficial, it takes place in superb surroundings. Take drinking water as there is none on the islands.

Taquile
ⓘ *US$1 to land. Contact Munay Taquile, the island's community-based travel agency, Titicaca 508, Puno, T351448, www.taquile.net*

Isla Taquile, 45 km from Puno, on which there are numerous pre-Inca and Inca ruins, and Inca terracing, is only about 1 km wide, but 6-7 km long. Ask for the (unmarked) **museum of traditional costumes**, which is on the plaza. There is a co-operative shop on the plaza that sells exceptional woollen goods, which are not cheap, but of very fine quality. Shops on the plaza sell postcards, water and dry goods. You are advised to take some food, particularly fruit, bread and vegetables, water, plenty of small-value notes, candles and a torch. Take precautions against sunburn. The principal festivals are from 2-7 June, and the *Fiesta de Santiago* from 25 July to 2 August, with many dances in between. Native guides in Taquile, some speaking English and/or German, charge US$3.40 for two-hour tours. It is worth spending a night on Taquile to observe the daily flurry of activity around the boatloads of tourists: demonstations of traditional dress and weaving techniques, the preapartion of trout to feed the hordes. When the boats leave, the island breathes a gentle sigh and people slowly return to their more traditional activities.

Amantaní
ⓘ *US$1 to land.*

Another island worth visiting, is Amantaní, very beautiful and peaceful. There are six villages and ruins on both of the island's peaks, **Pacha Tata** and **Pacha Mama**, from which there are excellent views. There are also temples and on the shore there is a throne carved out of stone, the **Inkatiana**. On both hills, a fiesta is celebrated on 15-20 January, *Pago a la Tierra or San Sebastián*. The festivities are very colourful, musical and hard-drinking. There is also a festival on 9 April, *Aniversario del Consejo* (of the local council), and a *Feria de Artesanías*, 8-16 August. The residents make beautiful textiles and sell them quite cheaply at the Artesanía Cooperativa. They also make basketwork and stoneware. The people are Quechua speakers, but understand Spanish. Islanders arrange dances for tour groups (independent travellers can join in), visitors dress up in local clothes and join the dances. Small shops sell water and snacks.

Anapia and Yuspique

In the Peruvian part of the Lago Menor are the islands of **Anapia**, a friendly, Aymara-speaking community, and **Yuspique**, on which are ruins and vicuñas. The community has organized committees for tourism, motor boats, sailing boats and accommodation with families (All Ways Travel, see page 83, arranges tours). To visit Anapia independently, take a colectivo from Yunguyo to Tinicachi and alight at Punta Hermosa, just after Unacachi. Boats to Anapia leave Punta Hermosa on Sunday and Thursday at 1300 (they leave Anapia for Yunguyo market on the same days at 0630); bus from Puno Sunday, Tuesday, Thursday, US$3. It's two hours each way by boat. On the island ask for José Flores, who is very knowledgeable about Anapia's history, flora and fauna. He sometimes acts as a guide.

The islands listings

For Sleeping and Eating price codes and other relevant information, see pages 10-14.

⊝ Sleeping

The Uros *p86*
Oscar Coyla, T051-951 824378 is the representative for the Uros community. Accommodation costs US$5 pp, simple meals are extra or US$10 pp full board including tour. **René Coyla Coila**, T051-951 743533 is an official tour guide who can advise on lodging and **Armando Suaña**, T051-951 341374 is another native guide offering accommodation in Kantati.

Taquile *p86*
The **Presidente del Comité Turístico de Taquile** is Leucario Huata Cruz, T051-951 830433. Lodging rates US$20-25 pp full board. Where possible try to support the communal system and ask the Jefe which families are in need of a visit from tourists. Since some families have become the favourites of tour groups they have been able to build better facilities (eg with showers and loos) and those which are in need of the income are often shunned as their facilities may be more basic. Instead of staying in the busy part around the main square, the Huayllano community is hosting visitors. This is on the south side of the island. Contact **Alipio Huatta Cruz**, T051-951 668551 or 951 615239 or you can arrange a visit with **All Ways Travel**.

Amantaní *p86*
The **Presidente del Comité Turístico de Amantaní** is Senón Tipo Huatta, T051-951 832 308. Rate is up to US$25 pp full board. If you are willing to walk to a more distant communities, you might get a better price and you are helping to share the income. Some families that one can contact are: **Kantuta Lodge**, T051-789290, 951 636172, www.kantutalodge.com; **Hospedaje Jorge Cari**, basic, but nice family, great view of lake from room, or **Ambrosio Mamani**, j.manani.cari@eudoramail. com; or **Familia Victoriano Calsin Quispe**, Casilla 312, Isla Amantaní, T051-360220 or 363320.

⊘ Eating

Taquile *p86*
There are many small restaurants around the plaza and on the track to the Puerto Principal (eg Gerardo Huatta's **La Flor de Cantuta**, on the steps; **El Inca** on the main plaza). Meals are generally fish, rice and chips, omelette and *fiambre*, a local stew. Meat is rarely available and drinks often run out. Breakfast consists of pancakes and bread.

Amantaní *p86*
There is 1 restaurant, **Samariy**. The artificially low price of tours allows families little scope for providing anything other than basic meals, so take your own supplies if you so wish.

⊖ Transport

The Uros *p86*
Boat **Asociación de Transporte los Uros**, at the port, T368024, aeuttal@hotmail.com, 0800-1600. Motorboat US$3.40, from 0600-1600 or whenever there are 10 people. Agencies charge US$7-10.

Taquile *p86*
Boats Centro de Operadores de Transporte Taquile, at the port, T205477, 0600-1100, 1400-1800. In high season, boats go at 0730 and 0800, returning at 1400 and 1430, in low season only one boat travels, US$4.50 one way. Organized tours cost US$10-16.

Amantaní *p86*
Boats Transportes Unificados Amantaní, at the port, T369714, 0800-1100. 2 daily boats at 0815, one direct, the 2nd one stops at Uros, they return at 0800 the next day, one direct to Puno, the 2nd one stops at Taquile. US$4.50 one way direct, US$10 return with stops at Uros and Taquile. Amantaní-Taquile costs US$2. If you stop in Taquile on the way back, you can continue to Puno at 1200 with the Amantaní boat or take a Taquile boat at 1400 (also 1430 in high season). Purchasing one way tickets gives you more flexibility if you wish to stay longer on the islands.

Puno to Cuzco: Sicuani *p85*
Bus To **Cuzco**, 137 km, US$1.25.

Contents

La Paz & around

La Paz and around

The minute you arrive in La Paz, the highest seat of government in the world, you realize this is no ordinary place. El Alto airport is at a staggering 4000 m above sea level. The sight of the city, lying 400 m below, at the bottom of a steep canyon and ringed by snow-peaked mountains, takes your breath away – literally. For at this altitude breathing can be a problem. The Spaniards chose this odd place for a city on 20 October 1548, to avoid the chill winds of the plateau, and because they had found gold in the Río Choqueyapu, which runs through the canyon. The centre of the city, Plaza Murillo, is at 3636 m, about 400 m below the level of the Altiplano and the sprawling city of El Alto, perched dramatically on the rim of the canyon.

Ins and outs → *Phone code: 02. Population: La Paz, 855,000, El Alto, 882,000.*

Getting there La Paz has the highest commercial **airport** in the world, at El Alto, high above the city at 4058 m; T281 0240. A taxi from the airport to the centre takes about 30 minutes, US$7, to the Zona Sur US$9. There are three main **bus terminals**; the bus station at Plaza Antofagasta, the cemetery district for Sorata, Copacabana and Tiwanaku, and Villa Fátima for the Yungas, including Coroico, and northern jungle. ▸▸ *See also Transport, page 112.*

Getting around There are two types of city bus: *micros* (small, old buses), which charge US$0.20 a journey; and the faster, more plentiful minibuses (small vans), US$0.15-0.30 depending on the journey. *Trufis* are fixed-route collective taxis, with a sign with their route on the windscreen, US$0.40 pp in the centre, US$0.50 outside. Taxis are often, but not always, white. There are three types: regular honest taxis which may take several passengers at once (US$0.85-1.10 for short trips), fake taxis which have been involved in robberies (see below), and radio taxis which take only one group of passengers at a time. Since it is impossible to distinguish between the first two, it is best to pay a bit more for a radio taxi which has a dome light and number and can be ordered by phone; note the number when getting in. Radio taxis charge US$1.10-1.40 in the centre, more to the suburbs.

Orientation The city's main street runs from **Plaza San Francisco** as Avenida Mariscal Santa Cruz, then changes to Avenida 16 de Julio (more commonly known as El Prado) and ends at **Plaza del Estudiante**. The business quarter, government offices, central university (UMSA) and many of the main hotels and restaurants are in this area. From the Plaza del Estudiante, Avenida Villazón splits into Avenida Arce, which runs southeast towards the wealthier residential districts of **Zona Sur**, in the valley,15 minutes away; and Avenida 6 de Agosto which runs through **Sopocachi**, an area full of restaurants, bars and clubs. Zona Sur has shopping centres, supermarkets with imported items and some of the best restaurants and bars in La Paz (see page 106). It begins after the bridge at La Florida beside the attractive Plaza Humboldt. The main road, Avenida Ballivián, begins at Calle 8 and continues up the hill to San Miguel on Calle 21 (about a 20-minute walk).

Sprawled around the rim of the canyon is **El Alto**, Bolivia's second-largest city (after Santa Cruz, La Paz is a close third). Its population of almost one million is mostly indigenous immigrants from the countryside and its political influence has grown rapidly. El Alto is connected to La Paz by motorway (toll US$0.25) and by a road to Obrajes and the Zona Sur. Minibuses from Plaza Eguino leave regularly for Plaza 16 de Julio, El Alto, more leave from Plaza Pérez Velasco for La Ceja, the edge of El Alto. Intercity buses to and from La Paz always stop at El Alto in an area called *terminal*, off Avenida 6 de Marzo, where transport companies have small offices. If not staying in La Paz, you can change buses here and save a couple of hours. There is accommodation in the area but it is not safe, especially at night.

Best time to visit Because of the altitude, nights are cold the year round. In the day, the sun is strong, but the moment you go into the shade or enter a building, the temperature falls. From December-March, the summer, it rains most afternoons, making it feel colder

① La Paz

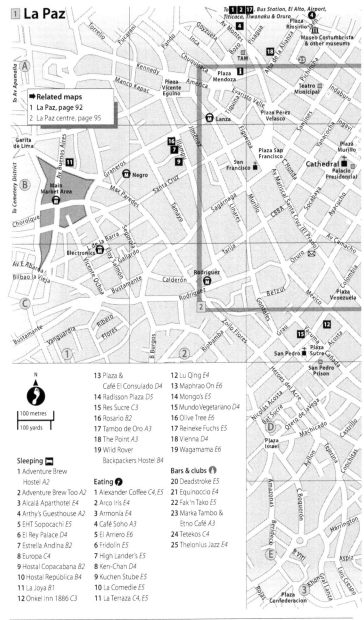

To **1 2 17**, Bus Station, El Alto, Airport,
Titicaca, Tiwanaku & Oruro

Plaza Riosinio

Museo Costumbrista & other museums

➡ Related maps
1 La Paz, page 92
2 La Paz centre, page 95

Related street labels (map): Torrello, Pucarani, Pando, Inca, Goyzueta, Av Montes, Rozo, Pisagua, Alto de Alianza, TAM, Kennedy, Manco Kapac, Plaza Vicente Eguino, America, Plaza Mendoza, Evaristo Valle, P.Chincha, Teatro Municipal, Indaburo, Tiquina, Plaza Pérez Velasco, Sanjines, Ingavi, Garita de Lima, Av Buenos Aires, Graneros, Jiménez, Illampu, Negro, Santa Cruz, San Francisco, Plaza San Francisco, Av Mariscal-Santa Cruz (El Prado), Plaza Murillo, Cathedral, Palacio Presidencial, Max Paredes, Tamayo, Sagarnaga, Linares, Murillo, CBBA, Socabaya, Ayacucho, Chorolque, Segunda, Tarija, Oruro, Av Camacho, Colombia, Electronics, Eloy Gallardo, Rodríguez, Calderón, Belzu, Mexico, Plaza Venezuela, Av E Abaroa, Vicente Ochoa, Bustamante, Rodríguez, Gonzales, Grau, Bilbao la Vieja, Ribero, Flores, B Burgos, Zoilo Flores, Riobamba, Yacuma, Acosta, Plaza Sucre, San Pedro Prison, Bustamante, Vanguardia, Ribero, Flores, San Pedro, Héroes del Acre, Nicolás Acosta, Bz Sucre, Machicado, Castrillo, Plaza Israel, Amazonas, Boquerón, Aytilon, Tejelna, Conchitas, Beliroco, B Viti, Harrington, Aspiz, Rojas, Gral Lanza, Plaza Confederación, Luis Crespo

Sleeping 🛏

1 Adventure Brew Hostel A2
2 Adventure Brew Too A2
3 Alcalá Aparthotel E4
4 Arthy's Guesthouse A2
5 EHT Sopocachi E5
6 El Rey Palace D4
7 Estrella Andina B2
8 Europa C4
9 Hostal Copacabana B2
10 Hostal República B4
11 La Joya B1
12 Onkel Inn 1886 C3
13 Plaza & Café El Consulado D4
14 Radisson Plaza D5
15 Res Sucre C3
16 Rosario B2
17 Tambo de Oro A3
18 The Point A3
19 Wild Rover Backpackers Hostel B4

Eating 🍴

1 Alexander Coffee C4, E5
2 Arco Iris E4
3 Armonía E4
4 Café Soho A3
5 El Arriero E6
6 Fridolin E5
7 High Lander's E5
8 Ken-Chan D4
9 Kuchen Stube E5
10 La Comedie E5
11 La Terraza C4, E5
12 Lu Qing E4
13 Maphrao On E6
14 Mongo's E5
15 Mundo Vegetariano D4
16 Olive Tree E6
17 Reineke Fuchs E5
18 Vienna D4
19 Wagamama E6

Bars & clubs 🍷

20 Deadstroke E5
21 Equinoccio E4
22 Fak'n Tako E5
23 Marka Tambo & Etno Café A3
24 Tetekos C4
25 Thelonius Jazz E4

N

100 metres
100 yards

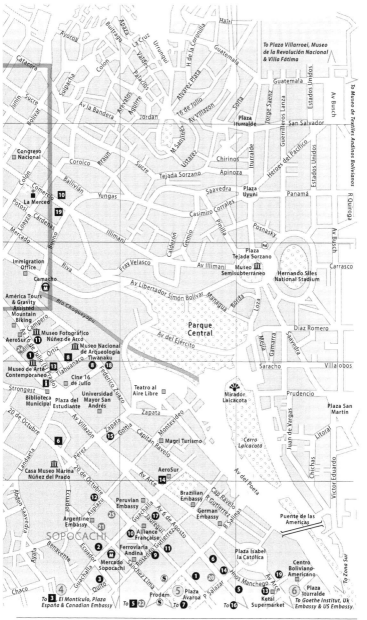

than it actually is. Temperatures are even lower in winter, June-August, when the sky is always clear. The two most important festivals, when the city gets particularly busy, are **Alasitas** (last week of January and first week of February) and **Festividad del Señor del Gran Poder** (end May/early June). See Festivals, page 107.

Tourist offices The Gobierno Municipal de La Paz ① *www.turismolapaz.travel* has information centres at: Plaza del Estudiante ① *at the lower end of El Prado between 16 de Julio and México, T237 1044, Mon-Fri 0830-1200, 1430-1900, Sat-Sun 0900-1300*, very helpful, English and French spoken. El Prado InfoTur ① *Mariscal Santa Cruz y Colombia, T265 1778, Mon-Fri 0830-1900, Sat-Sun 0930-1300.* Bus terminal ① *T228 5858, Mon-Fri 0600-2200, Sat 0800-1500, Sun 1400-2200, holidays 0800-1200, 1600-2000.* Angelo Colonial ① *C Linares y Sagárnaga (at the restaurant), T215 9632*, and Plaza Pérez Velasco ① *opposite San Francisco, under the pedestrian walkway.*Tourist office for **El Alto:** Dirección de Promoción Turística① *C 5 y Av 6 de Marzo, Edif Vela, p 5, also at arrivals in airport, T282 9281, Mon-Fri 0800-1200, 1400-1800*; the municipality is trying to attract visitors.

Safety The worst areas for crime are around Plaza Murillo and the Cemetery neighbourhood where local buses serve Copacabana and Tiwanaku. Tourist police (T222 5016) now patrol these bus stops during the daytime, making them safer than in the past, but caution is still advised. Other areas, particularly Sopocachi, are generally safer. **Warning for ATM users**: scams to get card numbers and PINs have flourished, especially in La Paz. The tourist police post warnings in hotels.▸▸ *See also Safety, page 19.*

Sights → *For listings, see pages 101-117.*

There are few colonial buildings left in La Paz; probably the best examples are in **Calle Jaén** (see below). Late 19th-, early 20th-century architecture, often displaying European influence, can be found in the streets around Plaza Murillo, but much of La Paz is modern. The **Plaza del Estudiante** (Plaza Franz Tamayo), or a bit above it, marks a contrast between old and new styles, between the commercial and the more elegant. The **Prado** itself is lined with high-rise blocks dating from the 1960s and 1970s.

Around Plaza Murillo

Plaza Murillo, three blocks north of the Prado, is the traditional centre. Facing its formal gardens are the Cathedral, the **Palacio Presidencial** in Italian renaissance style, known as the **Palacio Quemado** (burnt palace) twice gutted by fire in its stormy 130-year history, and, on the east side, the **Congreso Nacional**. In front of the Palacio Quemado is a statue of former President Gualberto Villarroel who was dragged into the plaza by a mob and hanged in 1946. Across from the Cathedral on Calle Socabaya is the **Palacio de los Condes de Arana** (built 1775), with beautiful exterior and patio. It houses the **Museo Nacional de Arte** ① *T240 8542, www.mna.org.bo, Tue-Sat 0900-1230, 1500-1900, Sun 0900-1330, US$1.50.* It has a fine collection of colonial paintings including many works by Melchor Pérez Holguín, considered one of the masters of Andean colonial art, and which also exhibits the works of contemporary local artists. Calle Comercio, running east-west across the Plaza, has most of the stores and shops. West of Plaza Murillo, at Ingavi 916, in the palace of the Marqueses de Villaverde, and undergoing renovation since 2005, is the

Museo Nacional de Etnografía y Folklore ① *T240 8640, Tue-Sat 0900-1230, 1500-1900, Sun 0900-1230, free.* Various sections show the cultural richness of Bolivia by region through textiles and other items. It has a *videoteca*.

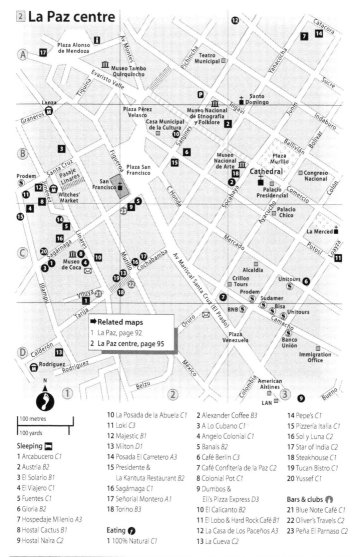

2 La Paz centre

➡ **Related maps**
1 La Paz, page 92
2 La Paz centre, page 95

100 metres
100 yards

Sleeping 🛏
1 Arcabucero *C1*
2 Austria *B2*
3 El Solario *B1*
4 El Viajero *C1*
5 Fuentes *C1*
6 Gloria *B2*
7 Hospedaje Milenio *A3*
8 Hostal Cactus *B1*
9 Hostal Naira *C2*
10 La Posada de la Abuela *C1*
11 Loki *C3*
12 Majestic *B1*
13 Milton *D1*
14 Posada El Carretero *A3*
15 Presidente &
   La Kantuta Restaurant *B2*
16 Sagárnaga *C1*
17 Señorial Montero *A1*
18 Torino *B3*

Eating 🍴
1 100% Natural *C1*
2 Alexander Coffee *B3*
3 A Lo Cubano *C1*
4 Angelo Colonial *C1*
5 Banais *B2*
6 Café Berlin *C3*
7 Café Confitería de la Paz *C2*
8 Colonial Pot *C1*
9 Dumbos &
   Eli's Pizza Express *D3*
10 El Calicanto *B2*
11 El Lobo & Hard Rock Café *B1*
12 La Casa de Los Paceños *A3*
13 La Cueva *C2*
14 Pepe's *C1*
15 Pizzería Italia *C1*
16 Sol y Luna *C2*
17 Star of India *C2*
18 Steakhouse *C1*
19 Tucan Bistro *C1*
20 Yussef *C1*

Bars & clubs 🍸
21 Blue Note Café *C1*
22 Oliver's Travels *C2*
23 Peña El Parnaso *C2*

Northwest of Plaza Murillo is **Calle Jaén**, a picturesque colonial street with a restaurant/ peña, a café, craft shops, good views and four museums (known as Museos Municipales) housed in colonial buildings ① *Tue-Fri 0930-1200, 1500-1900, Sat-Sun 0900-1300, US$0.15 each.* **Museo Costumbrista** ① *on Plaza Riosinio, at the top of Jaén, T228 0758, US$0.60*, has miniature displays depicting incidents in the history of La Paz and well-known Paceños, as well as miniature replicas of reed rafts used by the Norwegian Thor Heyerdahl, and the Spaniard Kitin Muñoz, to prove their theories of ancient migrations. **Museo del Litoral Boliviano** (T228 0758), has artefacts of the War of the Pacific, and interesting selection of old maps. **Museo de Metales Preciosos** (T228 0329), is well set out with Inca gold artefacts in basement vaults, also ceramics and archaeological exhibits, and **Museo Casa Murillo** (T228 0553), the erstwhile home of Pedro Domingo Murillo, one of the martyrs of the La Paz independence movement of 16 July 1809, has a good collection of paintings, furniture and national costumes. In addition to the Museos Municipales is the **Museo de Instrumentos Musicales** ① *Jaén 711 e Indaburo, T240 8177, daily 0930-1330, 1400-1830, US$0.75*, in a refurbished colonial house. **Museo Tambo Quirquincho** ① *C Evaristo Valle, south of Jaén, Plaza Alonso de Mendoza, T239 0969, Tue-Fri, 0930-1230, 1500-1900, Sat-Sun, 0900-1300, US$0.15*, displays modern painting and sculpture, carnival masks, silver, early 20th century photography and city plans, and is recommended.

Plaza San Francisco up to the cemetery district

At the upper end of Avenida Mcal Santa Cruz is the **Plaza San Francisco** with the **church and monastery of San Francisco** ① *open for Mass at 0700, 0900, 1100 and 1900, Mon-Sat, and also at 0800, 1000 and 1200 on Sun.* Dating from 1549, this is one of the finest examples of colonial religious architecture in South America and well worth seeing. The **Centro Cultural Museo San Francisco** ① *Plaza San Francisco 503, T231 8472, Mon-Sat 0900-1800, US$2.80, allow 1½-2 hrs, free guides available but tip appreciated, some speak English and French*, offers access to various areas of the church and convent which were previously off limits, including the choir, crypt (open 1400-1730), roof, various chapels and gardens. Fine art includes religious paintings from the 17th, 18th and 19th centuries, plus visiting exhibits and a hall devoted to the works of Tito Yupanqui, the indigenous sculptor of the Virgen de Copacabana. There is a pricey but good café at entrance. Behind the San Francisco church a network of narrow cobbled streets rise steeply up the canyon walls. Much of this area is a street market. Handicraft shops, travel agencies, hotels and restaurants line the lower part of **Calle Sagárnaga** (here you find the highest concentration of tourists and pick-pockets). The **Mercado de Brujas**, 'witchcraft market', on Calles Melchor Jiménez and Linares, which cross Santa Cruz above San Francisco, sells charms, herbs and more gruesome items like llama foetuses. The excellent **Museo de la Coca** ① *Linares 914, T231 1998, daily 1000-1900, US$1.50, shop with coca sweets for sale*, is devoted to the coca plant, its history, cultural significance, medical values and political implications, with explanations in Spanish and English. Nearby is the recommended **Museo de Arte Texil Andino Boliviano** ① *Linares 906, daily 1000-1900, Sun 1000-1700, US$1.20*, a small collection of old traditional weavings (not to be confused with the larger **Museo de Textiles Andinos Bolivianos** in Miraflores, see below).

Further up, from Illampu to Rodríguez and in neighbouring streets, is the produce-based **Rodríguez market** ① *daily, but best on Sun morning.* Turning right on Max

Paredes, heading north, is **Avenida Buenos Aires**, where small workshops turn out the costumes and masks for the Gran Poder festival, and with great of Illimani, especially at sunset. Continuing west along Max Paredes towards the **cemetery district**, the streets are crammed with stalls selling every imaginable item. Transport converges on the cemetery district (for more information see page 112). See also Safety, page 94.

The Prado, Sopocachi, Miraflores and Zona Sur

Museo de Arte Contemporáneo Plaza ① *Av 16 de Julio 1698, T233 5905, daily 0900-2100, US$2.* In a 19th-century house which has been declared a national monument, there is a selection of contemporary art from national and international artists. Just off the Prado (down the flight of stairs by the Hotel Plaza) is **Museo Nacional de Arqueología** or **Tiahuanaco** (Tiwanaku) ① *Tiwanacu 93 entre Bravo y F Zuazo, T231 1621, www.bolivian. com/arqueologia, closed for renovation in 2011.* It contains good collections of the arts and crafts of ancient Tiwanaku and items from the eastern jungles. It also has an exhibition of gold statuettes and objects found in Lake Titicaca. On Avenida Libertador Simón Bolívar, from where there are views of Mt Illimani, is the **Mercado Camacho** produce market, refurbished in 2010. In Sopocachi district, by Plaza España, is **El Montículo**, a park with great views of the city and Illimani. In the residential district of Miraflores, east of the centre, on Plaza Tejada Sorzano, outside the Hernán Siles national football stadium is the **Museo Semisubterráneo**, a sunken garden full of replicas of statues and artefacts from Tiwanaku, but difficult to get to because of the traffic. Further north, at Plaza Benito Juárez, is **Museo de Textiles Andinos Bolivianos** ① *Guatemala y Cuba, T224 3601, www.museodetextiles.org, Mon-Sat 0930-1200, 1500-1800, Sun 1000-1230, US$1.25,* with displays of textiles from around the country. At the north end of Av Busch are Plaza Villarroel and **Museo del la Revolución Nacional** ① *Tue-Fri 0930-1200, 1500-1800, Sat-Sun 1000-1200, US$0.15,* a memorial of the 1952 revolution and a mausoleum with tombs of former presidents.

Around La Paz → *For listings, see pages 101-117.*

South of La Paz

To the south of the city are dry hills of many colours, topped by the **Muela del Diablo**, a striking outcrop. Here is the **Valle de la Luna**, or 'Valley of the Moon' (US$2.10), with impressive eroded hills; the climate in this valley is always much warmer than in the city. For transport details see page 114. About 3 km from the bridge at Calacoto the road forks, get out of the minibus at the turning and walk a few minutes east to the Valle entrance, or get out at the football field which is by the entrance. Take good shoes and water, but do not go alone, armed robbery has occurred. Just past the Valle de la Luna is **Mallasa** where there are several small roadside restaurants and cafés and the **Hotel Oberland** (see page 104). The **zoo** ① *on the road to Río Abajo, entrance just past Mallasa, daily 0900-1700, US$0.50 adults, US$0.25 children,* in a beautiful, wide open park-like setting, conditions for the animals and birds are relatively good, but the public is allowed to feed the animals.

Tiwanaku

① *The site is open 0900-1700, US$11, including entry to museums. Allow 4 hrs to see the ruins and village. See also Transport, page 114.*

This remarkable archaeological site, 72 km west of La Paz, near the southern end of Lake Titicaca, takes its name from one of the most important pre-Columbian civilizations in South America. It is the most popular excursion from La Paz, with facilities being improved as a result. Many archaeologists believe that Tiwanaku existed as early as 1600 BC, while the complex visible today probably dates from the eight to the 10th centuries AD. The site may have been a ceremonial complex at the centre of an empire which covered almost half Bolivia, southern Peru, northern Chile and northwest Argentina. It was also a hub of trans-Andean trade. The demise of the Tiwanaku civilization, according to studies by Alan Kolata of the University of Illinois, could have been precipitated by the flooding of the area's extensive system of raised fields (*Sukakollu*), which were capable of sustaining a population of 20,000. The Pumapunku section, 1 km south of the main complex may have been a port, as the waters of the lake used to be much higher than they are today. The raised field system is once again being used in parts of the Titicaca area.

One of the main structures is the **Kalasasaya**, meaning 'standing stones', referring to the statues found in that part: two of them, the Ponce monolith (centre of inner patio) and the Fraile monolith (southwest corner), have been re-erected. In the northwest corner is the Puerta del Sol, originally at Pumapunku. Its carvings, interrupted by being out of context, are thought to be either a depiction of the creator god, or a calendar. The motifs are exactly the same as those around the Ponce monolith. The **Templo Semisubterráneo** is a sunken temple whose walls are lined with faces, all different, according to some theories depicting states of health, the temple being a house of healing; another theory is that the faces display all the ethnicities of the world. The **Akapana**, originally a pyramid (said to have been the second largest in the world, covering over 28,000 sq m), still has some ruins on it. Plastering of the Akapana's walls was halted in 2009 when UNESCO, among others, declared it inappropriate. At **Pumapunku**, some of whose blocks weigh between 100 and 150 tonnes, a natural disaster may have put a sudden end to the construction before it was finished. There is a small **Museo Lítico** at the ticket office, with several large stone pieces and, at the site, the **Museo Regional Arqueológico**, containing a well-illustrated explanation of the raised field system of agriculture. Many other artefacts are in the **Museo Nacional de Arqeología** in La Paz.

Written guide material is difficult to come by; hiring a guide costs US$8 for two hours, some speak English but don't be bullied into taking one if you prefer to go on your own. Locals sell copies of Tiwanaku figures; cheaper here than in La Paz.

Nearby **Tiwanaku village**, with several basic hotels and eateries, still has remnants from the time of independence and the 16th-century church used pre-Columbian masonry. In fact, Tiwanaku for a long while was the 'quarry' for the altiplano. For the **Willkakuti**, winter solstice festival on 21 June, there is an all-night vigil and colourful dances. There is also a colourful local festival on the Sunday after Carnival.

By road to Chile
The main route to Chile is via Tambo Quemado, but an alternative route, on which there are no trucks, is to go by good road direct from La Paz via Viacha to **Santiago de Machaco** (130 km, petrol); then 120 km on a very bad road to the border at **Charaña** (basic **Alojamiento Aranda**; immigration behind railway station). From Visviri, on the Chilean side of the frontier (no services), a regular road runs to Putre.

Trekking and climbing near La Paz

Four so-called 'Inca Trails' link the Altiplano with the Yungas, taking you from the high Andes to the sub-tropics, with dramatic changes in weather, temperature and vegetation. Each has excellent sections of stonework and they vary in difficulty from relatively straightforward to quite hard-going. In the rainy season going can be particularly tough. For details of how to reach the starting point of each trail, see Transport sections on page 115.

Takesi Trail Start at **Ventilla** (see below), walk up the valley for about three hours passing the village of Choquekhota until the track crosses the river and to the right of the road, there is a falling-down brick wall with a map painted on it. The Takesi and Alto Takesi trails start here, following the path to the right of the wall. The road continues to Mina San Francisco. In the first hour's climb from the wall is excellent stone paving which is Inca or pre-Inca, depending on who you believe, either side of the pass at 4630 m. There are camping possibilities at *Estancia Takesi* and in the village of Kakapi you can sleep at the **$ Kakapi Tourist Lodge**, 10 beds with good mattresses, solar shower and toilet. It is run by the local community and sponsored by Fundación Pueblo. It is also possible to camp. You also have to pass the unpleasant mining settlement of Chojlla, between which and Yanakachi is a gate where it is necessary to register and often pay a small 'fee'. Yanakachi has a number of good places to stay, several good hikes and an orphanage you can help at. The Fundación Pueblo office on the plaza has information. Buy a minibus ticket on arrival in Yanakachi or walk 45 minutes down to the La Paz-Chulumani road for transport. The trek can be done in one long day, especially if you organize a jeep to the start of the trail, but is more relaxing in two or three. If you take it slowly, though, you'll have to carry camping kit. Hire mules in Choquekhota for US$8 per day plus up to US$8 for the muleteer. A 2-3 day alternative is from Mina San Francisco to El Castillo and the village of Chaco on the La Paz-Chulumani road. This trek is called La Reconquistada and has the distinction of including a 200 m disused mining tunnel.

Choro Trail (La Cumbre to Coroico) Immediately before the road drops down from La Cumbre to start the descent to Las Yungas, there is a good dirt road leading up to the *apacheta* (narrow pass) where the trail starts properly. Cloud and bad weather are normal at La Cumbre (4660 m): you have to sign in at the Guardaparque post on the way to the pass. The trail passes Samaña Pampa (small shop, sign in again, camping US$0.60), Chucura (pay US$1.20 fee, another shop, camping), Challapampa (camping possible, US$0.60, small shop), the Choro bridge and the Río Jacun-Manini (fill up with water at both river crossings). At Sandillani it is possible to stay at the lodge or camp in the carefully tended garden of a Japanese man, Tamiji Hanamura, who keeps a book with the names of every passing traveller. He likes to see postcards and pictures from other countries. There is good paving down to Villa Esmeralda, after which is Chairo (lodging and camping), then to Yolosa. It takes three days to trek from La Cumbre to Chairo, from where you can take a truck to Puente Yolosita, the turn-off for Cocoico on the new road. From Puente Yolosita trucks run uphill to Coroico when they fill, US$0.70, 15 minutes. The Choro Trail has a reputation for unfriendliness and occasional robbery, take care.

Yunga Cruz (Chuñavi to Chulumani) The best, but hardest of the four 'Inca' trails, it has seen little use in recent years and may be badly overgrown; enquire in advance. From Chuñavi (3710 m) follow the path left (east) and contour gently up. Camping possible after two hours. Continue along the path staying on left hand side of the ridge to reach Cerro Khala Ciudad (literally, Stone City Mountain, you'll see why). Good paving brings you round the hill to join a path coming from Quircoma (on your right); continue, heading north, to Cerro Cuchillatuca and then Cerro Yunga Cruz, where there is water and camping is possible. After this point water and camping are difficult and normally impossible until you get down to Sikilini. The last water and camping possibilities are all within the next hour, take advantage of them. Each person should have at least two litres of water in bottles. Colectivos run from Sikilini to Chulumani. Starting in Chuñavi the trek takes three days. An alternative route is from Chuñavi to Irupana.

Huayna Potosí Huayna Potosí (6088 m) is normally climbed in two days, with one night in a basic shelter at 5300 m or camped on a glacier at 5600 m. Acclimatization and experience on ice are essential, and the mountain is dangerous out of season. There are four shelters: a community-run shelter 10 minutes up from the pass, one by the lake, very cold; *Refugio Huayna Potosí* at 4780 m, with toilets and shower, run by the operator of the same name, and a basic shelter at 5300 owned by the same operator. Average cost is US$100 per person for two-day tour for three people (US$200 for one) including all equipment except sleeping bag. The starting point for the normal route is at Zongo. A three-day trek in the area is also offered. See Climbing, hiking and trekking, page 109, for tour operators.

La Paz and around listings

For Sleeping and Eating price codes and other relevant information, see pages 10-14.

Around Plaza Murillo *p94,*
maps p92 and p95

$$$$-$$$ Presidente, Potosí 920 y Sanjines, T240 6666, www.hotelpresidente-bo.com. The 'highest 5-star in the world'. Includes breakfast, gym and sauna, pool, all open to non-residents, internet, Wi-Fi, bar, excellent service, comfortable, heating, good food.

$$ Gloria, Potosí 909, T240 7070, www.hotelgloria.com.bo. Modern, central, cable TV, price includes breakfast, 2 restaurants (1 of which vegetarian), internet, good food and service, run **Gloria Tours** (www.gloriatours.com.bo). Recommended.

$$ Señorial Montero, Av América 120, esq Plaza Alonso de Mendoza 120, T245 7300. Includes buffet breakfast, heating in rooms, cable TV, popular with tour groups; big, old-fashioned, comfortable hotel.

$ Adventure Brew Hostel, Av Montes 533, T246 1614, www.theadventurebrew hostel.com. With solar-heated showers, cheaper in dorm, on-site microbrewery, includes breakfast and beer every night, rooftop terrace with great views of the city and Illimani, nightly BBQs, use of kitchen, convenient to the bus station, associated with **Gravity Assisted Mountain Biking** (see Activities and tours, below). Also has

$ Adventure Brew Too, Av Montes 641, T228 4323. 8 or 12-bed dorms, with breakfast, internet, use of kitchen, free beer from microbrewery every night, garden patio with beer spa and jacuzzi, fantastic views of city, good value, popular meeting place.

$ pp Arthy's Guesthouse, Montes 693, T228 1439, http://arthyshouse.tripod.com. Shared bath, warm water, kitchen facilities, safe, helpful, popular with bikers, English spoken, 2400 curfew.

$ Austria, Yanacocha 531, T240 8540. Without bath, cheaper in shared room, basic, hot water but only three showers, safe deposit, laundry, TV lounge, use of kitchen, internet, luggage storage, no English spoken.

$ Bacoo, Calle Alto de la Alianza 693, T228 0679, infobacoo@gmail.com. Some rooms with private bath (cheaper in dorm), includes breakfast, Wi-Fi, jacuzzi, restaurant and bar, garden, ping pong and pool, arrange tours.

$ pp Hosp Milenio, Yanacocha 860, T228 1263, hospedajemilenio@hotmail.com. Shared bath, electric shower, basic, family house, homely and welcoming, popular, helpful owner, quiet, kitchen, breakfast extra, security boxes, internet, laundry service, great value.

$ Hostal República, Comercio 1455, T220 2742, www.hostalrepublica.com. Cheaper with shared bath, **$$** in apartment, old house of former president, hot water, luggage stored, laundry service, good café, quiet garden, free internet, Wi-Fi, book ahead and ask for room on upper floor.

$ Loki, Loayza 420, T211 9024, www.lokihostel.com. Old Hotel Vienna renovated as member of this chain of popular party hostels. Cheaper in 14-bed dorms (one dorm is girl-only), kitchen, includes breakfast, TV room, computer room and Wi-Fi, bar (serves dinner). Has tour operator.

$ Posada El Carretero, Catacora 1056, entre Yanacocha y Junín, T228 5271. Single and double rooms (cheaper with shared bath), also dorms, hot showers, kitchen, helpful staff, good atmosphere and value.

$ Tambo de Oro, Armentia 262, T228 1565. Near bus station, hot showers, good value if a bit run down, safe for luggage.

$ Torino, Socabaya 457, T240 6003, www.hoteltorino.com.bo. Ask for better rooms in new section, cheaper without bath, run-down rooms in old section. Popular with backpackers, free book exchange, cultural centre, travel agency, good service. Restaurant next door for breakfast and good-value lunch (Mon-Fri 1200-1500).

$ pp Wild Rover Backpackers Hostel, Comercio 1476, T211 6903, www.wildrover hostel.com. Party hostel in renovated colonial-style house with courtyard and high-ceilings, dorms with 6-10 beds and doubles with shared bath (cheaper), bar, TV room, book exchange, internet, serve dinner and breakfast, helpful staff speak English.

Plaza San Francisco up to the cemetery district *p96, maps p92 and p95*
$$ Estrella Andina, Illampu 716, T245 6421. Includes breakfast, **$** in low season, all rooms have a safe and are decorated individually, English spoken, family run, comfortable, tidy, helpful, Wi-Fi, roof terrace, heaters on loan, cable TV, laundry service, money exchange, very nice. Also owns **$$ Cruz de los Andes**, Aroma 216, T245 1401, same style but shares premises with a car garage.

$$ Hostal Naira, Sagárnaga 161, T235 5645, www.hostalnaira.com. Hot water, comfortable but pricey, rooms around courtyard, some are dark, price includes good buffet breakfast in **Café Banais**, safety deposit boxes, laundry service.

$$ La Posada de la Abuela, C Linares 947, T233 2285. Very pleasant inn, includes continental breakfast and Wi-Fi.

$$ Rosario, Illampu 704, T245 1658, www.hotelrosario.com. Good buffet breakfast, sauna, laundry, internet café **Jiwhaki** (free for guests, great view), Wi-Fi, good restaurant, stores luggage, very helpful staff, no smoking. Highly recommended. **Turisbus** travel agency downstairs (see Tour operators, page 111), Cultural Interpretation Centre explains items for sale in nearby 'witches' market'.

$$-$ Milton, Illampu 1126-1130, T236 8003, www.hotelmiltonbolivia.com. Hot water, includes breakfast, psychedelic 1970s style wallpaper in many rooms, restaurant,

expensive laundry, safe parking around corner, will store luggage, excellent views from roof, popular.

$ Arcabucero, C Viluyo 307 y Linares, T231 3473. Price rises in high season, pleasant new rooms in converted colonial house, excellent value but check the beds, breakfast extra.

$ El Solario, Murillo 776, T236 7963. Central, shared bath, luggage store, kitchen, internet, international phone calls, laundry and medical services, taxi and travel agency, good value, gets crowded.

$ El Viajero, Illampu 807, T245 1640, www.lobo.co.il. Cheaper without bath, cheaper in dorm, a reasonable hostel, decorated with plants, dorm has lockers.

$ Fuentes, Linares 888, T231 3966, www.hotel fuentesbolivia.com. Cheaper without bath, hot water, variety of rooms, includes breakfast, nice colonial style, comfortable, TV, internet, sauna, good value, family run, slow laundry service.

$ Hostal Cactus, Jiménez 818 y Santa Cruz, T245 1421. Shared electric showers, kitchen facilities, luggage store, poor beds and plumbing, don't leave valuables unattended, but peaceful, quiet, helpful, nice communal feel. **Coca Travels** agency downstairs, good.

$ Hostal Copacabana, Illampu 734, T245 1626, www.hostalcopacabana.com. Hot water, good showers, soft beds, includes breakfast, internet, fading but OK.

$ La Joya, Max Paredes 541, T245 3841, www.hotelajoya.com. Cheaper without bath, breakfast included, TV, modern and comfy, lift, laundry, area unsafe at night but provides transfers.

$ Majestic, Santa Cruz 359, T245 1628. Simple rooms with cable TV, breakfast included, restaurant, comfortable, laundry, safe.

$ Onkel Inn 1886, Colombia 257, T249 0456, www.onkel-inn-highlanders.com. Hostel in a remodelled 19th-century house, rooms with and without bath, doubles, triples and bunks, with breakfast. Jacuzzi, laundry facilities, internet, café and bar, HI affiliated.

$ Res Sucre, Colombia 340, on Plaza San Pedro, T249 2038. Cheaper without bath, quiet area, hot water, big rooms, kitchen and laundry facilities, luggage stored, helpful.

$ Sagárnaga, Sagárnaga 326, T235 0252, www.hotel-sagarnaga.com. Cheaper in plain rooms without TV, includes breakfast, solar-powered hot water, Wi-Fi, laundry, 2 ATMs, English spoken, *peña*.

The Prado, Sopocachi, Miraflores and Zona Sur *p97, map p92*

$$$$ Casa Grande, Av Ballivián 1000 y C 17, Calacoto, T279 5511, www.casa-grande.com.bo. Beautiful, top quality apartments, includes buffet breakfast, Wi-Fi, airport pickup, restaurant, very good service, US$4,200 per month.

$$$$ Europa, Tiahuanacu 64, T231 5656, www.hoteleuropa.com.bo. Next to the Museo Nacional de Arqueología. Excellent facilities and plenty of frills, internet in rooms, health club, several restaurants, parking. Recommended.

$$$$ Radisson Plaza, Av Arce 2177, T244 1111, www.radisson.com/lapazbo. 5-star hotel with all facilities, includes breakfast, gym, pool and sauna (also for guests of Plaza Hotel), Wi-Fi, excellent buffet in restaurant (see Eating, below).

$$$ El Rey Palace, Av 20 de Octubre 1947, T241 8541, www.hotelreypalace.com. Includes breakfast, large suites with heating, a/c and cable TV, internet, excellent restaurant, stylish.

$$$ Plaza, Av 16 de Julio 1789, T237 8311. Excellent hotel with good value restaurant (see below), includes breakfast, Wi-Fi, pool.

$$$-$$ Alcalá Aparthotel, Sanjinés 2662 at Plaza España, Sopocachi, T241 2336, www.alcalapartamentos.com. Comfortable, spacious, furnished apartments, includes breakfast, internet, 20% discount per month.

$$ A La Maison, Pasaje Muñoz Cornejo15, Sopocachi, T241 3704, www.alamaison-lapaz.com. Apart-hotel, brightly decorated, breakfast, laundry service, Wi-Fi, TV, kitchens in the larger flats, meals and tourist services can be arranged, daily and monthly rates available.

$$ EHT Sopocachi, Macario Pinilla 580 at the base of El Montículo, T241 0312. Spacious furnished apartments with kitchenette, good location and views, gym.

El Alto *p91*

$ Alexander, Av Jorge Carrasco 61 y C 3, Ceja, Zona 12 de Octubre, T282 3376. Modern, with breakfast, cheaper in dorm, parking, disco, cable TV.

$ Orquídea, C Dos 22 y Av 6 de Marzo, Villa Bolívar A, near bus terminals, T282 6487. Includes breakfast, comfortable heated rooms, cheaper with shared bath, electric showers, good value. Better than others in the area.

South of La Paz *p97*

$$$ Gloria Urmiri, Potosi 909, Urmiri, T240 7070, www.hotelgloria.com.bo. At hot springs 2 hrs from La Paz, price for 2 days, 1 night (price varies according to type of room), includes entry to pools, sauna and all facilities as well as 4 meals, lunch to lunch. Transport US$6.25 pp each way. Massage available, camping US$2.80, reservations required.

$$$-$$ Allkamari, near Valle de las Animas, 30 mins from town on the road to Palca, T279 1742, www.casalunaspa.com. Reservations required, cabins for up to 8 in a lovely valley between the Palca and La Animas canyons, a retreat with nice views of Illimani and Mururata, a place to relax and star-gaze, **$** pp in dorm, solar heating, jacuzzi included, meals on request, use of kitchen, horse and bike rentals, massage, shamanic rituals, taxi from Calacoto US$7, bus No 42 from the cemetery to Uni (7 daily weekdays, hourly weekends), get off at Iglesia de las Animas and walk 1 km.

$$ Oberland, Mallasa, El Agrario 3118, near main road, 12 km from La Paz centre, T274 5040, www.h-oberland.com. A Swiss-owned, chalet-style restaurant (excellent, not cheap) and hotel (also good) with older resort facilities, includes buffet breakfast, Wi-Fi, lovely gardens, spa, sauna, covered pool (open to public – US$2 – very hot water), volleyball, tennis. Permit camping with vehicle, US$4 pp. Recommended

❶ Eating

Around Plaza Murillo *p94, maps p92 and p95*
$$ La Casa de los Paceños, Sucre 814, also in San Miguel, C Juan Capriles. Open 1100-1600, 1800-2200. Tourist restaurant serving excellent Bolivian food, à la carte only.
$$ La Kantuta, in *Hotel Presidente*, Potosí 920, T240 6666. Excellent food, good service. La Bella Vista on the top floor is fancier.
$ El Calicanto, Sanjinés 467, T240 8008. Great regional specialities, renovated colonial house, live music on Fri. Mon-Sat 1100-1500, Mon-Fri 1830-2200.

Cafés
Alexander Coffee, Potosí 1091. Part of a chain, sandwiches, salads, coffee, pastries.
Café Berlin, Mercado 1377 y Loayza, and at Av Montenegro 708, San Miguel. 0800-2300. Coffee, omelettes, breakfast, popular with locals and smoky.
Café Confitería de la Paz, Camacho 1202, on the corner where Ayacucho joins Av Mcal Santa Cruz. Good if expensive tea room, traditional, great coffee and cakes but very smoky.

Plaza San Francisco up to the cemetery district *p96, maps p92 and p95*
$$ La Cueva, Tarija 210B, T231 4523, www.4cornerslapaz.com. Daily 1130-late. Small cozy mexican restaurant, quick service, wide selection of tequilas.

$$ Pizzería Italia, Illampu 840, T246 3152, and 809, 2nd floor, T245 0714. Thin-crust pizza, pasta and international food.
$$ Star of India, Cochabamba 170, T211 4409. British-run Indian curry house, will deliver, including to hotels. Recommended.
$$ Steakhouse, Tarija 243B, T231 0750, www.4cornerslapaz.com, daily 1500-2300. Good cuts of meat, large variety of sauces and a great salad bar in a modern environment.
$$ Tambo Colonial, in *Hotel Rosario* (see above). Excellent local and international cuisine, good salad bar, buffet breakfast, peña at weekend.
$$-$ Colonial Pot, Linares 906 y Sagárnaga. Bolivian dishes and a variety of main courses including vegetarian, all-day *menú* US$3.35 and à-la-carte, pastries, snacks, hot and cold drinks, quiet, homey, music, exceptional value.
$$-$ Sol y Luna, Murillo 999 y Cochabamba, T211 5323, www.solyluna-lapaz.com. Mon-Fri 0900-0100, Sat-Sun 1700-0100. Dutch run, breakfast, *almuerzo* and international menu, coffees and teas, full wine and cocktail list, live music Mon and Fri, movies, Wi-Fi, guide books for sale, book exchange, salsa lessons.
$$-$ Tucan Bistro, Tarija 725. Open daily 1600-2400. Varied international menu, good food in laid back atmosphere, US$2 for *almuerzo* Mon-Fri; wine bar. Bolivian/ Australian owned.
$$-$ Yussef, Sagárnaga 380, 2nd floor. Lebanese, mezze, good for vegetarians, good value and relaxed atmosphere.
$ 100% Natural, Sagárnaga 345. Range of healthy, tasty fast foods ranging from salads to burgers and llama meat, good breakfasts.
$ A Lo Cubano, Sagárnaga 357, entre Linares y Illampu, T245 1797. Open Mon-Sat 1200-2200. *Almuerzo* for US$2, but it runs out fast, also other choices of good Cuban food, good value.
$ Angelo Colonial, Linares 922, T215 9633. Vegetarian options, good music, internet access, open early for breakfast, can get busy

with slow service. Has a hostal at Av Santa
Cruz 1058, with hot water, safe, convenient.
$ El Lobo, Illampu y Santa Cruz. Israeli dishes,
good meeting place, noticeboard, popular.

Cafés
Banais, Sagárnaga 161, same entrance as
Hostal Naira. Coffee, sandwiches and juices,
buffet breakfast, laid-back music and
computer room.
Café Illampu, Linares 940, upstairs. La Paz
branch of the Swiss-run Sorata café known
for its sandwiches, bread and cakes.
Café Soho, Jaén 747. Cosy café with small
courtyard, inside and outside seating, local
artwork, open Mon-Sun 0930-2300.
Hard Rock Café, Santa Cruz 399 e Illampu,
T211 9318, www.hardrockcafebolivia.lobo
pages.com. Serves Hard Rock fair, turns into
nightclub around 2400, popular with locals
and tourists.
Pepe's, Pasaje Jiménez 894, off Linares.
All-day breakfasts, sandwiches, omelettes,
tables outside, cards and dominoes,
magazines and guidebooks.

**The Prado, Sopocachi, Miraflores and
Zona Sur** *p97, map p92*
$$$ Chalet la Suisse, Av Muñoz Reyes 1710,
Cota Cota, T279 3160, www.chaletlasuisse.
com. Serves excellent fondue, steaks,
booking is essential on Fri evening.
$$$-$$ La Comedie, Pasaje Medinacelli
2234, Sopocachi, T242 3561. 'Art café
restaurant', contemporary, with a French
menu, good salads, wine list and cocktails,
Mon-Fri 1200-2300, Sat-Sun opens at 1900.
$$$-$$ Maphrao On, Hnos Manchego
2586, near Plaza Isabela la Católica, T243
4682. Thai and South East Asian food,
warm atmosphere, good music.
$$ El Arriero, Av 6 de Agosto 2525 (Casa
Argentina), Sopocachi, T243 5060, also
Av Montenegro entre C 17 y 18, San Miguel,
T279 1907. The best Argentine *parrilla* in
the city, also daily *almuerzo* from US$5.

$$ El Consulado, Bravo 299 (behind Plaza
Hotel), T211 7706, http://cafeelconsulado.
com. In gorgeous setting with outdoor
seating and covered terrace, includes
high-end handicraft store, book exchange,
Wi-Fi, photo gallery, organic coffee and
food, pricey but worth it.
$$ High Lander's, Final Sánchez Lima 2667,
Sopocachi, T243 0023. Mon-Fri 1200-1500,
1700-2300, Sat 1900-2330, happy hour
Mon-Fri 1700-1900. Variable Tex-Mex fare,
nice atmosphere, good views from the end
of the street.
$$ Ken-Chan, Bat Colorado 98 y F Suazo,
p 2 of Japanese Cultural Center, T244 2292.
Open 1800-2300. Japanese restaurant with
wide variety of dishes, popular.
$$ La Quebecoise, 20 de Octubre
2387, Sopocachi. Good upmarket
international cuisine.
$$ La Tranquera, Capitán Ravelo 2123
next to Hotel Camino Real, T244 1103;
also at Hotel Camino Real, Calacoto,
T279 2323. Daily 1200-1600, 1900-2300.
International food, grill and salad bar.
$$ Reineke Fuchs, Pje Jáuregui 2241,
Sopocachi, T244 2979, and Av Montenegro y
C 18, San Miguel, T277 2103, www.reineke
fuchs.com/ Mon-Fri 1200-1430 and from 1900,
Sat from 1900 only. Many imported German
beers and food in a German-style bar.
$$ Suma Uru, Av Arce 2177 in Radisson
Plaza Hotel, T244 1111. Daily 1200-1500.
Excellent buffet in 5-star setting, friendly
to backpackers.
$$ Utama, in *Plaza* hotel, Av 16 de Julio
1789). 1700-2300. 2 restaurants: **Utama** on
the top floor, with the views, à la carte, and
Uma, on the ground floor, for breakfast and
lunch, buffet lunch US$6.15. Recommended.
$$ Vienna, Federico Zuazo 1905, T244 1660,
www.restaurantvienna.com. Open Mon-Fri
1200-1400, 1830-2200, Sun 1200-1430.
Excellent German, Austrian and local food,
great atmosphere and service, live piano
music, popular.

$$ Wagamama, Pasaje Pinilla 2557, T243 4911. Open Mon-Sat 1200-1400, 1900-2130 (closed Sun). Serves sushi, complimentary tea, excellent service, popular with ex-pats.

$$-$ Mongo's, Hnos Mancheqo 2444, near Plaza Isabela la Católica, T244 0714. Open 1830-0300. Live music Tue, excellent Mexican fare and steaks, open fires, bar (cocktails can be pricey), club after midnight, popular with gringos and locals.

$ Armonía, Ecuador 2286 y Quito. Mon-Sat 1200-1400. Nice vegetarian buffet lunch.

$ Eli's Pizza Express, Av 16 de Julio 1400 block (also at Comercio 914 and Av Montenegro y C 19, Zona Sur). Open daily including holidays. English spoken, very popular, maybe not the best pizza in La Paz, but certainly the largest omelettes.

$ Lu Qing, 20 de Octubre 2090 y Aspiazu, T242 4188. Mon-Sat 1130-1500, 1830-2300, Sun 1100-1530. Chinese food, large choice of dishes, set meals on weekdays.

$ Olive Tree, Campos 334, Edificio Iturri, T243 1552. Open Mon-Fri 1100-2200. Closed Sat evening and Sun, good salads, soups and sandwiches, attentive service.

Cafés

Alexander Coffee (Café Alex), Av 16 de Julio 1832, also at 20 de Octubre 2463 Plaza Avaroa, Av Montenegro 1336, Calacoto, and the airport. Open 0730-2400. Excellent coffee, smoothies, muffins, cakes and good salads and sandwiches, Wi-Fi. Recommended.

Arco Iris, F Guachalla 554 y Sánchez Lima, Sopocachi, T242 3009. Also in Achumani, C 16 by the market, T271 2577. Bakery and handicraft outlet of **Fundación Arco Iris** (www.arcoirisbolivia.org), which works with street children, good variety of breads, pastries, meats and cheeses.

Dumbos, Av 16 de Julio, near *Eli's* and Cinema. For meat and chicken *salteñas*, ice creams, look for the dancing furry animals outside.

Fridolin, Av 6 de Agosto 2415; and Prolongación Montenegro, San Miguel.

Empanadas, tamales, savoury and sweet (Austrian) pastries, coffee, breakfast, Wi-Fi.

Kuchen Stube, Rosendo Gutiérrez 461, Sopocachi. Mon -Fri 0800-2000, Sat-Sun 0800-1900. Excellent cakes, coffee and German specialities.

La Terraza, 16 de Julio 1615, T231 0701, 0630-0030; 20 de Octubre 2171 y Gutiérrez; and Av Montenegro 1576 y C 8, Calacoto, both 0730-2400. Excellent sandwiches and coffee, pancakes, breakfasts, Wi-Fi.

🎧 Bars and clubs

The epicentre for nightlife in La Paz is currently Plaza Avaroa in Sopocachi. Clubs are clustered around here and crowds gather Fri and Sat nights.

Around Plaza Murillo *p94, maps p92 and p95*

Etno Café, Jaén 722, T228 0343. Open Mon-Sat 1930-0300. Small café/bar with cultural programmes including readings, concerts, movies, popular, serves artisanal and fair trade drinks (alcoholic or not).

San Francisco up to the cemetery district *p96, maps p92 and p95*

Blue Note Café, Viluyo esq Plaza Gaston Velasco. Open Mon-Sat 1200-2400. Wine bar with light food, same owners as **Tucan Bistro**, interesting hat collection, good place to hang out for a coffee or glass of wine in relaxed atmosphere.

Oliver's Travels, Murillo y Tarija, T231 1574. Fake English pub serving breakfasts, curries, fish and chips, pasta, sports channels, music, travel agency.

The Prado, Sopocachi, Miraflores and Zona Sur *p97, map p92*

Deadstroke, Av 6 de Agosto 2460, Sopocachi, T243 3472. Opens 1700 (1900 on Sat). Bar/pool hall, café and billiards bar, food, drinks (good value for beer), billiards, pool and other games.

Equinoccio, Sánchez Lima 2191, Sopocachi. Thu-Sat. Top venue for live rock music and bar, cover charge US$2.10, or more for popular bands.

Fak'n Tako, Belisario Salinas opposite Presbitero Medina. Good place to get cheap drinks before going dancing at more expensive clubs, '80s style DJ, playing lots of reggaeton and Latin music.

Tetekos, C México 1553. Loud music, cheap drinks, popular with locals and backpackers.

Theolonius Jazz Bar, 20 de Octubre 2172, Sopocachi, T242 4405. Wed-Sat shows start at 2200. Renowned for jazz (what else?), cover charge US$1.40-2.80.

⊕ Entertainment

For up-to-the-minute information on cinemas and shows, check *La Prensa* or *La Razón* on Fri, or visit www.la-razon.com. Also look for *Kaos* and *Mañana*, 2 free monthly magazines with listings of concerts, exhibits, festivals, etc.

Around Plaza Murillo *p94, maps p92 and p95*

Bocaisapo, Indaburo 654 y Jaén. Open Thu-Fri 1900-0300. Live music in a bar; no cover charge, popular.

Marka Tambo, Jaén 710, T228 0041. Thu-Sat 2100-0200, also Mon-Sat 1230-1500 for lunch. US$6 for evening show, food and drinks extra, live shows with traditional dancing and music (peña), touristy but recommended.

Plaza San Francisco up to the cemetery district *p96, maps p92 and p95*

Peña Parnaso, Sagárnaga 189, T231 6827. Daily starting at 2030, meals available, purely for tourists but a good way to see local costumes and dancing.

Cinemas Films mainly in English with Spanish subtitles cost around US$3.50, see www.cineteatro16dejulio.com. Near Sopocachi is **Multicine**, Av Arce 2631,

11 modern cinemas, food court, gym, arcades; also **Megacenter** in the Zona Sur (see Shopping Malls, below).

Cinemateca Boliviana, Oscar Soria (prolong Federico Zuazo) y Rosendo Gutiérrez, T244 4090, info@cinemateca boliviana.org. Municipal theatre with emphasis on independent productions.

Theatre Teatro Municipal Alberto Saavedra Pérez has a regular schedule of plays, opera, ballet and classical concerts, at Sanjinés e Indaburo, T240 6183. The National Symphony Orchestra is very good and gives inexpensive concerts. Next door is the **Teatro Municipal de Cámara**, which shows dance, drama, music and poetry. **Casa Municipal de la Cultura 'Franz Tamayo'**, almost opposite Plaza San Francisco, hosts a variety of exhibitions, paintings, sculpture, photography, etc, mostly free. Free monthly guide to cultural events at information desk at entrance. The **Palacio Chico**, Ayacucho y Potosí, in old Correo, operated by the Secretaría Nacional de Cultura, also has exhibitions (good for modern art), concerts and ballet, Mon-Fri 0900-1230, 1500-1900, closed at weekends, free.

⊕ Festivals and events

La Paz *p90, maps p92 and p95*

Starting **24 Jan Alasitas**, in Parque Central up from Av del Ejército, also in Plaza Sucre/San Pedro, recommended. **Carnaval** usually in **Feb. End May/early Jun** Festividad del Señor de Gran Poder, the most important festival of the year, with a huge procession of costumed and masked dancers on the 3rd Sat after Trinity. **Jul** Fiestas de Julio, a month of concerts and performances at the Teatro Municipal, with a variety of music, including the University Folkloric Festival. **8 Dec**, festival around Plaza España, colourful and noisy. On **New Year's Eve** there are fireworks displays; view from higher up. See page 15 for national holidays and festivals outside La Paz.

La Paz *p90, maps p92 and p95*

Bookshops Los Amigos del Libro, Av Ballivián 1275, also Av Montenegro 1410, San Miguel and the airport, www.libros bolivia.com. Large stock of English, French and German books; also a few maps, expensive. **Gisbert**, Comercio 1270, and in San Miguel on a small lane opposite Café Alexander. Books, maps, stationery. **The Spitting Llama**, Linares 947 (inside Hostal La Posada de la Abuela), T7039 8720, www.thespittingllama.com. Issue ISIC cards, sell used books, guidebooks and camping gear including GPS units, English spoken, helpful; branches in Cochabamba and Copacabana. **Yachaywasi**, Pasaje Trigo 1971 y Av Villazón, on lane between Plaza del Estudiante and the university. Large selection, popular with students.

Camping equipment Kerosene for pressure stoves is available from a pump in Plaza Alexander, Pando e Inca. **Ayni Sport Bolivia**, Jiménez 806, open Mon-Sun 1030-2100. Rents and sometimes sells camping equipment and mountain gear (trekking shoes, fleeces, climbing equiment etc). **Caza y Pesca**, Edif Handal Center, No 9, Av Mcal Santa Cruz y Socabaya, T240 9209. English spoken. **Tatoo Bolivia**, Illampu 828, T245 1265, www.tatoo.ws. Tatoo clothing plus outdoor equipment including backpacks, shoes, etc. English and Dutch spoken. For camping stove fuel enquire at **Emita Tours** on Sagárnaga.

Handicrafts Above Plaza San Francisco (see page 96), up Sagárnaga, by the side of San Francisco church (behind which are many handicraft stalls in the Mercado Artesanal), are booths and small stores with interesting local items of all sorts. The lower end of Sagárnaga is best for antiques. **Galería Dorian**, Sagárnaga 177, is an entire gallery of handicraft shops; includes **Tejidos Wari**, unit 12, for high-quality alpaca goods, will make

to measure, English spoken. On Linares, between Sagárnaga and Santa Cruz, high quality alpaca goods are priced in US\$. Also in this area are many places making fleece jackets, gloves and hats, but shop around for value and service. **Alpaca Style**, C 22 No 14, T271 1233, Achumani. Upmarket shop selling alpaca and leather clothing. **Artesanía Sorata**, Linares 900 , T245 4728, and Sagárnaga 363. Specializes in dolls, sweaters and weavings. **Ayni**, Illampu 704, www.aynibolivia.com. Fair trade shop in Hotel Rosario, featuring Aymara work. **Comart Tukuypaj**, Linares 958, T231 2686, and C 21, Galería Centro de Moda, Local 4B, San Miguel, www.comart-tukuypaj.com. High-quality textiles from an artisan community association. **Incapallay**, Linares 958, p 2, www.incapallay.org. A weavers' cooperative from Tarabuco and Jalq'a communities, near Sucre. **Jiwitaki Art Shop**, Jaén 705, T7725 4042. Run by local artists selling sketches, paintings, sculptures, literature, etc. Open Mon-Fri 1100-1300, 1500-1800. **LAM** shops on Sagárnaga. Good quality alpaca goods. **Millma**, Sagárnaga 225, T231 1338, and Claudio Aliaga 1202, Bloque L-1, San Miguel, closed Sat afternoon and Sun. High-quality alpaca knitwear and woven items and, on the lower level of the San Miguel shop, a permanent exhibition of ceremonial 19th and 20th century Aymara and Quechua textiles (free). **Mother Earth**, Linares 870, T239 1911. 0930-1930 daily. High-quality alpaca sweaters with natural dyes. **Toshy** on Sagárnaga. Top-quality knitwear.

Jewellery There are good jewellery stores throughout the city: for example **Joyería King's**, Loayza 261, between Camacho and Mercado, T220 1331. Also Torre Ketal, C 15, Calacoto, T277 2542.

Maps IGM: head office at Estado Mayor, Av Saavedra 2303, Miraflores, T214 9484, Mon-Thu 0900-1200, 1500-1800, Fri 0900-1200, take passport to buy maps.

Also office in Edif Murillo, Final Rodríguez y Juan XXIII, T237 0116, Mon-Fri 0830-1230, 1430-1830, some stock or will get maps from HQ in 24 hrs. **Librería IMAS**, Av Mcal Santa Cruz entre Loayza y Colón, Edif Colón, T235 8234. Ask for the map collection and check what is in stock. Maps are also sold in the Post Office on the stalls opposite the Poste Restante counter.

Markets In addition to those mentioned in the Sights section (page 96), the 5-km sq **Feria 16 de Julio, El Alto** market is on Thu and Sun (the latter is bigger). Take any minibus that says La Ceja and get off at overpass after toll booth (follow crowd of people or tell driver you're going to La Feria), or take 16 de Julio minibus from Plaza Eguino. Arrive around 0900; most good items are sold by 1200. Goods are cheap, especially on Thu. Absolutely everything imaginable is sold here. Be watchful for pickpockets, just take a bin liner to carry your purchases. **Mercado Sopocachi**, Guachalla y Ecuador, a well-stocked covered market selling foodstuffs, kitchen supplies, etc.

Musical instruments Many shops on Pasaje Linares, the stairs off C Linares, also on Sagárnaga/Linares, for example **Walata 855**.

Shopping malls and supermarkets
Megacenter, Av Rafael Pabón, Irpavi, huge food court, 18 cinemas, bowling, banks, ATMs. **Shopping Norte**, Potosí y Socabaya. Modern mall with restaurants and expensive merchandise. **Supermercado Ketal**, Av Arce y Pinillo, near Plaza Isabel la Católica, Sopocachi, Av Busch y Villalobos, Miraflores, C 21, San Miguel, and Av Ballivián y C 15, Calacoto. Well-stocked supermarket.

▲▲ Activities and tours

La Paz *p90, maps p92 and p95*
City tours
Sightseeing, T279 1440, city tours on a double-decker bus, 2 circuits, downtown and Zona Sur with Valle de la Luna (1 morning and 1 afternoon departure to each), departs from Plaza Isabel la Católica and can hop on at Plaza San Francisco, tour recorded in 7 languages, US$6 for both circuits, Mon-Fri at 0830 and 1430, Sat-Sun at 0900 and 1430.

Climbing, hiking and trekking
Guides must be hired through a tour company. There is a mountain rescue group, **Socorro Andino Boliviano**, Calle 40 Villa Aérea, T246 5879, www.socorroandino.org.
Alberth Bolivia Tours, Illampu 713, T245 8018, www.hikingbolivia.com. Good for climbing and trekking, helpful, equipment rental.
Andean Summits, Muñoz Cornejo 1009 y Sotomayor, Sopocachi, T242 2106, www.andean summits.com. For mountaineering and other trips off the beaten track, contact in advance.
Bolivian Mountains, Rigoberto Paredes 1401 y Colombia, p 3, San Pedro, T249 2775, www.bolivian mountains.com (in UK T01273-746545). High-quality mountaineering outfit with experienced guides and good equipment, not cheap.
Climbing South America, Murillo 1014 y Rodríguez, Ed Provenzal PB, of 1, T215 2232, www.climbingsouthamerica.com. Climbing and trekking in Bolivia, Argentian and Chile, equipment rental, Australian run.
Refugio Huayna Potosí, Sagárnaga 308 e Illampu, T245 6717, www.huayna-potosi. com. Climbing and trekking tours, run 2 mountain shelters on Huayna Potosí and climbing school.
The Adventure Climbing Company, Av Jaimes Freyre 2950, Plaza Adela Zamudio, Sopocachi, T241 4197, www.adventureco-bo.com. Climbing, trekking and other adventures, equipment rental and sales, experienced guides.
Trek Bolivia, Sagárnaga 392, T231 7106. Organizes expeditions in the Cordillera.
For trekking Maps, see Essentials (page 42) and Shopping, above.

Football

Popular and played on Wed and Sun at the **Siles Stadium** in Miraflores (Micro A), which is shared by both La Paz's main teams, Bolívar and The Strongest. There are reserved seats.

Golf

Mallasilla is the world's highest golf course, at 3318 m. Non-members can play here on weekdays; no need to book. Club hire, green fee, balls and a caddy also costs US$37. There is also a course at Los Pinos in the Zona Sur.

Snooker/pool/other

Picco's, Edif 16 de Julio, Av 16 de Julio 1566. Good tables and friendly atmosphere.
YMCA sportsground and gym: opposite the UMSA University, Av Villazón, and clubhouse open to the public (table tennis, billiards, etc).

Tour operators

America Tours, Av 16 de Julio 1490 (El Prado), Edificio Avenida pb, No 9, T237 4204, www.america-ecotours.com. Cultural and ecotourism trips to many parts of the country (including Chalalán Lodge near Rurrenabaque and Parque Nacional Noel Kempff Mercado), rafting, trekking and horse-riding, English spoken. Highly professional and recommended.
Andean Epics, T7127 6685, www.andean epics.com. Innovative multi-day cycling trips, eg Sorata to Rurrenabaque, which include bike, boat and 4WD combinations. Owner Travis Gray is very knowledgeable and helpful.
Andean Base Camp, Illampu 863, T246 3782, info@andeanbasecamp.com. Overland tours throughout Bolivia, Swiss staff, good reports.
Andean Secrets, General Gonzales 1314 y Almirante Grau, San Pedro (Mon-Fri 1500-1900, Sat 0900-1730, Sun 1000-1400), T7729 4590, quimsacruz_bolivia@ hotmail.com, www.andean-secrets.com. Female mountain guide Denys Sanjines specializes in the Cordillera Quimsa Cruz.

Bolivian Journeys, Sagárnaga 363, p 2, T235 7848, www.bolivianjourneys.org. Camping, mountain bike tours, equipment rental, maps, English and French spoken, helpful.
B-Side Adventures, Linares 943, T211 4225, www.bside-adventures.com. Good for cycling to Coroico and other rides.
Colibrí, Alberto Ostria 1891 y J M Cáceres, Edif Isabelita p 4, Sopocachi Alto, T242 3246, www.colibri-adventures.com. Climbing, trekking, adventure tours, and more, helpful guides.
Crillon Tours, Av Camacho 1223, T233 7533, www.titicaca.com. With 24-hr ATM for cash on credit cards. A company with over 50 years experience. Joint scheduled tours with Lima arranged. Fixed departures to Salar de Uyuni, trips throughout Bolivia, including the Yungas, Sajama and Lauca, community and adventure tourism and much more. Recommended. Full details of their Lake Titicaca services on page 127.
Deep Rainforest, Galería Dorian, Sagárnaga 189, of. 9A, T215 0385, www.deep-rainforest. com. Off the beaten track trekking, climbing, canoe trips from Guanay to Rurrenabaque, rainforest and pampas trips.
Detour, Av Mcal Santa Cruz 1392, esq Colombia, T236 1626. Good for flight tickets.
Enjoy Bolivia, Plaza Isabel La Católica, Edif Presidente Bush, of 2, T243 5162, www.enjoybolivia.org. Wide selection of tours and transport service. Airport and bus terminal transfers, van service to Oruro (US$13 pp shared, US$90 private).
Fremen Creative Tours, Bernardo Trigo 447, p 2, Plaza del Estudiante, T244 2777, www.salar-amazon.com. Large well-established operator offering tours throughout Bolivia, including *Tayka* hotels around Salar de Uyuni, *El Puente Jungle Lodge* at Villa Tunari and *Reina de Enín* riverboat.
Gloria Tours/Hotel Gloria, Potosí 909, T240 7070, www.gloriatours.com.bo. Good service, see Sleeping, pages 101 and 103.

Gravity Bolivia, Av 16 de Julio 1490, Edif Avenida, PB, No 10, T231 3849, www.gravity bolivia.com. A wide variety of mountain biking tours throughout Bolivia, including the world-famous downhill ride to Coroico. Also offer a zipline at the end of the ride, or independently (www.ziplinebolivia.com). Also bike rides more challenging than Coroico, including single-track and high-speed dirt roads, with coaching and safety equipment. Sells guidebooks. Book on website in advance. Recommended.

Kanoo Tours, Illampu 832 entre Sagarnaga y Santa Cruz, T246 0003, www.kanootours.com. Also at Adventure Brew Hostel and Loki Hostel. Sells Gravity Bolivia tours (see above), plus Salar de Uyuni, Rurrenabaque jungle trips and Perú.

La Paz On Foot, C Pablo Sánchez 6981, Irpavi, T7153 9753, www.lapazonfoot.com. Walking city tours, walking and sailing trips on Titicaca and multi-day treks in the Yungas and Apolobamba. Recommended.

Lipiko Tours, Av Mariscal Santa Cruz, corner of Sagarnaga No 918, Galeria La República, T214 5129, www.travel-bolivia.co.uk. Tailor-made tours for all budgets, 4WD tours, trekking, climbing and adventure sport, trips to Amazon and national parks. Also cover Peru, Chile and Argentina.

Magri Turismo, Capitán Ravelo 2101, T244 2727, www.magriturismo.com. Recommended for tours throughout Bolivia, flight tickets. Own **La Estancia** hotel on the Isla del Sol.

Moto Andina, Urb La Colina N°6 Calle 25, Calacoto, T7129 9329, www.moto-andina. com (in French). Motorcycle tours of varying difficulty in Bolivia, contact Maurice Manco.

Mundo Quechua, Av Circunvalación 43, Achumani, Zona Sur, T279 6145, www.mundoquechua.com. Custom made climbing, trekking and 4WD tours

throughout Bolivia. Also extrensions to Peru and Argentina. English and French spoken, good service.

Queen Travel, Calle 18 7802, Calacoto, T279 5450, www.boliviatravel-queen.com. Offers a wide range of tours all over Bolivia, including Lake Titicaca, Salar de Uyuni, Northern Jungle and Eastern lowlands.

Topas Travel, Carlos Bravo 299 (behind Hotel Plaza), T211 1082, www.topas.bo. Joint venture of Akhamani Trek (Bolivia), Topas (Denmark) and the Danish embassy, offering trekking, overland truck trips, jungle trips, biking and climbing, English spoken, restaurant and *pensión*.

Transturin, Av Arce 2678, Sopocachi, T242 2222, www.transturin.com. Full travel services with tours in La Paz and throughout Bolivia. Details of their Lake Titicaca services on page 127.

Tupiza Tours, Villalobos 625 y Av Saavedra, Edif Girasoles, pb, Miraflores, T224 5254, www.tupizatours.com. La Paz office of the Tupiza agency. Specialize in the Salar and southwest Bolivia, but also offer tours around La Paz and throughout the country.

Turisbus, Av Illampu 704, T245 1341, www.turisbus.com. Lake Titicaca and Isla del Sol, Salar de Uyuni, Rurrenbaque, trekking and Bolivian tours. Also tours and tickets to Puno and Cuzco.

Turismo Balsa, Av 6 de Agosto 3 y Pinilla, T244 0620, www.turismobalsa.com. City and tours throughout Bolivia, see also under Puerto Pérez, page 124. Also international flight deals.

Vertigo Biking, Sagárnaga y Linares, T211 5220, www.vertigobiking.com. Mountain biking tours.

Xtreme Down Hill, Sagárnaga 392, T231 3310, www.xtremedownhill.com. Mountain biking tours.

La Paz *p90, maps p92 and p95*
Air
Cotranstur minibuses, T231 2032, white
with 'Cotranstur' and 'Aeropuerto' written
on the side and back, go from Plaza Isabel
La Católica, stopping all along the Prado and
Av Mcal Santa Cruz to the airport, 0615-2300,
US$0.55 (allow about 1 hr), best to buy an
extra seat for your luggage, departures every
4 mins. Shared transport from Plaza Isabel La
Católica, US$3.50 pp, carrying 4 passengers,
also private transfers from **Enjoy Bolivia**, see
Tour operators, page 110. Radio-taxi is US$7
to centre, US$9 to Zona Sur. Prices are
displayed at the airport terminal exit. There
is an **Info Tur** office in arrivals with a *casa de
cambio* next to it (dollars, euros cash and TCs,
poor rates; open 0530-1300, 1700-0300,
closed Sun evening – when closed try the
counter where departure taxes are paid).
Several ATMs in the departures hall. The
international and domestic departures hall
is the main concourse, with all check-in
desks. There are separate domestic and
international arrivals. Bar/restaurant and
café upstairs in departures. For details of
air services, see under destinations.

Bus
For information, T228 5858. Buses to: **Oruro**,
Potosí, **Sucre**, **Cochabamba**, **Santa Cruz**,
Tarija and **Villazón**, leave from the main
terminal at Plaza Antofagasta (micros 2, M,
CH or 130), see under each destination for
details. Taxi to central hotels, US$1.10. The
terminal (open 0400-2300) has a tourist
booth by the main entrance, ATMs, internet,
a post office, **Entel**, restaurant, luggage store,
near the main entrance and several private
kiosks at the rear, and travel agencies. Touts
find passengers the most convenient bus and
are paid commission by the bus company.
To **Oruro** van service with **Enjoy Bolivia**,

see Tour operators, page 110, US$13 pp
shared, US$90 private.

To **Copacabana**, several bus companies
(tourist service) pick-up travellers at their
hotels (in the centre) and also stop at the
main terminal, tickets from booths at the
terminal (cheaper) or agencies in town.
They all leave about 0800 (**Titicaca Bolivia**
also at 1400), 3½ hrs, US$3.60-4.50 one way,
return from Copacabana about 1330. When
there are not enough passengers for each
company, they pool them. **Diana Tours**
T228 2809, **Titicaca Bolivia**, T246 2655,
www.titicacabolivia.com.bo, **Turisbus**
T245 1341 (more expensive), many others.
You can also book this service all the way
to Puno, US$7.

Public buses to **Copacabana**,
Tiwanaku, **Desaguadero** (border with
Peru) and **Sorata**, leave from the Cemetery
district. To get there, take any bus or
minibus marked 'Cementerio' going up
C Santa Cruz (US$0.15-0.20). On Plaza Reyes
Ortiz are **Manco Capac**, and **2 de Febrero**
for **Copacabana** and **Tiquina**. From the
Plaza go up Av Kollasuyo and at the 2nd
street on the right (Manuel Bustillos) is
the terminal for minibuses to **Achacachi**,
Huatajata and **Huarina**, as well as **Trans
Unificada** and **Flor del Illampu** minibuses
for **Sorata**. Several micros (20, J, 10) and
minibuses (223, 252, 270, 7) go up
Kollasuyo. Taxi US$1 from downtown.
Buses to **Coroico, the Yungas and
northern jungle** leave from Villa Fátima
(25 mins by micros B, V, X, K, 131, 135, or
136, or *trufis* 2 or 9, which pass Pérez Velasco
coming down from Plaza Mendoza, and get
off at the *ex-gasolinera* YPFB, C Yanacachi
1434). See Safety, page 94.
International buses From Plaza
Antofagasta terminal: to **Buenos Aires**,
US$75, 2 a week with **Ormeño**, T228 1141,
54 hrs via Santa Cruz and Yacuiba; via Villazón
with **Río Paraguay**, 3 a week, US$75, or

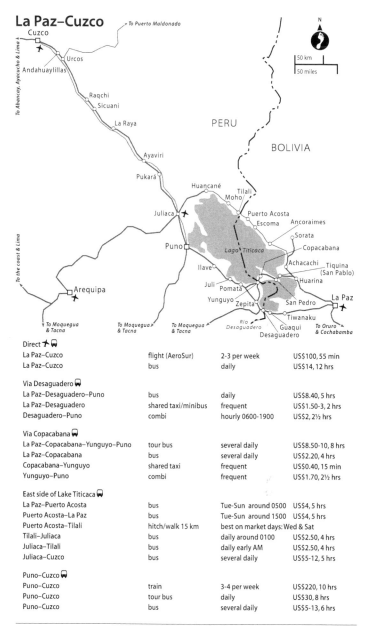

La Paz–Cuzco

Direct ✈ 🚌			
La Paz–Cuzco	flight (AeroSur)	2-3 per week	US$100, 55 min
La Paz–Cuzco	bus	daily	US$14, 12 hrs

Via Desaguadero 🚌			
La Paz–Desaguadero–Puno	bus	daily	US$8.40, 5 hrs
La Paz–Desaguadero	shared taxi/minibus	frequent	US$1.50-3, 2 hrs
Desaguadero–Puno	combi	hourly 0600-1900	US$2, 2½ hrs

Via Copacabana 🚌			
La Paz–Copacabana–Yunguyo–Puno	tour bus	several daily	US$8.50-10, 8 hrs
La Paz–Copacabana	bus	several daily	US$2.20, 4 hrs
Copacabana–Yunguyo	shared taxi	frequent	US$0.40, 15 min
Yunguyo–Puno	combi	frequent	US$1.70, 2½ hrs

East side of Lake Titicaca 🚌			
La Paz–Puerto Acosta	bus	Tue-Sun around 0500	US$4, 5 hrs
Puerto Acosta–La Paz	bus	Tue-Sun around 1500	US$4, 5 hrs
Puerto Acosta–Tilali	hitch/walk 15 km	best on market days: Wed & Sat	
Tilali–Juliaca	bus	daily around 0100	US$2.50, 4 hrs
Juliaca–Tilali	bus	daily early AM	US$2.50, 4 hrs
Juliaca–Cuzco	bus	several daily	US$5-12, 5 hrs

Puno–Cuzco 🚌			
Puno–Cuzco	train	3-4 per week	US$220, 10 hrs
Puno–Cuzco	tour bus	daily	US$30, 8 hrs
Puno–Cuzco	bus	several daily	US$5-13, 6 hrs

Trans Americano, US$85. Alternatively, go to Villazón and change buses in Argentina. To **Arica** via the frontier at Tambo Quemado and Chungará **Pullmanbus** at 0630 (good), **Cuevas** at 0700, **Zuleta** at 0600, **Nuevo Continente** at 1230 except Sat, **Litoral**, T228 1920, Sun-Thu 1230, US$14-18. Connecting service for Iquique or Santiago. To **Cuzco**: agencies to **Puno** where you change to a different company, most easily booked through travel agencies, US$14-22, but cheaper paying for each segment at a time. For luxury and other services to Puno see under Lake Titicaca below. Direct to Cuzco, 12 hrs with **Litoral**, US$14 via Desaguadero and Puno (5 hrs, US$8.40). To **Lima**, Ormeño daily at 1430, US$70, 27 hrs; **Nuevo Continente** at 0830, US$55, 26 hrs, via Desaguadero, change to **Cial** in Puno.

Car hire
Imbex, C 10 No 7812, Calacoto, T212 1010, www.imbex.com. Wide range of well-maintained vehicles; Suzuki jeeps from US$60 per day, including 200 km free for 4-person 4WD. Recommended. **Kolla Motors**, Rosendo Gutierrez 502 y Ecuador, Sopocachi, T241 9141, www.kollamotors.com. 6-seater 4WD Toyota jeeps, insurance and gasoline extra. **Petita Rent-a-car**, Valentín Abecia 2031, Sopocachi Alto, T242 0329, www.rentacar petita.com. Swiss owners Ernesto Hug and Aldo Rezzonico. Recommended for personalized service and well-maintained 4WD jeeps, minimum rental 1 week. Their vehicles can also be taken outside Bolivia. Also offer adventure tours (German, French, English spoken). Ernesto has a highly recommended garage for VW and other makes, Av Jaimes Freyre 2326, T241 5264.

Taxi
Standard taxis charge US$0.85-1.70 pp for short trips within city limits. A *trufi* US$0.40-0.50 pp in the centre. Taxi drivers are not tipped. At night, for safety, only take radio taxis (radio móvil), which are named as such, have a unique number and radio communication (eg **Gold** T241 1414 in the centre, 272 2722 in Zona Sur, **Servisur** T271 9999). They charge US$0.85-2.15 in centre, more to suburbs and at night. Also good value for tours for 3 people. **Oscar Vera**, Simón Aguirre 2158, Villa Copacabana, La Paz, T223 0453, specializes in trips to the Salar de Uyuni and the Western Cordillera.

Train
Ferroviaria Andina (FCA), Sánchez Lima 2199 y Fernando Guachalla, Sopocachi, T241 9770, www.fca.com.bo, Mon-Fri 0800-1600. Sells tickets for the **Oruro-Uyunui-Tupiza-Villazón** line. Tickets for *ejecutivo*class sold up to 2 weeks in advance, for *salón* 1 week. Must show passport to buy tickets. Also operate a **tourist train** from **El Alto** station, C 8, Villa Santiago I, by Cuartel Ingavi, the 2nd Sun of each month at 0800, to **Guaqui** via Tiwanaku; returning from Guaqui at 1500; US$6 *ejecutivo*, US$1.50 *popular*, confirm all details in advance.

South of La Paz *p97*
For Valle de la Luna, Minibuses 231, 273 and 902 can be caught on C México, the Prado or Av 6 de Agosto. Alternatively take Micro 11 ('Aranjuez' large, not small bus) or ones that say 'Mallasa' or 'Mallasilla' along the Prado or Av 6 de Agosto, US$0.65, and ask driver where to get off. Most of the travel agents organize tours to the Valle de la Luna. There are brief, 5 min stops for photos in a US$15 tour of La Paz and surroundings; taxis cost US$6, US$10 with a short wait.

Tiwanaku *p97*
To get to Tiwanaku, tours booked through agencies cost US$12 (not including entry fee or lunch). Otherwise take any **Micro** marked 'Cementerio' in La Paz, get out at Plaza Félix Reyes Ortiz, on Mariano Bautista (north side of

cemetery), go north up Aliaga, 1 block east of Asín to find Tiwanaku micros, US$2, 1½ hrs, every 30 mins, 0600 to 1500. Tickets can be bought in advance. **Taxi** costs about US$25-55 return (shop around), with 2 hrs at site. Some **buses** go on from Tiwanaku to Desaguadero; virtually all Desaguadero buses stop at the access road to Tiwanaku, 20-min walk from the site. Return buses (last back 1700) leave from south side of the Plaza in village. Minibuses (vans) to **Desaguadero**, from José María Asín y P Eyzaguirre (Cemetery district) US$2, 2 hrs, most movement on Tue and Fri when there is a market at the border. **Note** When returning from Tiwanaku (ruins or village) to La Paz, do not take a minibus if it has no other passengers. We have received reports of travellers being taken to El Alto and robbed at gun point. Wait for a public bus with paying passengers in it.

Takesi Trail *p99*
Take a **Líneas Ingavi** bus from C Gral Luis Lara esq Venacio Burgoa near Plaza Líbano, San Pedro going to **Pariguaya** (see Yunga Cruz below), daily at 0800, US$1, 2 hrs. On Sun, also mini-buses from C Gral Luis Lara y Boquerón, hourly 0700-1500. To **Mina San Francisco**: hire a **jeep** from La Paz; US$85, takes about 2 hrs. **Veloz del Norte** (T02-221 8279) leaves from Ocabaya 495 in Villa Fátima, T221 8279, 0900 daily, and 1400 Thu-Sun, US$2.10, 3½ hrs, continuing to Chojlla. From Chojlla to La Paz daily at 0500, 1300 also on Thu-Sun, passing **Yanakachi** 15 mins later.

Choro Trail *p99*
To the *apacheta* pass beyond **La Cumbre**, take a **taxi** from central La Paz for US$15, 45 mins, stopping to register at the Guardaparque hut. Buses from Villa Fátima to Coroico and Chulumani pass La Cumbre. Tell driver where you are going, US$2.10. The trail is signed.

Yunga Cruz Trail *p100*
Take the **bus** to **Pariguaya** (2 hrs past Chúñavi, see Takesi above), at 0800 Mon-Sat, 6 hrs to Chúñavi, US$2.25; 6½ hrs to Lambate (3 km further on). It's not possible to buy tickets in advance, be there at 0700. Also **Trans Río Abajo** to **Lambate** from C Gral Luis Lara y Romualdo Herrera, San Pedro, daily 0700-0800.

Huayna Potosí *p100*
The mountain can be reached by transport arranged through tourist agencies (US$100) or the refugio, **taxi** US$45. **Minibus Trans Zongo**, Av Chacaltaya e Ingavi, Ballivián, El Alto, daily 0600, 2½ hrs, US$1.80 to Zongo, check on return time. Also minibuses from the Ballivián area that leave when full; often return full (few on Sun). If camping in the Zongo Pass area, stay at the site near the white house above the cross.

① Directory

La Paz *p90, maps p92 and p95*
Airline offices Aerolíneas Argentinas, Edif Petrolero, 16 de Julio 1616, Mezanine, of 13, T235 1360. **Aerocon**, Av Arce 2549, p 1, T215 0093. **AeroSur**, Av Arce 2177, Hotel Radisson, p 5, T244 4930; also Av 16 de Julio 1616, T231 3233. **Amaszonas**, Av Saavedra 1649, Miraflores, T222 0848. **American Airlines**, Av 16 de Julio 1440, Edif Hermann and Galería Tellería, of 203, San Miguel, T237 2009, 800-100229. **Boliviana de Aviación (BoA)**, Camacho 1413 y Loayza, T211 7993, T901-105010. **Iberia**, Ayacucho 378, Edif Credinform p 5, T220 3911. **LAN**, Av 16 de Julio 1566, p 1, T235 8377, toll free T800-100521. **Lufthansa**, Av 6 de Agosto 2512 y P Salazar, T243 1717. **Sky Airline**, 16 de Julio 1459, Edif Avenida, p1, T211 0440, fly to northern Chile. **TACA**, edif Petrolero, 16 de Julio 1616 PB, and Av Montenegro 1420, San Miguel, T215 8200, toll free T800-108222. **TAM** (Mercosur), H Gutiérrez 2323, T244 3442. **Transportes Aéreo Militar (TAM)**,

Av Montes 738 y Bozo, T268 1111.
Banks See Money (page 17) for exchange
details. ATMs at many sites in the city. **Bisa**,
Camacho 1333 and Av Arce 2572, Sopocachi.
BNB,Camacho 1296 y Colón. **Banco Unión**,
Camacho 1416 y Loayza. **Prodem**, Camacho
1277 y Colón, Illampu 784 y Santa Cruz.
Exchange houses: Sudamer, Camacho
1311 y Colón, Mon-Fri 0830-1830, Sat
0900-1300 and C21 8179, San Miguel,
Mon-Fri 0900-1700, Sat 0930-1300.
Good rates for various currencies, 2%
commission on TCs into US$ cash, frequently
recommended. **Unitours**, Camacho 1389 y
Loayza, Mon-Fri 0830-1830, Sat 0900-1300.
Good rates for various currencies. Street
changers on corners around Plaza del
Estudiante, Camacho, Colón and Prado; rates
vary, watch out for tricks. **Cultural centres**
Alliance Française, Guachalla 399 esq Av 20
de Octubre T242 5005, http://lapaz.alianza
francesa.org.bo. French-Spanish library,
videos, newspapers, and cultural gatherings
information. Call for opening hours. **Centro
Boliviano Americano (CBA)**, Parque Zenón
Iturralde 121, T244 0650 (10 mins walk
from Plaza del Estudiante down Av Arce),
www.cba.edu.bo. Has public library and
recent US papers. **Goethe-Institut**, Av Arce
2708 esq Campos, T243 1916, www.goethe.
de/lapaz. Excellent library, recent papers
in German, CDs, cassettes and videos free
on loan, German books for sale. **Cycle
spares** See Gravity Assisted Mountain
Biking under Tour operators, page 111, very
knowledgeable, www.gravity bolivia.com.
Embassies and consulates Argentina,
Aspiazu 497, Sopocachi, T241 7737,
ebolv@mrecic.gov.ar. 24 hrs for visa,
0900-1330. **Brazil**, Av Arce 2739, Edif
Multicentro, T244 2148, embajadabrasil@
acelerate.com. 0900-1300, 1500-1800,
Mon-Fri (visas take 2 days). **Canada**, Edif
Barcelona p 2, Victor Sanjinés 2678, Plaza
España, T241 5141, lapaz@international.gc.ca,
Mon-Thu 0830-1700, Fri 0830-1400. **Danish**

Consulate, Av Arce 2799 y Cordero, Edif
Fortaleza, p 9, T243 2070, lpbamb@um.dk.
Mon-Fri, 0830-1600. **France**, Av Hernando
Siles 5390 y C 8, Obrajes, T214 9900,
www.ambafrance-bo.org, 0900-1230.
Germany, Av Arce 2395, T244 0066,
www.la-paz.diplo.de. Mon-Fri 0900-1200.
Italy, C 5 (Jordan Cuéllar) 458, Obrajes, T278
8506, www.amblapaz.esteri.it. Mon-Fri
0830-1300. **Netherlands Consulate**, Av 6
de Agosto 2455, Edif Hilda, p 7, T244 4040,
http://bolivia.nlambassade.org, 0900-1200.
Paraguay, Edif Illimani, p 1, Av 6 de Agosto y
P Salazar, T243 220, good visa service.
Mon-Fri 0830-1300, 1500-1730. **Peruvian
Consulate**, Av 6 de Agosto 2455, T244 0631,
open till 1600, visa issued same day if you go
early. **Spanish Consulate**, Av 6 de Agosto
2827 y Cordero, T243 0118, embespa@
entelnet.bo. Mon-Fri 0830-1500. **Swedish
Consulate**, Pasaje Villegas 1227, entre 20
de Octubre y 6 de Agosto, T214 6723,
sweconsul@kolla.net, open 0900-1200.
Switzerland, C 13 y 14 de Septiembre,
Obrajes, T275 1225, paz.vertretung@
eda.admin.ch. Mon-Fri 0900-1200. **UK**,
Av Arce 2732, T243 3424, http://ukinbolivia.
fco.gov.uk/en/. Mon-Thu 0830-1230,
1330-1700, Fri 0830-1330. **USA**, Av Arce
2780, T216 8000, http://bolivia.usembassy.
gov, Mon-Fri 0830-1730. **Internet** There
are many internet cafés in the centre of La
Paz, opening and shutting all the time. Cost
US$0.30-0.45 per hr, fast connections, long
hours, but many closed Sun. **Language
schools** Alliance Française (see also
above). **Instituto Exclusivo**, Av 20 de
Octubre 2315, Edif Mechita, T242 1072,
www.instituto-exclusivo.com. Spanish
lessons for individual and groups, accredited
by Ministry of Education. **Instituto de La
Lengua Española**, María Teresa Tejada,
C Aviador esq final 14, No 180, Achumani,
T279 6074, T7155 6735. One-to-one lessons
US$7 per hr. Recommended. **Speak Easy
Institute**, Av Arce 2047, between Goitía and

Montevideo, T244 1779, speakeasyinstitute@
yahoo.com. US$6 for one-to-one private
lessons, cheaper for groups and couples,
Spanish and English taught, very good.
Private Spanish lessons from: **Isabel Daza**,
Murillo 1046, p 3, T231 1471, T7062 8016.
US$4 per hr. **Enrique Eduardo Patzy**,
Méndez Arcos 1060, Sopocachi, T241 5501
or 776-22210, epatzy@hotmail.com. US$6
an hr one-to-one tuition, speaks English
and Japanese. Recommended. **Medical
services** For hospitals, doctors and dentists,
contact your consulate or the tourist office
for recommendations. **Health and hygiene:
Ministerio de Desarollo Humano, Secretaría
Nacional de Salud**, Av Arce, near *Radisson
Plaza*, yellow fever shot and certificate, rabies
and cholera shots, malaria pills, bring own
syringe. **Centro Piloto de Salva**, Av Montes y
Basces, T245 0026, 10 mins walk from Plaza
San Francisco, for malaria pills, helpful.
Laboratorios Illimani, Edif Alborada p 3,
of 304, Loayza y Juan de la Riva, T231 7290,
open 0900-1230, 1430-1700, fast, efficient,
hygienic. Tampons may be bought at most
farmacias and supermarkets. Daily papers list
pharmacies on duty (*de turno*). For contact

lenses, **Optalis**, Comercio 1089. **Post
offices** Correo Central, Av Mcal Santa Cruz
y Oruro, Mon-Fri 0800-2000, Sat 0830-1800.
Stamps are sold at post office and by some
hotels. *Poste Restante* keeps letters for 2
months, no charge. Check the letters filed
under all parts of your name. To collect
parcels costs US$0.15. Express postal service
(top floor) is expensive. **DHL**, Av 14 de
Septiembre 5351 y C7, Obrajes, T211 6161,
expensive and slow. **Telephones** Almost
every kiosk can make local calls and calls to
cell-phones. Also, call centres (**Cotel, Entel**
are the main ones) that allow for more
privacy and less street noise. For international
calls, lots of call centres in C Sagárnaga,
usually US$0.10 per min to Europe and North
America. **Useful addresses** Immigration:
to renew a visa go to **Migración Bolivia**,
Camacho 1468, T211 0960. Mon-Fri
0830-1230, 1430-1830, go early. Allow 48 hrs
for visa extensions. **Tourist Police:** C Hugo
Estrada 1354, Plaza Tejada Sorzano frente al
estadio, Miraflores, next to *Love City* Chinese
restaurant, T222 5016, toll free T800-108687.
Open 0830-1800, for police report for
insurance claims after theft.

Lake Titicaca

Lake Titicaca is two lakes joined by the Straits of Tiquina: the larger, northern lake (Lago Mayor, or Chucuito) contains the Islas del Sol and de la Luna; the smaller lake (Lago Menor, or Huiñamarca) has several small islands. The waters are a beautiful blue, reflecting the hills and the distant cordillera in the shallows of Huiñamarca, mirroring the sky in the rarified air and changing colour when it is cloudy or raining. A boat trip on the lake is a must.

Ins and outs

Getting there A paved road runs from La Paz to the Straits of Tiquina (114 km El Alto-San Pablo). ▶▶ *See also Transport, page 128.*

La Paz to Copacabana → *For listings, see pages 124-130.*

Puerto Pérez The closest point to the capital on Lake Titicaca, Puerto Pérez, 72 km from La Paz, was the original harbour for La Paz. It was founded in the 19th century by British navigators as a harbour for the first steam boat on the lake (the vessel was assembled piece by piece in Puno). Colourful fiestas are held on New Year's Day, Carnival, 3 May and 16 July (days may change each year). There are superb views of the lake and mountains.

Huatajata Further north along the east shore of the lake is Huatajata, with *Yacht Club Boliviano* (restaurant open to non-members, Saturday, Sunday lunch only, sailing for members only) and *Crillon Tours' International Hydroharbour* and *Inca Utama Hotel* (see below). Reed boats are still built and occasionally sail here for the tourist trade. There are several small but interesting exhibits of reed boats that were used on long ocean voyages. Beyond here is **Chúa**, where there is fishing, sailing and *Transturin's* catamaran dock (see below).

Islands of Lake Huiñamarca

On **Suriqui** (one hour from Huatajata) in Lake Huiñamarca, a southeasterly extension of Lake Titicaca, you can see reed *artesanías*. The late Thor Heyerdahl's *Ra II*, which sailed from Morocco to Barbados in 1970, his *Tigris* reed boat, and the balloon gondola for the Nasca (Peru) flight experiment, were also constructed by the craftsmen of Suriqui. Reed boats are still made on Suriqui, probably the last place where the art survives. On **Kalahuta** there are *chullpas* (burial towers), old buildings and the uninhabited town of Kewaya. On **Pariti** there is Inca terracing and the **Museo Señor de los Patos**, with weavings and Tiwanku-era ceramics.

From Chúa the main road reaches the east side of the Straits at **San Pablo** (clean restaurant in blue building, with good toilets). On the west side is San Pedro, the main Bolivian naval base, from where a paved road goes to Copacabana and the border. Vehicles are transported across on barges, US$5. Passengers cross separately, US$0.20 (not included in bus fares) and passports may be checked. Expect delays during rough weather, when it can get very cold.

Copacabana → *Phone code: 02. Population: 15,400. Altitude: 3850 m.*

A popular little resort town on Lake Titicaca, 158 km from La Paz by paved road, Copacabana is set on a lovely bay and surrounded by scenic hills. **Municipal tourist office** ① *16 de Julio y 6 de Agosto, Wed-Sun 0800-1200, 1400-1800.* **Red de Turismo Comunitario** ① *6 de Agosto y 16 de Julio, T7729 9088, rtiticaca@gmail.com, Mon-Sat 0800-1230, 1300-1900,* can arrange tours to nearby communities. At major holidays (Holy Week, 3 May, and 6 August), the town fills with visitors; beware of thieves and pickpockets at these times.

Copacabana has a heavily restored, Moorish-style **basilica**. ① *open 0700-2000; minimum 5 people at a time to visit museum, Tue-Sat 1000-1100, 1500-1600, Sun 1000-1100, US$1.50, no photos allowed.* It contains a famous 16th century miracle-working Virgen Morena (Dark Lady), also known as the Virgen de Candelaria, one of the patron saints of Bolivia. The basilica is clean, white, with coloured tiles decorating the exterior arches, cupolas and chapels. It is notable for its spacious atrium with four small chapels; the main chapel has one of the finest gilt altars in Bolivia. There are 17th- and 18th-century paintings and statues in the sanctuary. Vehicles decorated with flowers and confetti are blessed in front of the church.

On the headland which overlooks the town and port, **Cerro Calvario**, are the Stations of the Cross (a steep 45-minute climb – leave plenty of time if going to see the sunset). On the hill behind the town is the **Horca del Inca**, two pillars of rock with another laid across them; probably a sun clock, now covered in graffiti. There is a path marked by arrows, boys will offer to guide you: fix price in advance if you want their help.

There are many great hikes in the hills surrounding Copacabana. North of town is the **Yampupata Peninsula**. It is a beautiful 17 km (six hours) walk to the village of Yampupata at the tip of the peninsula, either via Sicuani on the west shore or Sampaya on the east shore, both picturesque little towns. There are also minibuses from Copacabana to Yampupata, where you can hire a motorboat or rowboat to Isla del Sol or Isla de la Luna; boats may also be available from Sampaya to Isla de la Luna.

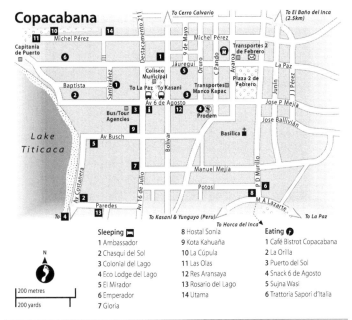

Copacabana

Lake Titicaca

200 metres
200 yards

Sleeping ☐		Eating ❶
1 Ambassador	8 Hostal Sonia	1 Café Bistrot Copacabana
2 Chasqui del Sol	9 Kota Kahuaña	2 La Orilla
3 Colonial del Lago	10 La Cúpula	3 Puerto del Sol
4 Eco Lodge del Lago	11 Las Olas	4 Snack 6 de Agosto
5 El Mirador	12 Res Aransaya	5 Sujna Wasi
6 Emperador	13 Rosario del Lago	6 Trattoria Sapori d'Italia
7 Gloria	14 Utama	

Isla del Sol

The site of the main Inca creation myth (there are other versions) is a place of exceptional natural beauty and spiritual interest. Legend has it that Viracocha, the creator god, had his children, Manco Kapac and Mama Ocllo, spring from the waters of the lake to found Cuzco and the Inca dynasty. A sacred rock at the island's northwest end is worshipped as their birthplace. Near the rock are the impressive ruins of **Chincana**, the labyrinth. At the south end of the island are the **Fuente del Inca**, a spring reached by Inca steps leading up from the lake, and the ruins of **Pilcocaina**, a two storey building with false domes and nice views over the water. Several restored pre-Columbian roads cross the island from north to south.

There are three communities on Isla del Sol: Challapampa, Challa and Yumani, from north to south. All have electricity (Yumani also has Internet), accommodation and simple places to eat. All charge visitors fees, US$0.75-$1.50, which allow entry to small museums or nearby archaeologic sites (keep tickets at hand). The island is heavily touristed and gets crowded in high season. Touts and beggars can be persistent, especially in Yumani. Tour operators in Copacabana offer half- and full-day 'tours' (many are just transport, see page 128) but at least an overnight stay is recommended to appreciate fully the island and to enjoy the spectacular walk from north to south (or vice-versa) at a comfortable pace. Note that it is a steep climb from the pier to the town of Yumani. Local guides are available in Challapampa and Yumani.

Southeast of Isla del Sol is the smaller **Isla de la Luna**, which may also be visited. The community of Coati is located on the west shore, an Inca temple and nunnery on the east shore.

Border with Peru

West side of Lake Titicaca The road goes from La Paz 91 km west to the former port of **Guaqui** (at the military checkpoint here, and other spots on the road, passports may be inspected). The road crosses the border at **Desaguadero** 22 km further west and runs along the shore of the lake to Puno. (There are three La Paz-Puno routes, see also page 75.) Bolivian immigration is just before the bridge, open 0830-2030 (Peru is one hour earlier than Bolivia). Get exit stamp, walk 200 m across the bridge then get entrance stamp on the other side. Get Peruvian visas in La Paz. There are a few hotels and restaurants on both sides of the border; very basic in Bolivia, slightly better in Peru. Money changers on Peruvian side give reasonable rates. Market days are Friday and Tuesday: otherwise the town is dead.

Via Copacabana From Copacabana a paved road leads 8 km south to the frontier at Kasani, then to Yunguyo, Peru. Do not photograph the border area. For La Paz tourist agency services on this route see International buses, page 114, and Activities and tours, page 127. The border is open 0730-1930 Bolivian time (one hour later than Peruvian time). International tourist buses stop at both sides of the border; if using local transport walk 300 m between the two posts. Do not be fooled into paying any unnecessary charges to police or immigration. Going to Peru, money can be changed at the Peruvian side of the border. Coming into Bolivia, the best rates are at Copacabana.

East side of Lake Titicaca

From Huarina, a road heads northwest to Achacachi (market Sunday; fiesta 14 September). Here, one road goes north across a tremendous marsh to **Warisata**, then crosses the altiplano to Sorata (see below). At Achacachi, another road runs roughly parallel to the shore of Lake Titicaca, through **Ancoraimes** (Sunday market, the church hosts a community project making dolls and alpaca sweaters, also has dorms), **Carabuco** (with colonial church), **Escoma**, which has an Aymara market every Sunday morning, to **Puerto Acosta**, 10 km from the Peruvian border. It is a pleasant, friendly town with a large plaza and several simple places to stay and eat. The area around Puerto Acosta is good walking country. From La Paz to Puerto Acosta the road is paved as far as Escoma, then good until Puerto Acosta (best in the dry season, approximately May to October). North of Puerto Acosta towards Peru the road deteriorates and should not be attempted except in the dry season. An obelisk marks the international frontier at Cerro Janko Janko, on a promontory high above the lake with magnificent views. Here are hundreds of small stone storerooms, deserted except during the busy Wednesday and Saturday smugglers' market, the only days when transport is plentiful. You should get an exit stamp in La Paz before heading to this border (only preliminary entrance stamps are given here). There is a Peruvian customs post 2 km from the border and 2 km before Tilali, but Peruvian immigration is in Puno.

Sorata → *Phone code: 02. Population: 8500. Altitude: 2700 m.*

Sorata, 163 km from La Paz (paved but for the last 15 km), is a beautiful colonial town nestled at the foot of Mount Illampu; all around it are views over steep lush valleys. The climate is milder and more humid compared to the *altiplano*. Nearby are some challenging long-distance treks as well as great day-hikes. The town has a charming plaza, with views of the snow-capped summit of Illampu on a clear day. **Tourist office** ① *in Alcaldía, Mon-Fri 0800-1200, 1400-1800, Sat 0830-1200*. The main fiesta is 14 September.

A popular excursion is to **San Pedro cave** ① *0800-1700, US$2, toilets at entrance*, beyond the village of San Pedro. The cave has an underground lake (no swimming allowed) and is lit. It is reached either by road, a 12 km walk (three hours each way), or by a path high above the the Río San Cristóbal (about four hours, impassable during the rainy season and not easy at any time). Get clear directions before setting out and take sun protection, food, water, etc. Taxis and pickups from the plaza, 0600-2200, US$7 with a 30-minute wait.

Trekking and climbing from Sorata

Sorata is the starting point for climbing **Illampu** and **Ancohuma**. All routes out of the town are difficult, owing to the number of paths in the area and the very steep ascent. Experience and full equipment are necessary. You can hire trekking guides and mules (see Activities and Tours, page 128). The 3-4 day trek to **Lagunas Chillata and Glaciar** is the most common and gets busy during high season. Laguna Chillata can also be reached by road or on a long day-hike with light gear, but mind the difficult navigation and take warm clothing. Laguna Chillata has been heavily impacted by tourism (remove all trash, do not throw it in the pits around the lake) and groups frequently camp there. The **Illampu Circuit**, a 6-7 day high-altitude trek (three passes over 4000 m, one over 5000 m) around Illampu, is excellent. It can get very cold and it is a hard walk, though very beautiful with nice campsites on the way. Some food can be bought in Cocoyo on the third day. You must be acclimatized before setting out. Another option is the **Trans-Cordillera Trek**, 10-12 days from Sorata to Huayna Potosí, or longer all the way to Illimani at the opposite (south) end of the Cordillera Real. Some communities charge visitors fees along the way and there have in the past been armed holdups near Laguna San Francisco but no incidents reported in recent years.

Cordillera Apolobamba

The Area Protegida Apolobamba forms part of the Cordillera Apolobamba, the north extension of the Cordillera Real. The range itself has many 5000 m-plus peaks, while the conservation area of some 483,744 ha protects herds of vicuña, huge flocks of flamingos and many condors. The area adjoins the Parque Nacional Madidi. This is great trekking country and the 4-6-day **Charazani to Pelechuco** (or vice versa) mountain trek is one of

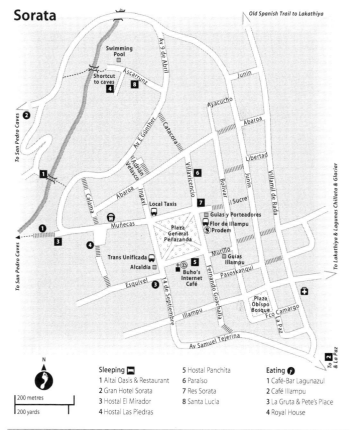

Sorata

Old Spanish Trail to Lakathiya

Sleeping		
1 Altai Oasis & Restaurant	5 Hostal Panchita	**Eating**
2 Gran Hotel Sorata	6 Paraíso	1 Café-Bar Lagunazul
3 Hostal El Mirador	7 Res Sorata	2 Café Illampu
4 Hostal Las Piedras	8 Santa Lucía	3 La Gruta & Pete's Place
		4 Royal House

200 metres
200 yards

the best in the country (see Footprint's *Bolivia Handbook* for details). It passes traditional villages and the peaks of the southern Cordillera Apolobamba.

Charazani is the biggest village in the region (3200 m), with hot springs (US$0.75). Its three-day fiesta is around 16 July. There are some **$** *alojamientos*, restaurants and shops. **Pelechuco** (3600 m) is a smaller village, also with **$** *alojamientos*, cafés and shops. The road to Pelechuco goes through the Area Protegida, passing the community of Ulla Ulla, 5 km outside of which are the reserve's HQ at La Cabaña. Visitors are welcome to see the orphaned vicuñas. There are community hostels (**$**) at the villages of Lagunillas and Agua Blanca. Basic food is available in the communities. For information, contact Trek Apolobamba (www.trekapolobamba.com) and SERNAP in La Paz (page 40).

Lake Titicaca listings

For Sleeping and Eating price codes and other relevant information, see pages 10-14.

○ Sleeping

La Paz to Copacabana *p119*
Puerto Pérez
$$$ Hotel Las Balsas, run by *Turismo Balsa* (see page 111, or T02-289 5147). In beautiful lakeside setting, views of the cordillera, all rooms have balcony over the lake, negotiate out of season, fitness facilities including pool, jacuzzi, sauna. Excellent restaurant with fixed price lunch or dinner.
$ Hostería Las Islas, nearby on the Plaza. Shared bath, hot water, heated rooms, comfortable but it can get crowded at times. There's a *Blue Note* jazz bar next door.

Huatajata
$$ Hotel Titicaca, between Huatajata and Huarina, Km 80 from La Paz, T289 5180 (in La Paz T220 3666). This place has beautiful views, sauna, pool, good restaurant. It's very quiet during the week.
$ Máximo Catari's Inti Karka hotel, on the lakeshore, T7197 8959, erikcatari@ hotmail.com. Cheaper with shared bath. Also restaurant, full menu, open daily, average prices.

Copacabana *p119, map p120*
$$ Ecolodge, 2 km south along the lakeshore, T862 2500 (or 245 1626 Hostal

Copacabana, La Paz). Small comfortable cabins in a quiet out-of-the way location, nice grounds. Includes breakfast (other meals not available), solar hot water, helpful owner.
$$ Gloria Copacabana, 16 de Julio y Manuel Mejía, T862 2094, La Paz T240 7070, www.hotelgloria.com.bo. Includes buffet breakfast, full board available, bar, café and restaurant with international and vegetarian food, Wi-Fi, gardens, parking. A classic resort hotel.
$$ Las Olas, lake-end of Pje Michel Pérez past La Cúpula, T7250 8668, www.olasbolivia.com. Tastefully decorated suites, each in its own style. All have kitchenettes, heaters, lovely grounds and views, outdoor solar-heated Jacuzzi, a special treat. Warmly recommended.
$$ Rosario del Lago, Rigoberto Paredes y Av Costanera, T862 2141, reservations T244 1756, www.hotelrosario.com/lago. Includes buffet breakfast, Wi-Fi, comfortable rooms with lake views, beautifully furnished, good restaurant, small museum, handicraft shop, *Turisbus* office (see Transport below), parking. Efficient and attentive service.
$$-$ La Cúpula, Pje Michel Pérez 1-3, 5 mins' walk from centre, T862 2029, www.hotel cupula.com. Variety of rooms and prices, cheaper with shared bath, reliable hot water, sitting room with TV and video, fully equipped kitchen, library, book exchange, attentive service, excellent restaurant (**$$** with vegetarian options,

great breakfast). Popular, advance booking advised. Highly recommended.

$ Chasqui del Sol, Av Costanera 55, T862 2343, www.chasquidelsol.com. Includes breakfast, lakeside hotel, café/breakfast room has great views, trips organized, video room, parking.

$ Colonial del Lago, Av 6 de Agosto y Av 16 de Julio, T862 2270. Some roms with lake view, cheaper without bath, hot water, garden, restaurant and *peña*.

$ Emperador, C Murillo 235, T862 2083. Cheaper without bath, electric showers, newer rooms at the back, popular, helpful, tours arranged.

$ Kotha Kahuaña, Av Busch 15, T862 2022. Cheaper without bath, simple kitchen facilities, quiet, hospitable, basic but clean and good value.

$ La Aldea del Inca, San Antonio 2, T862 2452, www.aldeadelinca.com. Includes breakfast, electric shower, snack bar, ample grounds, parking, opened in 2010.

$ Pacha, Bolívar y 6 de Agosto, T7658 5477. With electric shower, adequate rooms, bar/pizzeria downstairs, opened in 2010.

$ Sonia, Murillo 253, T862 2019. Cheaper without bath, good beds, big windows, roof terrace, laundry and kitchen facilities, breakfast in bed on request, very helpful, good value. Recommended.

$ Utama, Michel Pérez, T862 2013, www.utama hotel.com. With breakfast, hot water, good showers, comfy, restaurant, book exchange.

Isla del Sol *p121*
Yumani

Most of the posadas on the island are here. Quality varies; ignore the touts and shop around for yourself. Please conserve water, it is hauled up the steep hill by donkeys.

$$ Palla Khasa, 600 m north of town on the main trail to Challapampa, T7321 1585, pallakhasa@gmail.com. Includes good breakfast, large rooms, good beds, restaurant with fine views, nice location and grounds,

family run, solar electricity, changes US$ and other currencies. Book in advance.

$ Hostal Comunitario, half-way up the hill on the right, T7354 9898. With electric shower, simple rooms, pleasant common area, back yard.

$ Inti Kala, at the top of the hill, T7194 4013. Cheaper without bath, electric shower, fantastic views, serves good meals.

$ Templo del Sol, at the top of the hill, T7400 5417. Comfortable rooms, cheaper without bath, electric shower, great views, comfy beds, and a good restaurant.

Challa

Located mid-island on the east shore, about 200 m below the main north-south trail. Most hostels are on the beach, the town is uphill.

$ Inca Beach, on the beach, T7353 0309. Simple rooms with bath, electric shower, kitchen and laundry facilities, meals available, nice common area, camping possible, good value.

$ Qhumpuri, on hillside above beach, T7472 6525. Simple 2-room units with nice views, private toilet, shared electric shower, tasty meals available.

Challapampa

$ Cultural, one block from beach, T7190 0272. Cheaper without bath, clean rooms, nice terrace.

$ Manco Kapac, by the dock, T7128 8443. Shared bath, electrc shower, basic but clean and friendly, camping possible.

$ Wipala, 1 km north on trail to Chincana, T7257 0092. With electric shower, simple rooms, lovely quiet location.

Tour group accommodation

La Posada del Inca, a restored colonial hacienda, owned by **Crillon Tours**, only available as part of a tour with Crillon, see page 127. **Magri Turismo** also owns a hotel on the island, **La Estancia**, www.eco lodge-laketiticaca.com. See La Paz, Tour operators on page 111. See also **Transturin's** overnight options on page 127.

Sorata *p122, map p123*
$$ Altai Oasis, T213 3895, www.altai oasis.com. At the bottom of the valley in a beautiful setting, 15 min steep downhill walk from town, or taxi US$2. Cabins, rooms with bath (cheaper with shared bath), dorms (**$** pp) and camping (US$5 pp). Includes breakfast, very good restaurant (**$$**), bar, lovely grounds, pool, peaceful, very friendly and welcoming, family-run by the Resnikowskis, English and German spoken. Warmly recommended.
$ Hostal El Mirador, Muñecas 400, T7350 5453. Cheaper with shared bath, hot water, kitchen, laundry facilities, terrace.
$ Hostal Las Piedras, just off Ascarrunz, T7191 6341. Cheaper with shared bath, electric shower, very clean and nice, good breakfast available, basic kitchen facilities, very helpful, English and German spoken. Recommended.
$ Hostal Panchita, on plaza, T213 4242. Shared bath, electric shower, simple rooms, sunny courtyard, washing facilities, good value.
$ Paraíso, Villavicencio 117, T7327 5122. With electric shower, basic rooms, terrace, breakfast available.
$ Res Sorata, on plaza, T213 6672. Cheaper without bath, electric shower, restaurant, large but scruffy grounds, poor beds, a bit run down overall but still adequate.
$ Santa Lucía, Ascarrunz, T213 6686. Cheaper with shared bath, electric shower, carpeted rooms, patio, not always open.
$ Toro Bravo, below petrol station at entrance to town, T7197 1836. With electric shower, ample grounds and rooms (upstairs rooms are better), small pool, restaurant, a bit faded but good value.

Eating

Huatajata *p119*
$$-$ Inti Raymi, next to Inca Utama hotel. With fresh fish and boat trips. There are other restaurants of varying standard, most lively at weekends and in the high season.

Copacabana *p119, map p120*
Excellent restaurants at hotels **Rosario del Lago** and **La Cúpula**. Many touristy places on Av 6 de Agosto toward the lakeshore, all similar.
$$ Café Bistrot Copacabana, Cabo Zapana y 6 de Agosto, upstairs, daily 0730-2100. Varied menu, international dishes, vegetarian options, French and English spoken, friendly owner.
$$-$ La Orilla, Av 6 de Agosto, close to lake. Open daily 1000-2200 (usually), warm, atmospheric, tasty food with local and international choices.
$ Aransaya, Av 6 de Agosto 121. Good restaurant and café.
$ Puerta del Sol, Av 6 de Agosto. Good trout.
$ Snack 6 de Agosto, Av 6 de Agosto, 2 branches. Good trout, big portions, some vegetarian dishes, serves breakfast.
$ Sujna Wasi, Jaúregui 127, daily 0730-2300, serves breakfast, vegetarian lunch, wide range of books on Bolivia, slow service.

Sorata *p122, map p123*
Very good restaurant at **Altai Oasis**, see Sleeping above. There are several **$$-$** Italian places on the plaza, all quite similar.
$$-$ Café Illampu, 15 min walk on the way to San Pedro cave. Excellent sandwiches, bread and cakes, camping possible. Offers tours with own 4WD vehicle, Swiss-run, English and German spoken. Closed Tue and Dec-Mar.
$$-$ Jalisco, on plaza. Mexican and Italian dishes, sidewalk seating.
$ Royal House, off Muñecas by the market. Decent set lunch, friendly

Copacabana *p119, map p120*
Note: At these times hotel prices quadruple.
1-3 Feb Virgen de la Candelaria, massive procession, dancing, fireworks, bullfights. **Easter**, with candlelight procession on Good Friday. **23 Jun**, San Juan, also on Isla del Sol. **4-6 Aug**, La Virgen de Copacabana.

Sorata *p122, map p123*
14 Sep, Fiesta Patronal del Señor de la Columna, is the main festival.

⛰ Activities and tours

Lake Titicaca *p118*
Crillon Tours (address under La Paz, Tour operators, page 110) run a hydrofoil service on Lake Titicaca with excellent bilingual guides. Tours stop at their Andean Roots "Eco Village" at Huatajata. Very experienced company. The **Inca Utama Hotel and Spa (\$\$\$)** has a health spa based on natural remedies and Kallawaya medicine; the rooms are comfortable, with heating, electric blankets, good service, bar, restaurant, reservations through *Crillon Tours* in La Paz. *Crillon* is Bolivia's oldest travel agency and is consistently recommended. Also at *Inca Utama* is an observatory (*Alajpacha*) with 2 telescopes and retractable roof for viewing the night sky, an Altiplano Museum, a floating restaurant and bar on the lake (*La Choza Náutica*), a 252-sq m floating island and examples of different Altiplano cultures. Health, astronomical, mystic and ecological programmes are offered. The hydrofoil trips include visits to Andean Roots complex, Copacabana, Islas del Sol and de la Luna, Straits of Tiquina and past reed fishing boats. See Isla del Sol, Sleeping, for *La Posada del Inca*. Crillon has a sustainable tourism project with Urus-Iruitos people from the Río Desaguadero area on floating islands by the Isla Quewaya. Trips can be arranged to/from Puno and Juli (bus and hydrofoil excursion

to Isla del Sol) and from Copacabana via Isla del Sol to Cuzco and Machu Picchu. Other combinations of hydrofoil and land-based excursions can be arranged (also highland, Eastern lowland, jungle and adventure tours). See www.titicaca.com for full details. All facilities and modes of transport connected by radio.

Transturin (see also La Paz, Tour operators, page 110) run catamarans on Lake Titicaca, either for sightseeing or on the La Paz-Puno route. The catamarans are more leisurely than the hydrofoils of *Crillon* so there is more room and time for on-board meals and entertainment, with bar, video and sun deck. From their dock at Chúa, catamarans run day and day/night cruises starting either in La Paz or Copacabana. Puno may also be the starting point for trips. Overnight cruises involve staying in a cabin on the catamaran, moored at the Isla del Sol, with lots of activities. On the island, Transturin has the *Inti Wata* cultural complex which has restored Inca terraces, an Aymara house, the underground *Ekako* museum and cultural demonstrations and activities. There is also a 30-passenger totora reed boat for trips to the Pilcocaina Inca palace. All island-based activities are for catamaran clients only. Transturin runs through services to Puno without many of the formalities at the border. **Transturin** offers last minute, half-price deals for drop-in travellers (24-48 hrs in advance, take passport): sold in Copacabana only, half-day tour on the lake, continuing to Puno by bus, or La Paz; overnight Copacabana-Isla del Sol-Copacabana with possible extension to La Paz. Sold in La Paz only: La Paz-Isla del Sol-La Paz, or with overnight stay (extension to Puno possible on request).

Turisbus (www.turisbus.com, see La Paz, Tour operators page 110 and *Hoteles Rosario*, La Paz, and *Rosario del Lago*, Copacabana) offer guided tours in the fast launches *Titicaca Explorer I* (28 passengers) and *II* (8 passengers) to the Isla del Sol, returning to Copacabana via the Bahía de Sicuani for trips on traditional reed boats. Also La Paz-Puno, with boat excursion to Isla del Sol, boxed lunch and road transport, or with additional overnight at *Hotel Rosario del Lago*.

Copacabana *p119, map p120*
Town is filled with tour agencies, all offering excursions to floating islands on imitation reed vessels, and tours to Isla del Sol (see Transport, below). Kayak and pedal-boat rentals on the beach, US$3 per hr.

Sorata *p122, map p123*
Mountain biking
Andean Epics, T7127 6685, www.andeanepics.com. Biking and other tours, see La Paz Tour Operators, page 110.

Trekking guides
It may be cheaper to go to Sorata and arrange for trekking there than to book a trek with an agency in La Paz. Buy specialty foods and supplies in La Paz, Sorata shops have basic items. Asociación de Guías, Sucre 302 y Guachalla, leave message at **Res Sorata** (T213 6672); hires guides, porters and mules. Prices vary: guides approximately US$30 per day, mules US$15 per day. Porters take maximum 2 mules, remember you have to feed your guide/porter. **Eduardo Chura**, T7157 8671, guiasorata@yahoo.com, is an independent local trekking guide.

⊖ Transport

La Paz to Copacabana *p119*
Puerto Pérez
Bus Regular minibus service from **La Paz** Cementerio district: across from the cemetery, above the flower market, ask for buses to Batallas, US$0.75, but no public transport Batallas-Puerto Pérez.

Huatajata
Bus La Paz-Huatajata, US$1, frequent minibuses from Bustillos y Kollasuyo,

Cementerio district, daily 0400-1800, continuing to Tiquina.

Islands of Lago Huiñamarca *p119*
Boat Máximo Catari (see Huatajata, Sleeping, above) and Paulino Esteban (east end of town, T7196 7383) arrange regular boats to the islands in Lago Huiñamarca for US$15 per hr.

Copacabana *p119, map p120*
If arriving in Bolivia at Copacabana and going to La Paz, be sure to arrive there before dark. See also Safety on page 94.

Bus To/from **La Paz**, US$2 plus US$0.20 for Tiquina crossing, 4 hrs, throughout the day with **Manco Capac**, **2 de Febrero**. Both have offices on Copacabana's main plaza (but leave from Plaza Sucre) and in La Paz at Plaza Reyes Ortiz, opposite entrance to cemetery. Buy ticket in advance at weekends and on holidays. **Diana Tours**, **Milton Tours** and others daily at 1330, from Plaza Sucre, 16 de Julio y 6 de Agosto, US$3.50-4.50, take you to Sagárnaga e Illampu in the tourist district, but will not drop you off at your hotel. (See also Border with Peru via Copacabana, below.)

Isla del Sol *p121*
Boat Andes Amazonía and Titicaca Tours run motor boats to the island from Copacabana; offices on Av 6 de Agosto by the beach. These boats leave Copacabana daily at 0830 and 1330 (the latter only go to Yumani), returning at 1530 and arriving back around 1730. Fares vary, confirm all details in advance: US$2 one-way, US$3 if you return the same day; if you stay overnight or longer on the island, it is best to buy a separate ticket when you are ready to return, US$3-3.50. On a full-day tour you can be dropped off at Challapampa around 1100 and picked up at Yumani at 1530 (boats leave punctually, so you will have to walk quickly to see the ruins in the north and then hike south to Yumani).

Boats also run from Challa to Copacabana Wed, Sat, Sun at 0700, returning 1300, US$2.

From **Yampupata**: to Yumani by motorboat, US$13 per boat (US$3 pp by rowboat); to Isla de la Luna, US$26 per boat.

Border with Peru p121
Via Guaqui and Desaguadero
Bus Road paved all the way to Peru. Buses from La Paz to Guaqui and Desaguadero depart from J M Asín y P Eyzaguirre, Cementerio, from 0500, US$1.50, shared taxi US$3, 2 hrs. From Desaguadero to **La Paz** buses depart 4 blocks from bridge, last vehicle 2000.

Via Copacabana
Bus Several agencies go from La Paz to **Puno**, with a change of bus and stop for lunch at Copacabana, or with an open ticket for continuing to Puno later. They charge US$7 and depart La Paz 0800, pick-up from hotel. From Copacabana they continue to the Peruvian border at Kasani and on to Puno, stopping for immigration formalities and changing money (better rates in Puno). Both **Crillon Tours** and **Transturin** have direct services to Puno without a change of bus at the border. From Copacabana to Puno, **Trans Titicaca** (www.titicacabolivia.com) at 0900, 1330, 1830 and other agencies at 1330, offices on 6 de Agosto, US$3.50-4.50, 3 hrs. Also **Turisbus** (www.turisbus.com) to Puno from Hotel Rosario del Lago at 1330, US$9. To go to **Cuzco**, you will have to change in Puno where the tour company arranges connections, which may involve a long wait, check details. In high season, book at least a day in advance. It is always cheaper, if less convenient, to buy only the next segment of your journey directly from local bus companies and cross the border on your own. *Colectivo* Copacabana (Plaza Sucre)-**Kasani** US$0.50 pp, 15 mins, Kasani-**Yunguyo**, where Peruvian buses start, US$0.20 pp.

East side of Lake Titicaca *p122*
Bus La Paz (Reyes Cardona 772, Cancha Tejar, Cementerio district, T238 2239)-**Puerto Acosta**, 5 hrs, US$4, Tue-Sun 0500. Transport past Puerto Acosta only operates on market days, Wed and Sat, and is mostly cargo trucks. Bus Puerto Acosta-La Paz at about 1500. There are frequent minivans to La Paz from **Escoma**, 25 km from Puerto Acosta; trucks from the border may take you this far.

Sorata p122, map p123
Bus Minibuses throughout the day from **La Paz** with **Trans Unificada** (C Manuel Bustillos 683 y Av Kollasuyo in the Cementerio district, T238 1693); also **Perla del Illampu** (Manuel Bustillos 615, T238 0548), US$2.50, 3½ hrs. Booking recommended on Fri. To or from **Copacabana** and **Peru**, change buses at Huarina but they are often full so start early and be prepared for a long wait.

Jeeps run from La Paz (C Chorolque y Tarapacá, T245 0296, often full), via Sorata to **Santa Rosa** (US$15, 13 hrs), on the road to **Mapiri** and **Guanay**, a rough route with interesting vegetation and stunning scenery. Onward transport can be found in Santa Rosa. From Guanay private boats may be arranged to **Rurrenabaque**, and vehicles run to Caranavi and thence to Coroico. Sorata-Coroico by this route is excellent for offroad motorcycling. If travelling by public trasport it is easier to go La Paz – Coroico – Caranavi – Guanay – Santa Rosa – Sorata – La Paz, than vice versa.

Cordillera Apolobamba p124
Charazani
Bus From Calle Reyes Cardona 732, off Av Kollasuyo, Cemetery district, La Paz, daily with **Trans Altiplano**, T283 0859, and **Trans Provincias del Norte** (No 772, T238 2239), 0600-0630, 7 hrs, US$3.50, very crowded. Return to La Paz at 1800; **Altiplano** also has 0900 on Sat and 1200 Mon, Fri.

Pelechuco

Bus From **La Paz** Trans Provincias del **Norte** leaves daily 0600-0700 from Ex Tranca de Río Seco in El Alto, passing through Qutapampa, Ulla Ulla and Agua Blanca to Pelechuco, between 10-12 hrs, US$5, sometimes on sale 24 hrs before departure at the booking office in Calle Reyes Cardona. Return to La Paz between 0300 and 0400 most days.

❶ Directory

Copacabana *p119, map p120*
Banks No ATM in town, nearest one (Visa only) is in Yunguyo, Peru. **Prodem**, Av 6 de Agosto y Oruro, Tue 1430-1800, Wed-Fri 0830-1230, 1430-1800, Sat-Sun 0830-1500. **Café Bistrot Copacabana** (see Eating, above)

is a BCP agent, cash advances on Visa/MC, US$6 plus 5% commission, maximum advance US$200, take photocopy of passport. Many *cambios* on Av 6 de Agosto change US$ cash, sometimes TCs, Euros and soles, all at poor rates. **Internet** Several places along Av 6 de Agosto, US$1.50 per hr. **Post office** Plaza 2 de Febrero, open (in theory) Tue-Sat 0900-1200, 1430-1830, Sun 0900-1400.

Sorata *p122, map p123*
Banks No ATM in town, bring cash. **Prodem**, on main plaza, Tue-Fri 0830-1230, 1430-1800, Sat 0800-1500. **Internet** Several places in town, US$1.50 per hr. **Medical services** Hospital: Villamil de Rada e Illampu. **Post office** On the plaza, 0830-1230, 1500-1800.

Contents

Footnotes

Basic Spanish for travellers

Learning Spanish is a useful part of the preparation for a trip to Cuba and no volumes of dictionaries, phrase books or word lists will provide the same enjoyment as being able to communicate directly with the people of the country you are visiting. It is a good idea to make an effort to grasp the basics before you go. As you travel you will pick up more of the language and the more you know, the more you will benefit from your stay.

General pronunciation
Whether you have been taught the 'Castilian' pronunciation (*z* and *c* followed by *i* or *e* are pronounced as the *th* in think) or the 'American' pronunciation (they are pronounced as *s*), you will encounter little difficulty in understanding either. Regional accents and usages vary, but the basic language is essentially the same everywhere.

Vowels
a	as in English *cat*
e	as in English *best*
i	as the *ee* in English *feet*
o	as in English *shop*
u	as the *oo* in English *food*
ai	as the *i* in English *ride*
ei	as *ey* in English *they*
oi	as *oy* in English *toy*

Consonants
Most consonants can be pronounced more or less as they are in English. The exceptions are:

g	before *e* or *i* is the same as *j*
h	is always silent (except in *ch* as in *chair*)
j	as the *ch* in Scottish *loch*
ll	as the *y* in *yellow*
ñ	as the *ni* in English *onion*
rr	trilled much more than in English
x	depending on its location, pronounced *x, s, sh* or *j*

Spanish words and phrases

Greetings, courtesies

hello	*hola*	I don't speak Spanish	*no hablo español*
good morning	*buenos días*	do you speak English?	*¿habla inglés?*
good afternoon/	*buenas*	I don't understand	*no entiendo/*
evening/night	*tardes/noches*		*no comprendo*
goodbye	*adiós/chao*	please speak slowly	*hable despacio por*
pleased to meet you	*mucho gusto*		*favor*
see you later	*hasta luego*	I am very sorry	*lo siento mucho/*
how are you?	*¿cómo está?*		*disculpe*
	¿cómo estás?	what do you want?	*¿qué quiere?*
I'm fine, thanks	*estoy muy bien, gracias*		*¿qué quieres?*
I'm called...	*me llamo...*	I want	*quiero*
what is your name?	*¿cómo se llama?*	I don't want it	*no lo quiero*
	¿cómo te llamas?	leave me alone	*déjeme en paz/*
yes/no	*sí/no*		*no me moleste*
please	*por favor*	good/bad	*bueno/malo*
thank you (very much)	*(muchas) gracias*		

Questions and requests

Have you got a room for two people?	*¿Tiene una habitación para dos personas?*
How do I get to_?	*¿Cómo llego a_?*
How much does it cost?	*¿Cuánto cuesta? ¿cuánto es?*
I'd like to make a long-distance phone call	*Quisiera hacer una llamada de larga distancia*
Is service included?	*¿Está incluido el servicio?*
Is tax included?	*¿Están incluidos los impuestos?*
When does the bus leave (arrive)?	*¿A qué hora sale (llega) el autobús?*
When?	*¿Cuándo?*
Where is_?	*¿Dónde está_?*
Where can I buy tickets?	*¿Dónde puedo comprar boletos?*
Where is the nearest petrol station?	*¿Dónde está la gasolinera más cercana?*
Why?	*¿Por qué?*

Basics

bank	*el banco*	market	*el mercado*
bathroom/toilet	*el baño*	note/coin	*le billete/la moneda*
bill	*la factura/la cuenta*	police (policeman)	*la policía (el policía)*
cash	*el efectivo*	post office	*el correo*
cheap	*barato/a*	public telephone	*el teléfono público*
credit card	*la tarjeta de crédito*	supermarket	*el supermercado*
exchange house	*la casa de cambio*	ticket office	*la taquilla*
exchange rate	*el tipo de cambio*	traveller's cheques	*los cheques de viajero/*
expensive	*caro/a*		*los travelers*

Getting around

aeroplane	*el avión*	highway, main road	*la carretera*
airport	*el aeropuerto*	immigration	*la inmigración*
arrival/departure	*la llegada/salida*	insurance	*el seguro*
avenue	*la avenida*	insured person	*el/la asegurado/a*
block	*la cuadra*	to insure yourself against	*asegurarse contra*
border	*la frontera*		
bus station	*la terminal de autobuses/camiones*	luggage	*el equipaje*
		motorway, freeway	*el autopista/ la carretera*
bus	*el bus/el autobús/ el camión*	north, south, west, east	*norte, sur, oeste (occidente), este (oriente)*
collective/ fixed-route taxi	*el colectivo*		
corner	*la esquina*	oil	*el aceite*
customs	*la aduana*	to park	*estacionarse*
first/second class	*primera/segunda clase*	passport	*el pasaporte*
left/right	*izquierda/derecha*	petrol/gasoline	*la gasolina*
ticket	*el boleto*	puncture	*el pinchazo/ la ponchadura*
empty/full	*vacío/lleno*		

street	*la calle*	tyre	*la llanta*
that way	*por allí/por allá*	unleaded	*sin plomo*
this way	*por aquí/por acá*	to walk	*caminar/andar*
tourist card/visa	*la tarjeta de turista*		

Accommodation

air conditioning	*el aire acondicionado*	power cut	*el apagón/corte*
all-inclusive	*todo incluido*	restaurant	*el restaurante*
bathroom, private	*el baño privado*	room/bedroom	*el cuarto/la habitación*
bed, double/single	*la cama matrimonial/ sencilla*	sheets	*las sábanas*
		shower	*la ducha/regadera*
blankets	*las cobijas/mantas*	soap	*el jabón*
to clean	*limpiar*	toilet	*el sanitario/excusado*
dining room	*el comedor*	toilet paper	*el papel higiénico*
guesthouse	*la casa de huéspedes*	towels, clean/dirty	*las toallas limpias/ sucias*
hotel	*el hotel*		
noisy	*ruidoso*	water, hot/cold	*el agua caliente/fría*
pillows	*las almohadas*		

Health

aspirin	*la aspirina*	diarrhoea	*la diarrea*
blood	*la sangre*	doctor	*el médico*
chemist	*la farmacia*	fever/sweat	*la fiebre/el sudor*
condoms	*los preservativos, los condones*	pain	*el dolor*
		head	*la cabeza*
contact lenses	*los lentes de contacto*	period	*la regla*
contraceptives	*los anticonceptivos*	sanitary towels	*las toallas femeninas*
contraceptive pill	*la píldora anti- conceptiva*	stomach	*el estómago*
		altitude sickness	*el soroche*

Family

family	*la familia*	boyfriend/girlfriend	*el novio/la novia*
brother/sister	*el hermano/la hermana*	friend	*el amigo/la amiga*
daughter/son	*la hija/el hijo*	married	*casado/a*
father/mother	*el padre/la madre*	single/unmarried	*soltero/a*
husband/wife	*el esposo (marido)/ la esposa*		

Months, days and time

January	*enero*	June	*junio*
February	*febrero*	July	*julio*
March	*marzo*	August	*agosto*
April	*abril*	September	*septiembre*
May	*mayo*	October	*octubre*

November	*noviembre*	at one o'clock	*a la una*
December	*diciembre*	at half past two	*a las dos y media*
		at a quarter to three	*a cuarto para las tres/*
Monday	*lunes*		*a las tres menos quince*
Tuesday	*martes*	it's one o'clock	*es la una*
Wednesday	*miércoles*	it's seven o'clock	*son las siete*
Thursday	*jueves*	it's six twenty	*son las seis y veinte*
Friday	*viernes*	it's five to nine	*son las nueve menos*
Saturday	*sábado*		*cinco*
Sunday	*domingo*	in ten minutes	*en diez minutos*
		five hours	*cinco horas*
		does it take long?	*¿tarda mucho?*

Numbers

one	*uno/una*	sixteen	*dieciséis*
two	*dos*	seventeen	*diecisiete*
three	*tres*	eighteen	*dieciocho*
four	*cuatro*	nineteen	*diecinueve*
five	*cinco*	twenty	*veinte*
six	*seis*	twenty-one	*veintiuno*
seven	*siete*	thirty	*treinta*
eight	*ocho*	forty	*cuarenta*
nine	*nueve*	fifty	*cincuenta*
ten	*diez*	sixty	*sesenta*
eleven	*once*	seventy	*setenta*
twelve	*doce*	eighty	*ochenta*
thirteen	*trece*	ninety	*noventa*
fourteen	*catorce*	hundred	*cien/ciento*
fifteen	*quince*	thousand	*mil*

Food

avocado	*el aguacate*	chewing gum	*el chicle*
baked	*al horno*	chicken	*el pollo*
bakery	*la panadería*	chilli or green pepper	*el ají/pimiento*
banana	*el plátano*	clear soup, stock	*el caldo*
beans	*los frijoles/*	cooked	*cocido*
	las habichuelas	dining room	*el comedor*
beef	*la carne de res*	egg	*el huevo*
beef steak or pork fillet	*el bistec*	fish	*el pescado*
boiled rice	*el arroz blanco*	fork	*el tenedor*
bread	*el pan*	fried	*frito*
breakfast	*el desayuno*	garlic	*el ajo*
butter	*la mantequilla*	goat	*el chivo*
cake	*el pastel*	grapefruit	*la toronja/el pomelo*

grill	la parrilla	prawns	los camarones
grilled/griddled	a la plancha	raw	crudo
guava	la guayaba	restaurant	el restaurante
ham	el jamón	salad	la ensalada
hamburger	la hamburguesa	salt	la sal
hot, spicy	picante	sandwich	el bocadillo
ice cream	el helado	sauce	la salsa
jam	la mermelada	sausage	la longaniza/el chorizo
knife	el cuchillo	scrambled eggs	los huevos revueltos
lime	el limón	seafood	los mariscos
lobster	la langosta	soup	la sopa
lunch	el almuerzo/la comida	spoon	la cuchara
meal	la comida	squash	la calabaza
meat	la carne	squid	los calamares
minced meat	el picadillo	supper	la cena
onion	la cebolla	sweet	dulce
orange	la naranja	to eat	comer
pepper	el pimiento	toasted	tostado
pasty, turnover	la empanada/	turkey	el pavo
	el pastelito	vegetables	los legumbres/vegetales
pork	el cerdo	without meat	sin carne
potato	la papa	yam	el camote

Drink

beer	la cerveza	ice/without ice	el hielo/sin hielo
boiled	hervido/a	juice	el jugo
bottled	en botella	lemonade	la limonada
camomile tea	la manzanilla	milk	la leche
canned	en lata	mint	la menta
coffee	el café	rum	el ron
coffee, white	el café con leche	soft drink	el refresco
cold	frío	sugar	el azúcar
cup	la taza	tea	el té
drink	la bebida	to drink	beber/tomar
drunk	borracho/a	water	el agua
firewater	el aguardiente	water, carbonated	el agua mineral con gas
fruit milkshake	el batido/licuado	water, still mineral	el agua mineral sin gas
glass	el vaso	wine, red	el vino tinto
hot	caliente	wine, white	el vino blanco

Key verbs

to go — **ir**

I go	*voy*
you go (familiar)	*vas*
he, she, it goes, you (formal) go	*va*
we go	*vamos*
they, you (plural) go	*van*

to have (possess) — **tener**

I have	*tengo*
you (familiar) have	*tienes*
he, she, it, you (formal) have	*tiene*
we have	*tenemos*
they, you (plural) have	*tienen*

there is/are	*hay*
there isn't/aren't	*no hay*

to be — **ser estar**

	ser	estar
I am	soy	estoy
you are	eres	estás
he, she, it is, you (formal) are	es	está
we are	somos	estamos
they, you (plural) are	son	están

This section has been assembled on the basis of glossaries compiled by André de Mendonça and David Gilmour of South American Experience, London, and the Latin American Travel Advisor, No 9, March 1996

Index

Titles available in the Footprint *Focus* range

Latin America	UK RRP	US RRP
Bahia & Salvador	£7.99	$11.95
Buenos Aires & Pampas	£7.99	$11.95
Costa Rica	£8.99	$12.95
Cuzco, La Paz & Lake Titicaca	£8.99	$12.95
El Salvador	£5.99	$8.95
Guadalajara & Pacific Coast	£6.99	$9.95
Guatemala	£8.99	$12.95
Guyana, Guyane & Suriname	£5.99	$8.95
Havana	£6.99	$9.95
Honduras	£7.99	$11.95
Nicaragua	£7.99	$11.95
Paraguay	£5.99	$8.95
Quito & Galápagos Islands	£7.99	$11.95
Recife & Northeast Brazil	£7.99	$11.95
Rio de Janeiro	£8.99	$12.95
São Paulo	£5.99	$8.95
Uruguay	£6.99	$9.95
Venezuela	£8.99	$12.95
Yucatán Peninsula	£6.99	$9.95

Asia	UK RRP	US RRP
Angkor Wat	£5.99	$8.95
Bali & Lombok	£8.99	$12.95
Chennai & Tamil Nadu	£8.99	$12.95
Chiang Mai & Northern Thailand	£7.99	$11.95
Goa	£6.99	$9.95
Hanoi & Northern Vietnam	£8.99	$12.95
Ho Chi Minh City & Mekong Delta	£7.99	$11.95
Java	£7.99	$11.95
Kerala	£7.99	$11.95
Kolkata & West Bengal	£5.99	$8.95
Mumbai & Gujarat	£8.99	$12.95

Africa	UK RRP	US RRP
Beirut	£6.99	$9.95
Damascus	£5.99	$8.95
Durban & KwaZulu Natal	£8.99	$12.95
Fès & Northern Morocco	£8.99	$12.95
Jerusalem	£8.99	$12.95
Johannesburg & Kruger National Park	£7.99	$11.95
Kenya's beaches	£8.99	$12.95
Kilimanjaro & Northern Tanzania	£8.99	$12.95
Zanzibar & Pemba	£7.99	$11.95

Europe	UK RRP	US RRP
Bilbao & Basque Region	£6.99	$9.95
Granada & Sierra Nevada	£6.99	$9.95
Málaga	£5.99	$8.95
Orkney & Shetland Islands	£5.99	$8.95
Skye & Outer Hebrides	£6.99	$9.95

North America	UK RRP	US RRP
Vancouver & Rockies	£8.99	$12.95

Australasia	UK RRP	US RRP
Brisbane & Queensland	£8.99	$12.95
Perth	£7.99	$11.95

For the latest books, e-books and smart phone app releases, and a wealth of travel information, visit us at: www.footprinttravelguides.com.

footprinttravelguides.com

Join us on facebook for the latest travel news, product releases, offers and amazing competitions: www.facebook.com/footprintbooks.com.